Literature and Society

BY ALBERT GUÉRARD

FRENCH PROPHETS OF YESTERDAY

FIVE MASTERS OF FRENCH ROMANCE

FRENCH CIVILIZATION:

Volume I: From its Origins to the Close of the Middle Ages
Volume II: The Life and Death of an Ideal (The Classical Age)
Volume III: The Nineteenth Century
Volume IV: Contemporary France (in preparation)

THE INTERNATIONAL LANGUAGE MOVEMENT

REFLECTIONS ON THE NAPOLEONIC LEGEND

BEYOND HATRED

LITERATURE AND SOCIETY

In French

HONORÉ DE BALZAC

L'AVENIR DE PARIS

LITERATURE
AND
SOCIETY

by

Albert *Leon* Guérard

*Professor of General and
Comparative Literature
Stanford University*

NEW YORK
Cooper Square Publishers, Inc.
1970

Copyright © 1935 and Renewed 1963 by Albert Guerard
Reprinted by Permission of William Morrow and Co.
Published 1970 by Cooper Square Publishers, Inc.
59 Fourth Avenue, New York, N. Y. 10003
International Standard Book No. 0-8154-0364-X
Library of Congress Catalog Card No. 74-135271

Printed in the United States of America

*To Emile Legouis
and Fernand Baldensperger
Who Pointed the Way*

FOREWORD

THIS book attempts to state a problem and to define a method. The problem is: to what extent is Literature conditioned by Society? The method is resolutely pragmatic and comparative.

The work may be used as an introduction; it may be considered as a challenge; it is decidedly not a cyclopædia. The author's aim has been to trace the relation between literary facts and other facts of a non-literary nature. It has not been to supply exhaustive information, still less to offer a final solution. The facts themselves are presented only as illustrations; the bibliographical notes are confessedly the merest signposts. Every student of literature must do his own thinking in terms of his own experience.

That experience, even in the case of the average reader, is by no means limited to books of straight Anglo-Saxon origin. Indeed such books would be hard to find: those writers who are almost chemically pure Americans have probably been exposed to such non-American influences as the Bible. The author happens to be, not merely a teacher of General and Comparative Literature, but a believer in it. He borrows his instances from the common fund of our Western civilization, not from a single national hoard. He does so, not because cosmopolitan references sound more erudite, but because they are more accessible. It is safer, in an argument, to adduce Homer, Dante, Goethe or Tolstoy than Charles Brockden Brown or even E. P. Whipple. On the other hand, Walt Whitman and Hermann Melville will serve much better than Palfurius Sura or Julius Tryfonianus. Greatness ignores the accident of political boundaries.

The problems treated in this book do not depend upon the greatness of the writers under discussion. Mediocrity, as a rule, is more "typical" of a civilization than is genius. Quite apart from the question of artistic merit, foreign examples are frequently more telling than their domestic equivalents. We examine them with a mind freer from preconceived ideas. The remoteness, the strangeness of the environment blot out minor issues, and help us focus the main problem more sharply. The purpose of this book remains *the study of literature by Americans and for Americans:* but restricting ourselves to American authors would not be the best way of serving that purpose. "Seeing others," which is comparatively easy, may lead us to that most difficult achievement, "seeing ourselves." There are motes in European eyes, plainly visible across the Atlantic. This is the very essence of the comparative method: some aspects of our own selves — perhaps the most American of all — are best revealed through a German or Italian mirror.

This book, therefore, quotes freely from the most obvious European sources. The author wishes he might have included Asiatic literature as well. But he is no Irving Babbitt: Sanskrit and Chinese are hermetically sealed to him. It happens that a large number of these instances are borrowed from the French. Only a slight effort would have been needed to alter the proportion: Italian, Spanish and German authorities are easily available. The author has preferred to face the accusation of partiality, and preserve the spontaneity and individuality of his work. The terms he uses are those of his own experience, which is mainly Anglo-Franco-American: criticism inevitably contains elements of autobiography.

But he could defend his course on more objective grounds. No supremacy is claimed for French literature: the choice of French examples was not dictated by blind admiration. But it is a fact that the cultural life of England and that of France have been inseparably mingled for eight hundred years. *The Romance of the Rose*, Montaigne's *Essays*, Voltaire's *Candide*, Flaubert's *Madame Bovary*, *Les Misérables*, are in no sense foreign masterpieces. They are less foreign than the home-grown best-seller of yesteryear.

Then it has ever been the ideal of French civilization to *elucidate*. The origins of great movements may be traced to many countries: the neatest formula is usually written down in Paris. Protestantism is by no means France's gift to the world: but it needed a Calvin. The Enlightenment arose in England: but it had to be disseminated through Montesquieu and Voltaire. England muddles through, gloriously, and her achievements are beyond compare, for they can be reduced to no system and to no common measure. It is France's part to evolve the clear-cut Doctrine, the organized School, the definite Institution, through which unconscious trends are at last made manifest.

Although this book is chiefly concerned with the present

and the future of our own literature, all concrete examples had naturally to be sought in the past: who, in the instantaneous present, could tell a lasting trend from a mere eddy? Now our own national past is brief; our literary world has never been fully organized; neither, for that matter, has our "Society." Cincinnati offers no equivalent for the Hôtel de Rambouillet; Chicago has no Academy quite so venerable as the Académie Française; the White House has never filled, in the literary scene, exactly the same place as Versailles under Louis XIV. Our pragmatism compelled us to acknowledge these facts. Our study of the European past implies no superstitious reverence; and, in our last pages, we face the American future without a trace of dismay.

ALBERT GUÉRARD

CONTENTS

xi

CONTENTS

Part III   The Public

Part IV   To-morrow

Part I

The Background of Literature
Race, Environment and Time

Chapter 1

THE PROBLEM

I

ART is the expression of a unique personality; yet there is no literature, not even the wildest Prophetic Books of Blake, that is not, in some measure, the joint production of author and public. He who "voyages through strange seas of thought alone" is not acclaimed as a poet until he returns. How could the critic of literature take cognizance of "the mute inglorious Milton"? As Martial said nineteen centuries ago, "He does not write at all, whose poems are read by none." Shakespeare exists for us because he is acknowledged. Literature may be the reflection of Eternal Beauty: empirically, it is, first of all, the reflection of Public Taste. For the Pragmatist, the corpus, the canon, of literature is determined solely by the fact of recognition. To say: "This man is great" means: "He is accepted by the right people." And who are "the right people"? This is the question that the present book will attempt to answer, concisely, in about a hundred thousand words.

On this pragmatic basis, literature is a social product. It implies language, a means of communication: the One can express himself only in terms accessible to the Many.

Language itself is a set of symbols which embody, beyond their plain, literal meaning, all the customs, feelings, beliefs of the group. *King*, for instance, had a different connotation for the seventeenth century absolutist, for the eighteenth century liberal, for the nineteenth century democrat. The throng of images that the word may evoke to-day ranges from the Vicar of God on earth to a comic-opera puppet. A language is not an algebraic code: with the best dictionaries at your command, you literally can not understand an author if you are wholly out of touch with his civilization.

This conception is hoary with age. Implicit in Herder's *Ideen* *, it was already clear in Madame de Staël's work, *On Literature considered in its Relations with Social Institutions,* which appeared in 1800. Its application was codified by Taine, in his *Introduction to the History of English Literature,* with the magic formula *Race, Environment and Time.* Taine himself may be antiquated: his method is still with us. It does not tell the whole truth, nor perhaps the essential truth: but the truth that it tells is far from negligible.

Race, it seems, can not be exorcised from the literary field. Even to-day, reputable critics will speak of "Latins", "Celts" or "Slavs", as if the words had some bearing on the interpretation of masterpieces. Mrs. Gertrude Atherton tells us that human nature is largely a matter of the cephalic index; that *The Scarlet Letter* is incompatible with brachycephaly; and that our dismal naturalism is due to the resurgence of the plebeian Alpine. If a critic

* Herder, J. G.: *Ideen zur Philosophie der Geschichte der Menschheit,* 1784–1791.

4

has never indulged in such racial fantasies, let him cast the first stone.

The concept of *Race* is somewhat enfeebled at present —the nemesis of its own excess; that of *Environment* is as lusty as ever. Environment means more than the physical climate, the geographical habitat: it includes political, social, economic conditions. When Irving Babbitt ascribes to a false conception of democracy the low state of our culture, he is using the method of Taine, just as much as the Critics of the Extreme Left, when they interpret literary history in the light of Karl Marx's Communism.

It might be interesting, therefore, to re-state Taine's famous principles in terms of modern experience; and, as we re-state them, to submit them to the most searching criticism. We have no desire to "explode" Race, Environment and Time: we only want to understand. We all feel that there is "something" to them: but what is that something, and how much of it is there? We have no faith whatever in the holiness of the vague; and we entertain but scant respect for prejudice camouflaging as pseudo-science.

Race, Environment and Time are, roughly speaking, common to author and reader, and affect them very much in the same fashion. They account for folklore, "floating literature", or, in the parlance of to-day, *folkways* and *folksay*. They explain Jack Brown and his favorite pulp magazines even more definitely than they explain Branch Cabell. But literature in the stricter sense, literature as conscious craft, implies a dissociation: the few who are vocal, the many who listen. Authors are, in some very important respects, different from the mass. The laws of civilization, if there be such, do not apply to them with exactly the same incidence. We shall have to consider a series of problems about the Man of Letters as such, the natural gifts which constitute his vocation, the deformations, the aberrations which are his professional risks. Coal miners are exposed to melanosis, white-lead workers to necrosis, writers to various forms of graphitis. A psychological and social study of *Homo Scriptor* may yield curious results.

The dissociation, however, is never complete. The author remains linked with his public—else the Ivory Tower would be his tomb. Every book is a dialogue in which the silent interlocutor, the Reader, can not be ignored. Literature is written for a public, large or small, even when it is written for the express purpose of exasperating that public. It is a reflection, however distorted, of the public mind; and the works that survive for posterity give a fairly accurate definition of the best public taste. But that common word *public* is as elusive as it is convenient. Is there such a thing as a clear, spontaneous *vox populi?* Is not "the public mind" a myth? In literature as in politics, the "public mind" is made up by conscious, vocal, energetic minorities. The masses are offered merely a choice between the rival groups which assume leadership and claim authority.

If we could determine what these centers of influence are, many problems of literature would be elucidated. But we should bear in mind that the "Phantom Public" is evolving: the solutions of yesterday fail to meet present conditions. In the classical age, whose shadow lingers in

Europe, and even, very faint but unmistakable, in the United States, these active minorities were essentially emanations of *Society* in the narrower sense: the Court as the supreme drawing-room, the Salon as a miniature private Court, the Tavern or the Café as an impromptu Bohemian salon, the Academies as the most exclusive of Clubs, the Universities as those places where "gentlemen" were trained. Literature ranked with horsemanship, dancing and table manners among the possessions and distinctive marks of a social élite. This "genteel tradition", as Santayana called it, is no longer "at bay": it is gone. The Neo-Humanists are mourning over a tomb. The disruption of the ancient social hierarchy has destroyed the old scale of literary values. We shall restore "standards" if we restore to their primacy the Monarchy, the Church, the Aristocracy. In spite of such prophets as Charles Maurras and T. S. Eliot, the chances for such a restoration are dim.

In our pluto-democracy, literature may be roughly defined in terms of the book industry. Manuscripts that can not possibly sell are not printed; if printed, they are stillborn. But this affords no key to our problem: the book industry does not know the rules of its own game, and publishers are the first to realize that their trade is a gamble. They do not know enough about our civilization to "give the public what they want." In their own interest, they are eager to know more about the laws of public taste. They would like to possess the infallible recipe for a best-seller; and they dream, not only of the short-lived best-seller, but of the perennial good-seller, i.e. the *classic*. How can classics be told? Forecasting is the

7

test of science as well as the key to successful production. In literature, forecasting is Criticism. The critic should be able to tell: "Such a book will appeal to such a class of readers, in such numbers." He should be: but he is not, to the despair of authors, publishers and public alike. The chaos of our competitive economics is reflected in the chaos of our literary mart.

How can literature transcend such a chaos—the road back to yesterday being irremediably closed? How can it supply the needs of the general public, without the waste, surfeit and spiritual starvation which we are experiencing to-day? *Society* lies in ruins: will our community become a genuine society again, conscious of its organic unity? And can it achieve such a consciousness without becoming a Leviathan, and crushing out of existence all cultural minorities? What chances of life are there under the present dispensation, what chances will there be to-morrow, for the unpopular book, adventurous, subtle, cryptic, or simply unobtrusive and gentle? Now that the élite no longer have a common center and a consolidated prestige, how can the scattered lovers of things rare and delicate be integrated into *a* public without merging altogether with *the* Public?

Literature as one of the elements of a civilization, conditioned if not determined by social life as a whole, reacting upon social life in its turn: such is the problem which we propose to discuss in this book. We do not claim that this is the sole possible approach to literature. As a matter of fact, much of our effort will consist in marking the limits of the sociological method: this work, not committed to materialistic determinism, will never

8

be used as a text book in the schools of Soviet Russia. All aspects of civilization, while they are part of an organic whole, do enjoy a measure of autonomy; and in no case is this autonomy larger than in the case of literature. This other side of the question—the refusal of the artist to bow down, to conform, to serve; the defiant assertion of the Unique against the laws of the herd,— we hope to study in a companion volume on *The Doctrine of Art for Art's Sake*.

II

"What was the largest island in the world before Australia was discovered?"—Why, Australia, of course. Translate this conundrum into literary terms: "Who was the greatest American poet before Jefferson Aloysius Kegelbahn was discovered?" Was it Jefferson Aloysius Kegelbahn?

We are reluctant to admit that, in art any more than in geography, discovery amounts to creation. Discovery is a fortunate incident. The thing is there, even if no human eyes have seen it: remote continent, forgotten civilization, mysterious chemical element, star beyond our ken, *unknown masterpiece*. If Shakespeare's *Hamlet* existed only in a single manuscript, never communicated to living man, buried in some vault at Stratford, would it be any the less *Hamlet?* The question is plain: the answer, be it yes or no, will sound paradoxical or even absurd.

Tradition commits us to the view that there is something intrinsic, essential, eternal, about the masterpiece. Its quality partakes of the supreme *I am that I am*. The masterpiece is such because it reflects some element of absolute truth and beauty. This principle underlies all teaching and all discussion of literature. We take it for granted that there are *standards,* even though we might be embarrassed to define them. By these standards, individual and collective taste should be ruled. You must *learn* to enjoy the Beautiful, just as you must bow to the True and follow the Good. If you do not like what you should like, it argues your own perversity of taste, your unsoundness of mind, your moral depravity. If there be such a thing as essential *Rightness* in literature, it can be taught, and our duty is to submit.

Do not believe that such an attitude is a professor's trick. The average professor is far more sceptical than the most sophisticated sophomore. Pedantry is bred, not by those who crave to teach, but by those who crave to be caught. "Tell us what is *real literature*": and unless you are ready with an orthodoxy, that of Aristotle or the latest Greenwich Village brand, you are despised as spineless or flippant.

This conception may be called *idealistic,* both in the common acceptation of the term and in the more specifically Platonic. Idealism always implies a certain loftiness—the uplifted gaze, the waving *Excelsior!* banner. And it means, more strictly, a belief in a world of permanent values, a world of which our common life is but the broken and distorted shadow. It is a term much abused by its foes, and even more by its friends: we should be glad to find a less ambiguous one. But *absolutism* also has equivocal connotations, and so have *fundamentalism* and *dogmatism*. Whatever the name, we hope the principle is clear.

The notion of permanent values is eminently classical: but it is by no means identical with classicism. In all schools, at all times, the idea of absolute Beauty has been maintained. Certainly the most ardent Romanticists, such as Blake and Shelley, held it more firmly than Pope himself. Romanticism rebelled against conventions, not against verities. It believed that imagination and passion were direct avenues to living truth, while common sense was but the rationalization of prejudice. Before Abraham was, Beauty *is*. The vision of it is *true*. The failure of the average man to see it only proves his infirmity. The Romanticist is a mystic: the individual reaches directly beyond the realm of tame consent. But what he reaches is no less absolute, no less universal, than the dogmas of Classicism.

And the Realist also believes in a world anterior and superior to the individual mind. He also preaches that, when the objective truth is attained, our duty is to submit, or we stand condemned. His method of approach is that of science: observation, experimentation. It differs from the abstract reason of the Classicist, from the passionate imagination of the Romanticist, but his goal is the same: a world of eternal values. Flaubert and Zola are dogmatists: in the name of their orthodoxy, they curse and excommunicate without hesitation.

Dogmatism is almost irresistibly attractive. Away from it, there can be no solid spiritual comfort. We need to be constantly assured that we are right; we are eager to follow the guide who promises the words of eternal life.

Scepticism may bring release and relief for a while: but it offers no resting place. There were positive creeds behind the smile of Montaigne and the grin of Voltaire.

So we should all love to throw ourselves at the feet of the Pontiffs. Unfortunately, there have been, there are still, far too many Pontiffs. We can not worship all the gods: a Pantheon is the temple of the atheist. We must either mutilate our souls in the service of our orthodoxy or recognize that there are many *doxies* with very substantial claims. The Pontiffs keep excommunicating, most impressively, in the name of standards: but the standards remain conveniently vague. And when a standard is so unguarded as to clash with a masterpiece, the standard comes out badly crumpled: Rymer did little damage to Shakespeare. The only safe standard is Catholicity of Taste, the denial of all orthodoxies. The only safe altar in literature is that to the Unknown God.

Thus we are, with deep reluctance and constant hankerings, driven from the dogmatic position. At the other pole of thought, we find *Radical Individualism* ready to welcome us. After striving to conform, to admire the Highest, to enjoy the Best, reproving ourselves for every irrepressible nod or yawn, always fearful lest we be missing just the right thing, and the right shade of the right meaning,—what a pleasure it is to relax, and be frankly, openly, cynically *ourselves!* In homely parlance: "I know what I like when I like it." I am I: why should I be ashamed? I can not add a cubit to my stature, nor think the thoughts of Gertrude Stein. Is this giving up the good fight? No: there is virtue in our apparent capitulation. No literary appreciation can be valid unless it be genuine. We may nod our heads wisely before a "master-piece", and be fooled, like the courtiers in Andersen's Fairy Tale, who went into ecstasies over the King's invisible cloak. If we happen to like *The Shepherd of the Hills* and not *The Faerie Queene,* we should stand heroically, like Luther: "So help me God, I can not otherwise!" Taste is the artistic conscience, and conscience will brook no dictation.

It is difficult to escape from Individualism. It attracts us because it is candid, not because it is easy. Try it for yourself for twenty-four hours: it is the most difficult thing in the world. You will constantly catch yourself using stock judgments, conventional phrases, shibboleths. Do I really like Shakespeare? How can I tell? My conscious mind is a mass of preconceived ideas. I heard his name uttered with bated breath before I could read him; I was taught to admire before I could understand. Is it possible to enjoy any high literature without a corresponding education? Even a virgin mind would have to know Shakespeare's language, and could not understand his English without some familiarity with the civilization he represents. I am blissfully free from bias concerning the Chinese drama: but, as a consequence, an untranslated Chinese play means nothing to me; a translated one, not much more. And what is an education,—culture in Matthew Arnold's sense, the knowledge of the best that has been thought and said—but the transmission of the "right" prejudices?

So we are led to doubt whether *radical individualism* is even a possibility. Every man must follow his own taste in art, his own conscience in moral life. But taste and conscience are never purely his own. They are fashioned by environment, of which education is a part. One man's conscience will tell him that it is wicked to eat steak on Friday. "Superstition!" exclaims his neighbor, whose conscience will tell him it is wrong to doubt the story of Jonah. Taste and conscience are historical and social products.

This is particularly true of literature. With a generous imagination, you may conceive that every human being, under the same circumstances, will be prompted aright by his conscience; you might even admit that every one will respond to the same perfect piece of statuary. But in literature we encounter the boundaries of language, and within these, the further limitation of *availability*. I may have an inborn taste for our mythical Kegelbahn: but, if I never come across his works or even his name, my potential admiration will remain decidedly abstract and tenuous. My taste can exercise itself only within the range of my experience. The books that are not published, not advertised, not recommended by critics, not talked about, not offered in bookstalls, not found on library shelves, do not exist for me. A universal conspiracy forces Shakespeare upon me and withholds Kegelbahn. But for that, I am—partly—free.

Absolute Individualism can not therefore be severed from the social element. What *you* like is an individual choice within a social choice. What is liked by one isolated man, and by that man only, does not take its place in literature. Every poet is great in his own conceit; and at the time of writing at any rate, he feels that what he has to say had never been said before, or never so well.

Self-satisfaction is no sufficient warrant of excellence. A poem is only a candidate to literature: literary rank is conferred from without.

Poets, no doubt, will demur. Yet the history of literature is written in no other terms—including that contemporary history which is called criticism. If Chaucer, Spenser, Milton; if Ezra Pound, Hart Crane, E. E. Cummings exist at all, it is not on their own recognizances, but on the basis of public recognition. By whom? Obviously not by the mob exclusively; still less by the clique exclusively. Neither the best-seller nor the esoteric enigma can be assured of a place in literature. Recognition means the suffrage of a fairly extensive intelligent class.

How large must that class be? That depends upon the period, and the kind of writing. Tolstoy, alone among genuine artists, wanted to include the masses; Stendhal dedicated his work (a master stroke of salesmanship!) *To the Happy Few*. Poetry can do with a very small public; the novel must be of wider appeal; the curse of the talkie is that it must please the million, or fail utterly.

In all cases, the applause of a public, large or small, will not create literary standing, unless the effect be prolonged. Six months hence, the nine-day wonder will not even be a curiosity; and the *cognoscenti* are notoriously more fickle than the crowd. Literature exists *in time,* and the test of time is the most reliable of all. Trifles may endure through the centuries, like the frail flowers of the Greek *Anthology*. Massive epics may crumble, like Bailey's *Festus*. Are the Laureates of the eighteenth century *literature?* No: for they have not survived, except for a scholar like Kemper Broadus. Is Alexander Dumas *literature?* Before you say no, consider that a third and a fourth generation of readers young and old are devouring his romantic tales. Is *Abie's Irish Rose literature?* I am inclined to think, with Professor Baker, that "such popularity must be deserved": but let us wait a while before committing ourselves. Molière's extravaganza, *The Tricks of Scapin,* was frowned upon by Boileau, as unworthy: but it is alive. There is horseplay in *The Taming of the Shrew* and *The Merry Wives of Windsor;* there is a situation both hackneyed and improbable in *The Comedy of Errors;* there is rank melodrama in *Œdipus Tyrannus.* Are they *literature?* Certainly, since they live as literature.

"Time will tell": aye, but will it tell the truth? Few works last long if there is no life in them: but how many potential masterpieces are nipped by unkindly fate?

What we have been discussing is a frankly *pragmatic* conception of literature: literature as the history of reputations. It is hard to put that conception into definite words. "Literature is that which is recognized as such by a sufficient number of people over a sufficient period of time": vagueness in such a case is the beginning of wisdom. I know that such pragmatism is not idealistic: but is there any study of literature that is not based upon it? Every standard textbook includes the names of men whose theories you do not share, whose work you do not enjoy, and yet whom you can not ignore. Why? They had, or still have, a following: *they count.*

Many great ideas, which once were stated in clear-cut terms, require now more elastic definitions. What is

"Religion"? What is "the State"? Do I envy those who can answer with a brief formula, or do I pity them?

Between the pragmatic conception and the individual-istic, there is no conflict. Collective opinion is the sum total of private opinions; private opinions are limited and guided by collective factors. Literature is a Club: it has a corporate existence, yet it exists only through its members and for their sakes. You join the group because you find it congenial; but you are ready to sacrifice some of your minor idiosyncrasies. Even if you do not strive to conform, you are unconsciously modeled by your chosen environment; you grow more perfect in the group psychology, which was, to start with, in harmony with your own. Within the group, you have a certain leeway. Once you are fully accepted, you would have to grow frankly obnoxious before you were kicked out. You may influence, perceptibly, the thought of your fellow members. I joined the Homer-Dante-Shakespeare Club because the members I knew, my elders, my teachers, my betters, seemed to me desirable associates. I am free to resign at any time: but I am comfortable in the Club— a trifle lazy perhaps, and maybe a little snobbish. This is the best club in our civilization, so why should I give it up? But do not ask me for the "principles" of the Club: I hold them as Mr. Branch Cabell holds the Thirty Nine Articles of his Church, with my eyes closed. All I know is that it is an association of fine fellows, "ripe and mellow scholars" and thorough gentlemen; and I am proud to belong.

The comparison with the Church may be carried fur-ther. For most people, the Church is first of all a congenial Club with a spiritual tinge. As a rule, you do not join the Presbyterian Church because you believe in Presbyterianism: you believe in Presbyterianism because you are a member of the Presbyterian Church. And what is true of the traditional Churches is truer still of the historical parties. But although principles or beliefs are indeed quite secondary, like the colors of a flag, they will be defended with the utmost vigor, even though they may be utterly beyond the grasp of the average member.

In the same way, the Literary Club secretes, as it were, its own orthodoxy. There *must* be a right and a wrong in literature, since there are right and wrong people; and it happens that we are on the right side. The result is a pseudo-dogmatism, a semi-rationalization of our intellectual habits. The supremacy of Shakespeare is obvious in our eyes; we are sane people; therefore all sane people must admit Shakespeare's supremacy. And you have a definite tenet which, if challenged, will be upheld at all cost. This tendency is hard to resist. I remember telling a group of students: *"No man in his senses* would maintain that Art has progressed since the Greeks." As I had been warning them earnestly against all sweeping assertions, they broke into a unanimous smile. I had to correct myself: *"No man in my senses . . ."*

Eternal Verities; spontaneous personal opinions; the custom of the tribe: it is more hopeless to draw boundaries between them than to trace a sensible frontier between Poland and Germany. Impressionism is the basic fact: "I feel, therefore I am." What I do not feel does not count for me. But my impressions have a tendency to

organize themselves into a code. What are these abstract ideas? Are they illusions, myths, symbols, or ultimate realities? I know not: at any rate, they are fascinating building blocks for the maturer minds. Radical
individualism, dogmatism, may have their sphere of validity. Certain it is that all the literature we can talk
about and write about is a social product: the selection
and manifestation of a group and of an age, an integral
part of our civilization.

III

Etymology, at times a capricious guide, but sensible
enough in this case, tells us that *literature* means *writing*
(Letters). To be sure, there may be unwritten literature
and unliterary writing: but let that pass. Writing remains the standard method of recording, more retentive
than memory, and, even to-day, more convenient than
the gramophone. When we speak of the "literature" of
a subject, we mean everything written about that subject; and I am deluged with "literature" about tooth-
paste, hosiery, automobiles, free silver and the Shakespeare folios.

Needless to say that this all-embracing acception is
of little interest to the *literary* student. Yet, even for him,
it is not quite negligible. For one thing, scholarship,
his goddess, tends to efface the line between writing that
is an art, and writing in general. The classical archeolo-
gist, the medieval philologist, will pounce eagerly upon
any text that pertains to their period, even though, in
subject or form, it has not the slightest claim to literary
interest. Nay, they will rather scorn "literary interest"

as amateurish and almost frivolous. Our practical, but wholly artificial division of knowledge into *Departments* should not blur the fact that linguistics and some aspects of literary history are historical sciences, and not æsthetic studies at all.

In another respect, the all-inclusive definition of literature is of greater importance. It is a commonplace of criticism that "literature is the mirror of civilization"; and, because it is such a commonplace, we shall not let it pass unchallenged. We expect to show that *artistic* literature is a dangerously distorting mirror: the Coolidgian régime of Louis-Philippe, in France, found its expression in the wildest romanticism. If you want a truer reflection of life, you will have to include the second- and third-raters, and, beyond them, those writers who have no literary standing at all. A critic like Sainte-Beuve, because he was an observer of life,—a passionately cool observer—devoted many of his *Causeries* to people who did not in the least count *as literature*.

If we want to extract from that loose mass of mere writing that which is properly literature, we shall find one delicate criterion after another breaking in our hands. There is no form, there is no theme, there is no mood and no intention that will inevitably stamp a piece of writing as sterling literature. Watch a lake by moonlight: you are persuaded that the long silver ray on the water has an objective existence. Yet the whole lake is illumined, and the shaft of light that reaches to your feet is a delusion. More precisely: it is not the light that is a delusion, but the darkness beyond. All writing is potential literature: the narrow gleaming ribbon moves with the observer.

Our conscious selves are conditioned by the subconscious and the unconscious; and, between the three stages, there are no impassable barriers. A distinct thought, an act of will, may after a time sink below the threshold; an obscure tendency may work its way up to the light. Similarly, the *literature* that emerges as such is not radically different from the *sub-literature* and the *un-literature* which lurk, amorphous, beneath.

Instead of *literature* and *sub-literature,* I have frequently used the terms proposed by Professor Richard G. Moulton: *fixed* and *floating.* Words which have not attained undisputed currency are apt to be misleading: when I asked for an example of *floating* literature, I was answered: "The novels of Joseph Conrad." Again I wish we had at our service more perspicuous expressions; but, in attempting to discriminate between them, we may clear up our own thought.

By *fixed* literature, I mean that kind which is inseparable from a definite authorship and a definite text. An anonymous work may belong to fixed literature: whoever "Junius" may be, we are conscious that there was a man who penned those *Letters.* A corrupt or chaotic text is a text all the same: it is hard for editors to agree on the presentation of Pascal's *Thoughts;* still every page bears Pascal's imperious mark.

If, on the contrary, the actual author and the literal text are matters of indifference, then we have *floating* literature. The first example that will come to mind is that of folklore. We—rather loosely—admit that those popular traditions came to life and grew by a process of spontaneous generation; and although the theme may be definite enough, the details and the wording may vary *ad libitum*. Take a modern form of folklore, the jokes that fill the best page of *The Literary Digest*. Here is a well-known sample: a man was falling from the twentieth story, and, as he passed the tenth, he was asked: "How goes it?"—"All right so far," was the cheerful reply. Now this profound parable was used by Prosper Mérimée, who took it from Voltaire, who had it from Fontenelle. But it does not matter in the least who said it first: our own guess is that it goes back to that ill-fated skyscraper, the Tower of Babel. It matters even less whether the building had six stories or sixty, whether the victim was an Irishman or a Negro, whether he shouted back: "All right so far" or "So far so good." (Under somewhat similar circumstances, Madame Laetitia, Napoleon's mother, used the words: *"Pourvu que cela dure!"*) It is *floating* literature.

Fixed and floating do not correspond to written and unwritten. Not a few Homeric scholars believe that the *Iliad* was fixed before it was put down in writing; and publication in *The Literary Digest* does not moor a "floating" story to an immovable quay wall. The difference is not the same as that between *permanent* and *ephemeral*. Every day sees an enormous batch of new books that are "fixed" enough according to our definition, but will be forgotten to-morrow, while folklore motives are the most enduring element in literature: Aurelio Macedonio Espinosa has traced *The Tar Baby* almost to the Earthly Paradise. Still less does the distinction imply *good* or *bad*. Atrocious foolishness has found its way into print, with the author's name proudly flaunted on the title page, while the homely wisdom and mother-wit of the ages, as well as many tender or tragic stories, may remain "floating" for ever.

We may think that our civilization is too grown-up for folklore. Nothing of the kind. The mind of modern man has not been struck with barrenness. Stories still originate, in smoking compartment, pool room or board meeting, which, if they were found among the Zyrians and the Trobrianders, would be fit subjects for Doctoral Dissertations. Jokes, anecdotes, situations, types, are teeming as much as ever: Senator Sorghum, Farmer Corntossel, Moronia the Office Flapper, Pat and Abie, are authentic products of the popular imagination, no less than the Werewolf, the Ogre, Tom Thumb and Reynard the Fox. Some students of literature and some alert editors are at last making the tremendous discovery that American folks are not wholly dumb. There is in this country a *vox populi* which might be heard, if the professionals did not attempt to drown it. If we followed that line of thought with any consistency, the future of literature would be in the hands of the illiterate.

Language, the warp and woof of literature, affords striking instances of folk creation. Language, and particularly the American language, is constantly renewed through the quaint figures of speech which go by the name of slang. For one picturesque expression deliberately coined by a licensed wisecracker and duly credited to him, there are a hundred that sprang mysteriously from the myriad lips of Demos. No one is accountable for "the cat's meow" and such felicities of speech.

It "springs to the eyes" that floating literature is the store from which fixed literature is constantly drawing. Racine's harmonious lines were written in an idiom derived, however remotely, from the slang of soldiers and traders. Molière confessedly borrowed right and left, not exclusively from the known writers of Greece, ancient Rome, Italy and Spain, but from the inexhaustible fund of Gallic tradition. The most profound of philosophical dramas, *Faust,* was once a puppet show. The rarest flowers of art need a rich popular humus.

With this idea we are in full sympathy: leave literature to the professionals, and it will soon die in their hands, as Latin died when the Humanists vowed to restore Vergilian purity. But it can easily be carried to an absurd extreme. In the eighteenth century, as a reaction against an excessively sophisticated culture, there began a romantic extolling of the primitive, the barbaric, *i.e.* the subconscious and unconscious in literature. Vico, that lonely forerunner, then Herder and all the pioneers of Romanticism, were eagerly listening for "folk's voices." The readers of *Ossian* were enraptured by the "primitiveness" of those poems: the name Macpherson seems linked by fate with sensational hoaxes. In the same line of thought came the theories dissolving Homer into a loose heap of folk tradition. The definite medieval epic, of which the *Song of Roland* is the type, *must* have been preceded by a rich ballad literature, a French *Romancero* of which no trace is to be found. For many scholars, it was a heresy that anything should ever have originated with one definite author: the subconsc·ous held undisputed sway.

Now the wheel has turned again. We are no longer so certain about the poetic power of the collective mind. We believe that the relations between fixed and floating literature are not so one-sided. If conscious individual works constantly arise out of the indeterminate mass, that mass is no less constantly renewed by individual works as they lose their "fixity." The whole process is not a steady ascent, but a *circulus*.

The "just growed" theory is a lazy explanation. It does not stand to reason; neither is it confirmed by experience. It is far more likely that everything that survives in folklore—theme, character, name or phrase—had a beginning, definite although forgotten. Some one invented the Tar Baby; some one was actually the first to mention Paul Bunyan; some one started the joke about the Ford that went to heaven on high. Those creations may have been altered in transmission, contaminated by other creations of the same kind: but they were creations all the same.

We have seen popular slang rising into formal literature: conversely, formal literature unceasingly enriches the vernacular. We use the word *to pander* without remembering the story of *Troilus and Cressida*. We say: *to curry favor,* unconscious that *favor* is really *Favel* or *Fauvel,* the roan horse symbolical of human vanity in a medieval poem. *Renard,* the hero of the satirical folk epic, has entirely displaced the old French word for fox (*goupil*). When we say *quixotic,* we need not be thinking of Cervantes. French working men will refer

25

to a particularly noxious kind of hypocrite as a *tartuffe,* even though they have not read Molière's masterpiece. I was surprised recently to find that many young people, using the word a *babbitt* very freely, did not know Sinclair Lewis.

In the walls of peasants' huts, near Roman ruins, you will find imbedded some half-effaced inscription, some barely recognizable fragment of a classic figure: in like fashion is common speech strewn with blurred and broken literary allusions.

This leads us to wonder whether popular traditions really did spring from the untutored masses, or whether they represent the dim and degraded memories of a vanished formal art. We know that the courtly romances of the later Middle Ages lost caste, and finally reached the villages in debased form: had the process gone a little farther, we might easily have lost sight of their sophisticated origins, and considered *The Four Sons of Aymon* or *Fierabras* as authentic folk tales. There are traces of a Roland Tradition throughout Europe: but, says Professor Hugh Smith, the *Song of Roland* was not the elaboration of preëxisting legends: it was a conscious piece of work, a new departure; it started the vogue for Carolingian epics; and ultimately the story, in vague outline, reached the people.

The *circulus* goes on under our very eyes. Goethe took the Faust motive from floating literature, and turned it, for all time, into one of the major works of fixed literature. For all time? Yes, so far as scholars are concerned. For the average man, Faust is floating again. Almost everybody knows the name, and remembers Gretchen

26

and Mephistopheles: but very little more. The memories evoked by the title *Faust* seldom go deeper than Gounod's opera or Emil Jannings's picture. We have already seen how *Babbitt* has gone floating. Scholars in distant ages will dispute: (a) whether Babbitt was an historical character or a solar myth; (b) whether there was an actual book (an *Ur-Babbitt*) by that name; (c) whether our present text was a late version of the popular Babbitt Saga or Cycle; (d) what on earth it had to do with the mysterious cult known as Humanism.

The problem, it will readily be seen, is a delicate one. Even at present, we are deeply influenced, in history and literature, by the romantic craze for the primitive. The Romanticists loved the past so dearly that they manufactured it to satisfy their desire. Just as they built faked ruins in their gardens, they made up faked "popular traditions" in poetry. In the *Lorelei,* Heine can not drive out of his mind "a legend from most ancient time": but the legend was of recent fabrication, like some of the horrific instruments of torture in the Nürnberg Museum.

A curious aspect of the question is offered by the Napoleonic Legend. It is taken for granted that the Emperor's saga arose from the very hearts of the people; much later, conscious poets, such as Victor Hugo, would take hold of that epic material and shape it into formal narratives. A song of Béranger, *The Memories of the People,* a chapter in Balzac, *The Story of Napoleon told in a Barn,* are accepted as honest transcriptions of Napoleonic folklore. On closer inspection, the evidence dissolves. We know for certain that Napoleon was far from popular during the last years of his reign and immediately after his fall. His *Legend* was started after his death, deliberately; it became one of the great Romantic myths, like Prometheus, Don Juan, Faust, Ahasverus. Neither Béranger nor Balzac was a peasant, nor in close touch with the peasantry. In his *Memories of the People,* Béranger does not even claim to represent actual facts: his song is a prophecy: *"Fifty years hence, they will be talking of his glory . . ."* From 1825 to 1840, Napoleonism was in vogue among the *bourgeoisie* and with some of the Romanticists, for political or æsthetic reasons. King Louis-Philippe himself found it shrewd policy to foster it; the common people came to it but slowly. No doubt, by 1848, when the Emperor's nephew was triumphantly elected President of the Republic, Napoleonism had at last reached the masses: but it did not originate with the masses. Victor Hugo, Béranger, Thiers, Balzac, were the tutors, not the mouthpieces, of the nation. "Artless" memoirs like those of the *grognard* Captain Coignet, were written long after the events, and only because Napoleon-worship had become the fashion. It is interesting to note that those writers who sprang directly from the people, like Michelet and Veuillot, and not from the *bourgeoisie,* were definitely anti-Napoleonic.

We may apply the distinction between *fixed* and *floating* even to evangelical literature. Stories about the Lord, reports of His sayings (*logia*), were at first transmitted orally, without any thought of definite authorship. The gospel "according to" Matthew or Mark, meant a certain line of tradition, not an invariable text. Luke, a conscious author, tells us how he organized these floating elements into a definite whole. John, a supreme poet and philosopher, scorned the task of mere compilation, and gave us a Gospel that bears the marks of his genius. There were many other narratives "afloat": some based on vague hearsay, some tinged with imagination, or slightly twisted so as to serve some particular doctrine, some deliberate although pious frauds. In this mass of edifying literature, the Church operated a selection. Four versions alone were recognized as canonical, and not one jot or tittle of their text could be altered. In theory, no work could be more "fixed" than the Gospel: in fact, the sacred story has returned to the people, has become "floating" again. Only prize pupils in Sunday schools know their gospel narratives in proper sequence, and could give chapter and verse for every quotation. For most of us, it must be confessed that the outlines are blurred and the wording far from certain, as in the case of folklore.

Not only does a theme thus pass from fixed to floating, from floating to fixed, and back again: but, at any moment, it may be fixed or floating according to the experience of the individual reader. *Faust* is not the same to the Goethean scholar and to the man in the street. The Gospel is not the same to the orthodox minister and to the vaguely deistic humanitarian.

Literature may be likened to a saturated solution into which water and chemicals are constantly poured. Crystals are formed, and dissolve again. The crystals are different from the solution in which they are immersed; yet, in essence, they are not different. Thus do masterpieces concentrate the soul of a people, and merge into that soul again.

This opens up a problem which we can only state in naked terms for the present. In former ages, when a literary work was a rare and difficult achievement, when it was polished for many years, transcribed at great expense on the most durable material, accessible only to a few, in constant danger of annihilation, and for all those reasons preserved jealously in the treasure house of mankind, *fixity* in all senses of the word was the ideal. Today, floating literature has innumerable channels of expression: not merely the pulpit, the forum, the gossip of the market place, private correspondence, but the cheap ephemeral book, the magazine, the newspaper, the talkie, the radio. Under these unprecedented circumstances, is fixity possible, is it even desirable? The individual time-defying masterpiece might well be a thing of the past; would its disappearance entail an irremediable loss?

Be this as it may: literature is never a foreign substance erratically imbedded in the body of a civilization: it is part of the general life, it is a function of the general organism. The indifference of the "practical man" to æsthetic values—whether frankly contemptuous or under a veil of frigid reverence — is a needless self-inflicted mutilation. But the aloofness of the mere bookman—author, critic, scholar—in his Ivory Tower is even more deadly to the soul.

Chapter 2

RACE

I

The criticism which is mere fault-finding went into the discard with our last literary code. The criticism which consists in exclaiming over "beauties" is voted amiably vapid. Impressionism pure and simple has never achieved authority: "Who are you," says the ungentle reader, "that I should bother about your impressions? Have I not impressions of my own?" So, driven from their ancient judgment seats, the critics must find refuge in the temple of the latest idol, Science. They will no longer attempt to condemn or to praise, but only to understand. And, in that vast temple, they seek the very latest altar: young goddesses are most eager to perform miracles, or, in homely parlance, new brooms sweep clean. Hence the favor enjoyed by the New, the Newer, the Newest Criticism, the Sociological kind. A touch of Muscovite red imparts a rich glow to what might easily be a dismal study. And we are offered "the Materialistic Interpretation of Literature" according to the doctrine of Karl Marx.

Perhaps the broom is not quite so new as the sweepers

believe. As early as 1800, the intimate connection between civilization and literature was clearly seen by that formidable blue-stocking Madame de Staël: the very title of her book, *On Literature considered in its Relations with Social Institutions,* is illuminating. It was she, in particular, who sought to establish that "the North" was essentially Romantic and Protestant, while "the South" was Classical and Catholic: one of those dazzling half-truths far more dangerous than palpable errors. Herder had already expounded similar conceptions, with a wealth of undigested information and a fine frenzy of Idealism. Voltaire himself, in his *Century of Louis XIV,* had given an all-embracing survey of a society, in which literature took its natural place. So Messrs. V. F. Calverton and Granville Hicks can boast of a distinguished ancestry.

It was Taine, however, who, with the abstract logic he professed to despise, hardened a tendency of modern thought into a doctrine, and expressed the doctrine in masterful formulæ. Ever since his *Introduction to the History of English Literature* (1863), the magic words *Race, Environment and Time* have been piously repeated. The latest works of the Sociological Critics do not go far beyond the impressive theories of Taine.

The whole *History of English Literature* was written as a demonstration of the principles promulgated in the *Introduction,* and the whole work might close with Q. E.D. It belongs exactly to the same generation as Karl Marx's *Capital,* and, like *Capital,* it shows unmistakable signs of age. Even in its prime, it never was fully reliable; and few pieces of scholarship retain their authority after threescore and ten. As a demonstration, the *Literary History of the English People,* by the late Ambassador J. J. Jusserand, is far more convincing. Taine's continued appeal is due solely to his vigorous talent: but, as a writer no less than as a scholar, he *dates,* fully as much as his contemporary Matthew Arnold, vastly more than Sainte-Beuve, Renan or Walter Pater. Much of his imperious logic is forced; much of his brilliancy strikes us as glitter. Let us not forget that he was writing under the Second Empire, whose masterpiece was Garnier's gaudy Opera, and that he, the ascetic scholar, collaborated to *La Vie Parisienne.*

Most antiquated of all is the "positivism" of Taine, his naïve worship of facts, facts, facts. It is antiquated because it did not represent the man himself: it was the *Zeitgeist* of Scientific Realism speaking through a sensitive, tormented soul. His phrase: "Vice and virtue are products like vitriol and sugar," is often quoted as an example of crass materialism. Determinism, yes; materialism, no. Taine does not even suggest that vice and virtue are *chemicals;* he only asserts that they are *products,* and this no conservative moralist will deny. If we insist upon the importance of education, a wholesome atmosphere, the avoidance of dangerous associations, it is because we believe, with Taine, that the law of cause and effect is valid even on the ethical plane. On the whole, however, the general impression is not wrong: Taine was committed to the materialistic interpretation of history, including, as a by-product, the history of literature.

We were taught our letters by faithful disciples of Taine. We rebelled against him, because he had been captured by the reactionaries. But these word-battles of the past century are now one with Nineveh and Tyre. Taine is just receding beyond the awkward stage when a writer no longer possesses the liveliness of a contemporary, and has not quite attained the dignity of a classic. We may now come to grips with his thought without awe and without animosity.

His Race, Environment and Time still afford, we believe, a convenient classification. Every one of the three terms is ambiguous, and, in our own study of French Civilization, we adopted in preference the words People, Habitat, Tradition, which seemed to us, at the time, not so cynically question-begging. We must repeat that all such words have no dogmatic value. We shall use them only as points of departure: their full meaning, and the indispensable corrections or qualifications, will appear as the result of the discussion itself.

II

The notion of *Race,* applied to literature, does not belong exclusively to Taine and his followers: it is ubiquitous, and correspondingly loose. Guarded as you may swear to be, you will catch yourself asserting that Yeats's dreaminess, for instance, or Anatole France's clarity, or d'Annunzio's sensuousness, are "racial" traits; and, in so doing, you will be in excellent company, including, among our contemporaries, Mesdames Edith Wharton and Gertrude Atherton. The present writer has been waging his thirty years' war agains the race phantom. This, in itself, is sufficient evidence of his "Latin" blood: no "Anglo-Saxon" would worry so long about a theory.

Taine himself defines Race as "those innate and hereditary dispositions which man brings with him at his
birth, and which, as a rule, are linked with marked differences in temperament and bodily structure. They vary
with the peoples. Nature offers varieties of men as well
as of bulls and horses, some brave and intelligent, others
timid and dull. . . ."

A race, therefore, is an example of collective heredity,
a strain, a breed, a large family. The qualities it implies
are "in the blood": training can work only within the
limits of hereditary capacities. Treat a dray horse as
though he were a race horse, you will not turn him into
a race horse.

Taine does not assert that races are immutable: but
he maintains that, if they change at all, it is with infinite slowness. The "primordial characteristics" of a race
are the results of "perhaps myriads of centuries." Against
such a vast accumulation of forces, the influence of a lifetime is insignificant; even the influence of historical ages
—a paltry half dozen of millennia—is barely perceptible.
For all practical purposes, the race may be considered
as an absolutely fixed element. In other terms, acquired
characteristics, including those due to environment, are
either not transmitted at all, or are transmitted to an infinitesimal degree. All this is orthodox enough, although
Lamarck is raising his head again, and although there
is a breed of rats at Stanford University striving hard
to establish the transmissibility of acquired characteristics.

Race implies again, although Taine does not say so,
that only certain combinations are biologically possible.

In many cases, miscegenation means immediate barrenness; in others, the new breed is neither stable nor, *a fortiori*, permanent. Hybrids die out, or revert to the original *true* types. If it were not so, there would be no *races* in the strict sense of the term. Every chance union between different breeds might start a new variety, and the essential notions of distinctness and permanence would be lost. We confess that, however true this may be in the simple world of Mendel's sweet peas, we do not know to what extent it holds good in the case of human varieties.

Another implication is that members of the same group are fundamentally more alike than members of two different groups could possibly be. Here again, we are not fully convinced. Even in the physical sense, we have seen the boundaries between groups waver and practically disappear. We have known white Mediterraneans with dark skins and curly hair, who seemed a great deal closer to the Negro than to the Scandinavian; and other "white" men, in Auvergne, who were curiously akin to some Mongolians and some Red Indians.

Finally—and now we transcend Mendel's realm to pass into the more shadowy world of Gobineau, Chamberlain and Madison Grant—Taine admits that "as a rule", certain physical traits imply corresponding intellectual, moral and spiritual traits. There is a kind of science, of poetry, of virtue, of religion, that goes with a flat nose, and another kind that belongs to aquiline features. We shall see how eagerly Mrs. Atherton swallowed that theory: we may be forgiven if we withhold our assent yet awhile.

So far, we have defined race in the abstract, and contented ourselves with the assertion that there are races among men. If we are challenged to enumerate these races, and to discriminate between them, we shall get ourselves into a very pretty tangle. All the more so because, in literature, the classic and undeniable distinction according to the color of the skin is of little avail. Our field, even though in our conceit we call it *world* literature, is almost exclusively *white* literature. The contribution of the red man is negligible; that of the negro is secondary; and the vast production of the Mongolian is barely beginning to influence ours. The "races" of Taine must be subdivisions of the Indo-European.

Taine evades the difficulty neatly by not defining concrete races at all. In the course of his five volumes, he frequently refers to "the English race" or to "the Anglo-Saxon race." Therein lies a fallacy which is as obvious as it is indestructible.

For, as a rule, when we say *race,* we mean *language group*. We speak of the Latin, the Germanic, the Slavic *races,* while the corresponding realities are the Latin, Germanic, Slavic linguistic families. These terms do not refer to biological kinship: only to affinities in speech. A dusky sergeant, at the time when things were looking gloomy for the Allies, boasted: "Wait till we Anglo-Saxons get into this fight!" He was thoroughly justified. An English-speaking Negro is an Anglo-Saxon in the same sense as Mr. Lloyd George the Welshman. A Zapoteca like Porfirio Diaz becomes a "Latin" just like the Breton, Fleming or Basque who happens to speak French, and like the Bessarabian Jew who has adopted Rumanian. Of two brothers in Upper Silesia, one may turn into a Teuton, the other into a Slav.

We have no desire to minimize the influence of language on thought and literature. In spite of such a miraculous exception as Switzerland, language groups are far more potent realities than are political units. Language is the only true frontier: the one that can not be altered by a stroke of the pen, nor ignored by aëroplane and radio, the one also that levies the heaviest toll on foreign goods. Community of language means even more than ease of communication: it implies a common background of education, common patterns of thought, a common cultural heritage. But, essential as it may be, language is not race; indeed it may have very little to do with race.

France is a "Latin" country: very few genuine Romans settled in Gaul. The soldiers were recruited from all parts of the Empire, and not from Latium alone; the auxiliaries were Barbarians; the traders were mostly Greeks. It was in speech and culture only that the country was "Latinized." Language is most decidedly an acquired characteristic. In this respect, at any rate, we know that our melting pot does melt: the children of immigrants speak the vernacular as purely as Ring Lardner himself. Between 1918 and 1931, the number of French-speaking Alsatians increased threefold; and, in a single generation, our guardianship of the Filipinos has turned a million Malays from "Latins" to "Anglo-Saxons."

We shall have to allude more than once to the Celtic imbroglio. There are definite Celtic languages, all in danger of being shoved over, like Cornish, into the Western sea. A "Celt", small and dark, burly and reddish, melancholy or joyous, is presumably the descendant of people who once spoke a Celtic dialect. But a Protestant from Yorkshire like G. B. Shaw, with very few words of Gaelic at his command, is not seldom referred to as a Celt.

I have often heard, with mild exasperation, that "the French" were congenitally incapable of this or that— fault or virtue, it does not matter. Here, *race* is identified with *nation,* not with language: there are few nations that coincide with a language area. We, for instance, are only a part of the English-speaking world; French spills over several of the political frontiers of France, while Flemings, Alsatians, Bretons, Basques, Catalans, Corsicans, are Frenchmen whose home language is not French.

I am far from denying the existence of national types. You can usually tell a Frenchman from an Englishman, even though both should happen to be tall and blond. To be sure, "Frenchiness" and "Britishness" are to some extent sartorial and tonsorial affairs. A close shave, a Hart, Schaffner and Marx suit, a pair of Harold Lloyd spectacles, will turn Monsieur Gaston Durand into a very acceptable George F. Babbitt. But, even *in naturalibus* or under the same uniform, the difference would persist. Intonation, gestures, glances and smiles, are indelible labels. And to these superficial idiosyncrasies correspond elusive yet unmistakable twists of thought and qualities of feeling. It has been the curse of international life ever since the Great War that France and America, both with the most excellent intentions, could not be brought to think and feel alike.

But again, however potent a force nationality may be, it is not "in the blood", it is not *race*. France and America have marked psychological traits, and act as units, more so perhaps than any other nation: yet neither is a race. There are quite a few prominent Jews and Irishmen, Slavs and Latins, in this country who consider themselves *bona fide* American citizens. France likewise is a melting pot which, at work for twenty centuries at least, has not stopped operations. On the roll of French worthies, we may pick out at random such names as Bonaparte, Brazza, Zola, Gambetta, Galliéni, Antonetti, Giovanninelli; as Kleber, Kellermann, Scherer, Schrader, Zurlinden, Siegfried, Hirschauer; as Clarke, Macdonald, Mac-Mahon, Hennessy, Thompson, Archdeacon, Viele Griffin, Stuart Merrill; as Zyromski, Strowski, José-Maria de Heredia, Zamacois, Psichari and Papadiamantopoulos.

A small isolated country may, in the course of centuries, become literally one great family: it is pretty certain that all Corsicans are cousins. In a much vaguer fashion, this holds true even of England. David Starr Jordan found amusement in the thought that he and a surprising number of noted Americans were all the descendants of Isabelle de Vermandois, who, in her turn, claimed Charlemagne as her ancestor. But, even in the tight little island, the blood relationship between Lady Clara Vere de Vere and Sarah Gamp requires no small amount of faith.

Curiously enough, the most nationalistic element in

all countries is the aristocracy, which is also the most cosmopolitan. A patriotic French Count will marry his daughter to a man with an Austrian or an Italian title, rather than to a plain French *poilu*. The royal "race" of France, symbol of the country's unity, is a hodgepodge of Spanish, Italian, Austrian and German ingredients.

Nationality is not race: it can be acquired. Not through a mere formal document, a treaty or naturalization papers: but through consent, education, environment. Yes, you can tell a Frenchman from an American. But you can likewise tell a French Negro from an American Negro: both bear, beyond cavil, the stamp of their nationality. America and France are usually conceded greater powers of assimilation than most other countries. I have seen on the Boul' Mich' Chinese students who were almost ludicrously French.

The national type is a fact: but it is far more superficial than we are frequently asked to believe. There is more reality in the provinces or sections than in the country as a whole: if an Irishman is not an Englishman, neither is a Catalan a Spaniard, neither is a Breton a Frenchman. Even the *local* type, although more definite, is not the average, but the exception, the extreme, the caricature. We are all aware that the stage Southern Colonel as well as the stage Minnesota Swede have little validity except on the boards. A Frenchman of fair size, who wears no goatee, is not voluble, does not gesticulate, does not kiss ladies' hands, is satisfied with one slice of bread, and is not decorated with the Legion of Honor, is not a *typical* Frenchman at all: only there are millions upon millions like him.

The national type, however real, is less real than the *period* type. Look at old photographs: you can tell at a glance whether they belong to the nineties or the sixties, but closer attention will be needed before you can locate the originals in Scotland, Germany or Pennsylvania. A family portrait strikes you first of all as eighteenth century, before it strikes you as French or English. This is not merely a matter of costume, but also of attitude, expression and even physical traits. There were moments when, throughout Europe, it was fashionable for ladies to have opulent charms; moments (happy moments!) when every one wore the keen and courtly smile so well caught by La Tour; moments when our most solid great-grandmothers were languishing, and our most stodgy great-granduncles looked inspired. The period is a self-determined country of the soul more real than any political area. Fashion is thicker than blood.

We may add that, at least in the old countries, the professional or social type also is more deeply imprinted than the national. Priests, soldiers, business men, professors, mechanics, peasants, sailors, come to look the part of their occupation, even during off-hours. There are therefore many resemblances which imply no blood relationship: they are the result of environment and tradition, not of race.*

Is there a safer criterion of race than either language or nationality? Could it not be found in the "marked differences in bodily structure" mentioned by Taine?

---

*The study of Nationalism and Literature will therefore be reserved for later chapters on Environment and Tradition.

These, at any rate, are plainly hereditary. To be sure, Taine was satisfied with a very general hint: anthropology was still in swaddling clothes at the time. In the last seventy years, these differences have been investigated, measured, classified; and we feel that we are on scientific ground at last.

Anthropology has exercised such a fascination on the literary mind that it might almost be called a branch of literature. The "Nordic Myth", a vague heritage of Romanticism, has been hardened into pseudo-scientific consistency by men of whom Count de Gobineau is the archetype. Diplomat, *littérateur,* philosopher, Orientalist, Gobineau was a near-genius in every line, and has achieved a kind of twilight celebrity in every country but his native France. To the same school of thought belonged Vacher de Lapouge, who punctuated pages of statistical tables with outbursts of somber eloquence, and Houston Stewart Chamberlain, the Anglo-German Wagnerian who won the Iron Cross for his services to German culture. The literature of race philosophy is enormous; it attained genuine and not undeserved popularity in the works of Madison Grant and Lothrop Stoddard, not to mention those of the fantastic Chinese General, Homer Lea. All these books are marked by traits which were already found in Taine: all, in the same trenchant tone, profess the same love for "science", the same contempt for "sentiment", the same stern and virile "realism"; all reveal the same aristocratic haughtiness toward lesser breeds and mongrels; all rejoice in the same Cassandra-like prophecies of doom, for pessimism has always been a source of morose delectation.

As a rule, anthropology is applied to literature, not directly, but through sociology. *The Passing of the Great Race,* the recurrent theme of the authors we have mentioned, will leave a society in which universal dullness or futility must prevail: the "redoubtable Pan-Baeotia" with which Renan threatened us. France, in destroying her Nordic aristocracy, has committed spiritual suicide; the formal graces of her civilization can not veil its fundamental decadence. Undeterred, England, Russia, America, are traveling the same road to the abyss:

> Lo! Thy dread Empire, CHAOS!, is restored;
> Light dies before thy uncreating word:
> Thy hand, great anarch! lets the curtain fall;
> And universal darkness buries all.

A few bolder critics have definitely asserted the direct influence of race upon art and literature. A passage from *A Motor Flight through France,* by Mrs. Edith Wharton, offers a notable example of racial determinism in the æsthetic field: Taine would have nodded approval. The author is describing the scene of Salome's dance, as carved in Amiens Cathedral. There is a dog present —an irrelevant element introduced, in the teeth of logic, solely for naturalism and picturesqueness:

"Of composition there is none. . . . And thus one is brought back to the perpetually recurrent fact that all northern art is anecdotic, and has always been so; and that, for instance, all the elaborate theories of dramatic construction worked out to explain why Shakespeare crowded his stage with subordinate figures and unnecessary incidents, and would certainly, in relating the story

44

of Saint John, have included Herod's 'Tray and Sweet-heart' among the dramatis personæ—that such theories are but an unprofitable evasion of the ancient ethnological fact *that the Goth has always told his story in that way.*"

Unfortunately, the argument reposes on an unconscious pun. There is no evidence that Gothic art had anything to do with the Goths. It originated in Northern France half a millennium after the great invasions, at a time when the Pre-Gallic, Gallic, Roman and Teutonic elements in the population had become thoroughly fused. It was known then not as Gothic, but simply as the *new* or the *French* style—*opus francigenum.* Gothic was later applied to it by the Italians as a term of contempt: even in classical French, *Gothique* preserved the meaning of uncouth or barbarous. We may add that in thus insisting on the discursive and episodical character of Gothic, Mrs. Wharton is overlooking the magnificent simplicity and unity of the general plan. Amiens, Rheims, and especially Paris, offer elements of serene logic and even of majestic symmetry which might very well be termed classical. Early Gothic, in particular, is far less fantastic and exuberant than Italian or Spanish Barocco.

Mrs. Wharton herself, by the way, is presumably a Goth, and, in this very involved sentence, tried to write like one. As a rule, however, her art is scrupulously Latin in its economy and neatness; it challenges comparison with Paul Bourget's rather than with Shakespeare's.

Mrs. Gertrude Atherton is more systematic, and more rigorous in her scientific terminology. Her critical essay, "The Alpine School of Fiction" (*Bookman,* March, 1922),

a valuable and delightful document, is based on the standard division of European races: the Nordic, the Alpine
and the Mediterranean. Nordics are tall, slender, blond,
long-headed; Alpines are medium-sized, stocky, varying in coloring but inclined to the darker shades, and
round-headed; Mediterraneans are slight, dark and long-
headed. The proportion between length and breadth
of head is called the *cephalic index*. Stature and coloring may vary to an appreciable extent within the same
race and even within the same family: but the cephalic
index can be trusted. And with the cephalic index go
literary gifts or deficiencies: "Fancy a round head writing *The Scarlet Letter!*" (The Puritans, by the way,
were known as Roundheads: but that was only one of
those tonsorial facts we mentioned before.) There are
breeds of poets, biologically, not metaphorically speaking,
as there are breeds of bulls and horses. No man with a
cephalic index above 75 can be trusted to write decent
lyrics. This is "scientific criticism" with a vengeance.

The literary mind, eager to escape from its own impressionism, ascribes to everything "scientific" a degree
of certainty and fixity that true scientists would never
claim. Anthropology is a great science: but it is a very
young science, still toddling uncertainly. (The older
sciences, by the way, are at present just as much "in the
making" as their infant sisters.) Its rough and ready
classifications are not the law of the Medes and the
Persians. If most of the elementary textbooks and secondary authorities adopt without question the division
Nordic-Alpine-Mediterranean, many workers at first
hand have classifications of their own. Vacher de La-

pouge, himself a believer in the Standard Three, recognized that pure types are a minority in Europe. There are tall blonds with round heads that will not fit into the tripartite scheme. That great administrator, Dr. Ray Lyman Wilbur, is too tall for a Mediterranean and too dark for a Nordic. The Cro-Magnons, the curious fossil race still alive in the Dordogne region, have a peculiar head shape.

"You can not get away from the cephalic index," quoth Mrs. Atherton. This called for the obvious retort: "You can not get away with the cephalic index." Jews are supposed to be a race, and certainly have a well marked physical type: yet there are broad-headed Jews and long-headed Jews. A Spanish Basque looks for all the world like a French Basque: but their cephalic indices are different. Franz Boas has cast serious doubts on the cephalic index as a race criterion. It may join the phrenology of Lavater and the facial angle of three generations ago on the great junk pile of science. Hair structure and blood counts are more fashionable criteria to-day.

The tests of comparative racial ability, carried on in some of our large cities, and by Dr. Porteus in Hawaii, are not conclusive, because they start with a loose definition of race. The groups they are comparing have a linguistic, national, social, rather than a biological unity. In Hawaii, for instance, the Portuguese and the Porto-Ricans are listed separately and are indeed different. But there is no Portuguese race and no Porto-Rican race: in both cases, we have to deal with an Iberian-Negroid mixture, in various proportions. All tests, any way, show a wide zone of overlapping. Statistically, the average Greek may be brighter than the average Lapp, or *vice versa:* but you can not tell in advance, from the color of the skin, which child is going to stand higher in the scale. Now literature does not deal with averages, but with individual achievements.

Even if *race* should be entirely a superstition, we know that superstitions are potent factors—tragically so. There are therefore racial themes in literature: works about the Negro and the Jew, works by race-conscious Negroes and Jews. We can not ignore Burghardt Du Bois and Ludwig Lewisohn. The problem, however, is social, cultural, not biological. If you find a "racial" Hebraic tang to some of our smart-set journals, remember that the New York ultra-sophisticate belongs to the same "race" as Spinoza and Jesus. Nordics enjoy Heine, Schnitzler, Wassermann, Bergson, André Maurois, without thinking of their racial origins; and the American students upon whom *L'Abbé Constantin* is so frequently inflicted are apt to entertain the delusion that Ludovic Halévy was a Catholic. Few among the innumerable readers of Alexander Dumas are conscious of the fact that he was a quadroon. René Mayran, the Negro author of *Batouala,* wrote about Central Africa from the point of view of an educated Frenchman. The book belongs to Negro literature exactly in the same sense as *The Magic Isle.*

Need we repeat that we are not denying *heredity?* But heredity is difficult enough to trace, even in the case of a single family: when we come to those vast and loose agglomerations called *races,* the collective heritage carried in the blood becomes extremely elusive. We might admit, for the sake of argument, that Alexander Dumas Fils had inborn capacities for writing, because his father was himself a gifted writer: this is *heredity*. But we have no right to say that he turned into a talented dramatist because his father was a quadroon.

Anthropology is a fascinating science, and may prove a very useful one. But, at the present stage, the "marked differences in bodily structure" suggested by Taine have not been organized into an irrefutable system; still less have the relations between physical and mental traits been satisfactorily established. So far as literature is concerned, cultural elements—language, the political, economic and social régime, a liberal or restrictive tradition, educational opportunities—are vastly more important than race.

Chapter 3

ENVIRONMENT: CLIMATE

"MAN is not alone in the world: nature envelops him, and other men surround him." These external influences which hinder or strengthen man's inborn tendencies constitute his environment (*milieu*). Taine classifies them under three heads: climate, political circumstances, social circumstances.

Climate means more than meteorological conditions: it embraces all geographical factors. Taine had probably borrowed the term from Montesquieu, who had it from Jean Bodin: but no Taine and no Montesquieu were needed to tell us that a gloomy climate spreads gloom, that a harsh climate challenges our energy, that a sunny climate is joyous, a mild climate relaxing, a sultry climate oppressive. It is—or it seems—a fact of common experience. It may be a string of metaphors and a version of the pathetic fallacy.

Montesquieu had said that the mountains breed freedom; Milton before him had spoken of "the Mountain Nymph, sweet Liberty"; whereupon Voltaire remarked that not all the Alpine dwellers were free, while the freest population in Europe, the Dutch, lived below sea-level. An apt lesson in method. General ideas are frequently attractive; but we must not allow ourselves to be seduced. Every one of them is to be treated as a working hypothesis, which requires the support of definite facts.

It would be interesting to collect an Atlas of Literature, devoting one map to the Mystics, another to the Pessimists, another to the great Love Poets, and so on with every important type of genius; and then to confront these maps with others which indicate the standard geographical data—heat, humidity, orography, coast line, rivers. We wonder whether we could scientifically trace the isotherms of melancholy, or the hypsometric contours of wit. We confess that we have not made such a systematic test. A few random attempts, however, may serve as indications of the method.

It seems fairly safe to say that literature thrives best in the temperate zone: the torrid belt and the arctic regions, in comparison, are barren. There have been centers of literary production within the tropics: Cuba, the French West Indies and Réunion, Central America, the northern countries of South America. But, for one thing, they are colonial, not indigenous; and in every case, the effect of latitude is corrected by maritime or mountain influences. The Equator is deadly to the muse. To be sure, India is sweltering in raging heat, and her literature is not to be despised, for all we are so woefully ignorant of it. In our own times, it has given the world Kipling and Tagore. The Ganges holds out a promise to the Niger, the Congo and the Amazon. On the other hand, temperate Australia and New Zealand have not achieved greatness.

The case against the cold countries is not so evident. Northern Germany, Scotland, vast stretches of Russia, the whole Scandinavian world, have decidedly rigorous climates, and stand second to none in literary production. Iceland, within the Arctic circle, has played its very creditable part. In proportion to its population, the frozen North is far more fertile for the spirit than the rank tropics. It must be noted that the North enjoys at least a few weeks of summer heat, whereas the tropics afford no corresponding relief.

The hygrometry of literature is hard to trace. Greece is dry, England is damp, and both have bred great writers. Further still on either side, we find the narrative and poetical wealth of the Arabian desert, and the no less remarkable flowering of song and romance in sodden Ireland.

The influence of sunshine on literature seems to be mostly moonshine. Taine does not fail to contrast the gloomy North and the radiant South, as if the typical product of the Mediterranean world were the Neapolitan tarentella, while the North was constantly keyed up to Young's *Night Thoughts*. Human joy and despair seem to be curiously independent of Nature's alleged mood. The sunny Mediterranean belt gave rise to the Hebrew Scriptures, earnest and terrible rather than lighthearted. Neither *Prometheus* nor *Œdipus* can be called cheerful. Lucretius seems to have closed his eyes to the smiling heavens. In Italy, a strain of deep seriousness and even of despair is no less marked than the joyous acceptance of life. Dante and Michael Angelo are anything but gay; Ugo Foscolo is among the most somber of the Romanticists; Leopardi reaches the nadir of pessimism.

On the other hand, England, in her eternal fog, was justly known as Merrie England, until the Continental Reformation spread its pall of gloom; Shakespeare could write *Hamlet* and *Lear,* but also the *Merry Wives.* Let us go deeper into Cimmerian darkness: in Scotland, when the summer visitor asks the native: "Does it *always* rain here?", he gets the comforting reply: "Oh, no! It sometimes snows." Now medieval and Renaissance Scotland was like England a land of jollity, until a Frenchman, Calvin, cast his spell upon her. Take typical Scots: Robert Burns, Sir Walter, Robert Louis Stevenson, Sir J. M. Barrie: they are not lacking in good cheer. No doubt Carlyle was a Scot, and Carlyle was grumpy: but was the chief cause of his temper geographical? Was it not rather dyspepsia? Or was it Mrs. Carlyle? *

There is no absurdity in this apparent paradox. An unfavorable environment is a challenge: we never feel more keenly alive than when we are going to battle. When we reach home after fighting our way through blustering wind, sleet or snow, the plainest lamplit room will give us a sense of comfort and peace, deeper than a serene sunset over a placid sea. Our reaction against the climate may thus be at least as effective as the expected direct

---

* Statistics of suicide are notoriously unreliable; but figures do not confirm the impression that England has a larger proportion of suicides than France; whereas, in this respect, sunny California tops the list of the States. If a man is unhappy elsewhere, he still has the hope of going to California; if he is unhappy in California, he knows his ills are beyond cure.

action. The net scientific result is that "you never can tell."

Taine alludes also to the physical features of the country—its picturesqueness or its monotony, its rugged or smiling beauty, the graciousness of well-shaped hills, the squalid and sullen look of marshland and mud flats. There again, the literary imagination, with a dash of semi-science, is apt to run amok. The awful majesty of the desert is monotheistic, said Renan (forgetting that monotheism was a late achievement among the Arabs); the epics of ancient India are as overwhelmingly luxuriant as her vegetation; Greek thought is clear-cut like a bare promontory outlined on a limpid sky; English literature has the tang of the sea; France has the reasonableness of her moderate hills and gentle gray heavens; and so on *ad infinitum*. Metaphors again, expressing truths so vague that they cease to be even vaguely true. For, as in the case of heat or cold, we find that literature is surprisingly independent of such circumstances.

Neither the Alps nor the Pyrenees have been the centers of great poetical production. Jean-Jacques Rousseau discovered the beauty of mountains: but that was after he had lived in Paris. On the other hand, Russian literature, a literature of the plains, does not lack massive power; with Dostojewski at any rate, it attains a weird and abrupt intensity which reminds us of stupendous crags rather than of the illimitable steppe. America had Joaquin Miller, the poet of the Sierras: but Chicago, the North West, the whole Mississipi valley, need not despair. Chaucer, Spenser, Shakespeare, Milton, fair representatives of English genius, are only very incidentally poets of the sea. The greatest modern sea writer in English is Joseph Conrad, who came from landlocked Poland. The same is true of France: if Loti came from Rochefort and became a naval officer, Michelet and Victor Hugo, the greatest painters and lovers of the sea, were both landlubbers.

Here again, there is a reason. Literature is not the expression of those daily experiences that we take for granted: intense realization needs the thrill of discovery. The captain who takes his ship once a month through the Panama Canal is not filled with the same awe and wild surmise as "stout Cortez", or was it Balboa? The beauty of Nature is a conquest, not a habit.

Poetical psychology operates in more than one way. Thousands of potential poets of the sea will never sing, because they were born in the heart of a massive continent; whereas every English child has a chance to see the supreme wonder with his own eyes. We may thus distinguish three zones on our literary map. First, the actual mountain, the actual coast line, where familiarity is likely to benumb lyric effusion. Then the areas within easy access of mountain or sea: there opportunities for literature will be abundant, but so abundant that commonplaceness may be the result. Finally, remoter parts, where ocean and peaks are known but dimly, and akin to fairy tales. Supreme poets may appear in any of the three zones: possibly they have their best chance in the third. Our next Laureate of the Atlantic may come from Kansas City as well as from Cape Cod.

Perhaps the most important geographical factor in

literature is *accessibility vs. isolation*. Afghanistan and Abyssinia are seriously handicapped; it would be rash to promise a great cultural future to Kamchatka or the Kerguelen Islands. On the contrary, Honolulu, at the crossroads of the Pacific, is well favored in this respect. There are apparent exceptions: Iceland exists on the map of the epic: but it is as an outpost of a seafaring civilization. R. G. Caldwell told us how romantically remote Santa Fé de Bogotá was in his youth. The stern-wheelers paddled their painful way up the Magdalena river for nearly a fortnight; then followed days on a mule trail; and finally the Athens of South America was reached, renowned for the purity of its language, the graces of its society, its interest in literature. It was a miraculous survival of aristocratic Castilian culture, isolated on the high plateaus of a distant continent.

But with the idea of accessibility, we are introducing another element: the human, the social factor. Physical geography merges imperceptibly into economic and political geography.

Chapter 4

THE ECONOMIC ENVIRONMENT

WE have no lack of critics in America who are offering us an economic (I stand corrected: *the* economic) interpretation of literature. V. F. Calverton is getting to be a veteran in that school; and the latest recruit, Granville Hicks, has managed to attract favorable attention with his *Great Tradition*. A blessing on Karl Marx and all his disciples! Literary knowledge is forever getting cluttered up with the dim and dusty masterpieces of yesterday, with desiccated names of whilom favorites, with toothless theories and outlooks long sightless. Any new method is at any rate a challenge. It goes through our critical lumber room like a devastating housemaid, with powerful Scandinavian arms and a purpose inscrutable to man. When the turmoil is over, things may be a little worse than they were before, but at least they will never be quite the same again.

Saith the prophet, Friedrich Engels: "Marx discovered the simple fact (heretofore hidden beneath ideological overgrowths) that human beings must have food, drink, clothing and shelter first of all, before they can interest themselves in politics, science, art, religion, and the like. This implies that the production of the immediately requisite material means of subsistence, and therewith the existing phase of development of a nation or an epoch, constitute the foundation upon which the state institutions, the legal outlooks, the artistic, and even the religious ideas are built up. It implies that these latter must be explained out of the former, whereas the former have usually been explained as issuing from the latter." *

This passage, involved in style but elementary in thought, shows what a fine, elusive line may at times separate a truism from a fallacy. "One must live": at any rate, no writer can write unless he is alive. *Primo vivere, deinde philosophari:* these words of wisdom were spoken ages before the days of Karl Marx. Engels might have added that man needs a solid earth under his feet, and therefore that geology is the indispensable foundation of all art and all religion. We might further agree that geology is not to be explained in terms of art or religion, although the orthodox have made brave efforts in that line. All this is so obvious that it becomes inane. If we attempt to think with greater precision, then the doctrine propounded by Marx and Engels ceases to be even roughly true.

As man is assured of food and shelter, even of the scantiest, he is free to ponder, to enjoy, and to dream. No doubt his dreaming is to a large extent conditioned by the material world he leaves behind: the literature of conscious protest and wilful escape mirrors the very

*Quoted by Max Eastman, Introduction to Modern Library Edition of *Capital and Other Writings,* p. 12.

conditions that it spurns. But, as soon as his bodily wants are satisfied, man is released from immediate necessity. Forgetting for a while appetite and toil, he faces those problems which are beyond any economic régime— the whence and the whither, Nature and the beyond, love and death. He uses symbols, words and illustrations which belong to his age, tribe or class: but they are merely the garments of his thought.

All this may sound like idealistic nonsense: it is literally and pragmatically true. There are moments when I feel at one with Ecclesiastes or Voltaire, although their economic worlds were radically different from mine. There are moments when I am not in perfect harmony with Harold Bell Wright and Gertrude Stein, although both are the "inevitable" products of the civilization which is also responsible for me. When I settle down to enjoy music, I blissfully forget whether Beethoven was the child of capitalism or communism, and whether I myself am a *bourgeois* or a bolshevist. If our critics of the extreme left need sociology before they are able to appreciate Homer, Fielding, or Ogden Nash, it simply proves that they remain on the hither side of literature.

Obviously, physical conditions determine economic development, which, in its turn, influences culture. If the land is too barren to support even a scanty population, no "idealism" will suffice to create the amenities of civilized life. There may be abundant literature *about* the Sahara and the North Pole: we hardly expect literature to take root in arctic ice or desert sand. To this extent, we are as "deterministic" as Taine or Engels.

But, no less obviously, this is true only in extreme cases. In civilization, the human factor is supreme. Many countries, far more richly endowed than Ireland, Scotland or Scandinavia, have contributed far less to culture. Venice and Holland are classical examples of the human will conquering nature. Between material opportunities and human development, the connection is not always inevitable. Between prosperity and cultural achievements, there may be an abyss. Physical geography and economics do not tell the whole tale.

The Economic Interpretation of Literature evokes at once the idea of a debate between Capitalism and Communism. Our pragmatic method prevents us from using these familiar terms. Communism has not "arrived", even in Soviet Russia, and it is far too early to study its influence upon literature. The term Capitalism does not adequately define our composite régime. Speaking with necessary and pardonable roughness, we may recognize, for our purpose, four economic states: the pastoral, the agricultural, the commercial and the industrial.

The first is a great favorite with literary men; the *Pastoral,* the bucolic poem or story, has never been wholly out of fashion for thousands of years. But its greatest vogue is invariably in sophisticated ages: the Alexandrian period, Imperial Rome, the Renaissance, first in Italy, then throughout Europe, the eve of the French Revolution. To the end of the classical era, it was a favorite trick of courtly poets to masquerade as shepherds.

The Hebrew Patriarchs led the pastoral life, and King David, to whom are ascribed some of the greatest lyrics in any language, was himself a shepherd. As we invariably fashion God in our own image, "the Good Shepherd", the One who leadeth us in green pastures, has remained the most permanent picture of the Deity. The Child Jesus was hailed by the Wise Men of the East, but also by humble shepherds. It was felt that tending His flock was not beneath the dignity of God Himself. In every other comparison with some human trade, there would lurk an element of sacrilege: even Mr. Bruce Barton would hardly dare to speak of "the Supreme Realtor."

But Hebrew literature, such as it has come down to us, is essentially the product of the city, Jerusalem, rather than of the tent. The patriarchal age was exalted as a retrospective Utopia: whether it had left authentic traces in narrative and song is far from certain. Even at present, we may find among the Arabs, from Irak to Morocco, dignified and picturesque characters who evoke the memory of Abraham: but their contribution to literature is meager. Genuine Arabic masterpieces are the fruit of the trader's life: they bring the atmosphere of the city mart, the street, the wharf, the court, not the desert.

In European literature, actual shepherds occupy no favored position. He of Ettrick, James Hogg, remains an exception, and not a very significant one. In America, the cowboys have their lyric lore, which was collected by Professor Lomax. It is a minor curiosity, nothing more: the animal stories and the Spirituals of the Negroes rank definitely higher. Samuel Butler was for a while a sheep rancher in New Zealand: but that hardly confers a genuine pastoral character to *Erewhon* or *The Way of All Flesh*.

So we are afraid that the spontaneous literature of the pastoral age is a delusion, although it is a very ancient one. The shepherd's life appeals strangely to the jaded city dweller:, it is ample, silent, wind-swept, free. The shepherd moves with the season, like migratory birds and multimillionaires; and he seems to possess the greatest of all luxuries, the one most indispensable to art: *leisure*. The Bucolic is a return to the Golden Age; its attraction is a form of the nostalgic primitivism which has never ceased haunting civilized man. We all dream of Arcady: but Arcady as the best "environment" for literature is a myth.

In the agricultural state, men till the soil and live in permanent homes. Their free wanderings, their spacious leisure, are over; and with them, their noble independence. Peasant democracies are an exception: for untold ages, the serf or even the slave, at best the tenant farmer, formed the majority of the rural element. The full emancipation of the peasantry was achieved in Western Europe only at the end of the eighteenth century or early in the nineteenth; in Russia, two generations later.

As compared with the shepherd, the peasant ceased to be a full man. He was attached to the glebe; the nature of his work made him a perpetual hostage; and his work was never done. Even if he did not sink to the tragic degradation described by La Bruyère, he lacked the variety of experience, the freedom of attitude, the leisure, that would release the poetry in his soul.

The popular literature of the Middle Ages was entirely urban in character, much as it may have lacked in urbanity. In the tales and the farces, the peasant is invariably treated with bitter scorn. *Villein* (villanus, villager) became in French *vilain,* mean and ugly; in English, *villain.* "Thrall, boor, hind, bumpkin, hayseed": the peasant has always been despised as well as maltreated. We hear of literature "springing from the earth": it is doubtful whether the folklore collected among the peasants is purely of peasant origin. Songs or tales came to the village through itinerant minstrels, through an occasional pilgrimage, through a rare visit to some important fair: in all cases, from the town.

Unrelieved by other elements, rural life would be heavily dumb. There is no lack of vivacity among Italian peasants: but the country is so thickly populated, so liberally bestrewn with active townships, so heavily fraught with cultural traditions, that it does not represent the bucolic mind in its awful simplicity. France was until yesterday predominantly an agricultural country, and has brought her full quota to world literature. Predominantly, but never exclusively. French culture has ever been urban, courtly, and, in the last three hundred years, metropolitan: the classical centuries almost forgot Nature altogether. France has no peasant-poet to compare with Burns. Robert Burns was indeed racy of the soil, using village tales as his themes, and the episodes of the ploughed field: yet Robert Burns had received an urban culture. Ireland is a nation of farmers, and has achieved surprising greatness in literature: but would there have been an Irish Renaissance without Dublin—

and London? Our farmers, in these days of universal schooling, the daily press, the automobile, the radio, live under radically different circumstances from those of European peasants a few generations ago. Yet even they, it must be admitted, are almost perfect non-conductors of literature. Poets may arise from the farm, but they have to leave the farm. Vachel Lindsay, with his "ballads exchanged for bread", attempted a back-to-the-land movement: but it was a wilful oddity, and it left no permanent trace.

All this may seem deliberately insulting to the largest and the most indispensable element in society. But it should be remembered that literature is not the whole of life. In essentials,—health, contentment, moral stamina—the derided bumpkin may be far superior to Baudelaire or Oscar Wilde. We do not believe in the congenital and irremediable inferiority of the peasant type: Zola's worst book, *The Soil,* is a tragic and revolting caricature. In his famous poem on Millet's *Man with the Hoe,* Edwin Markham arraigns the oppressors, who have defaced God's image and reduced that living soul to brutishness.* David Starr Jordan, on the contrary, believed that the Man with the Hoe was biologically such. He had not been forced down, or even kept down: his breed was incapable of rising, and race is a more fundamental factor than environment. No one can accuse Jordan of haughtiness, or lack of human sympathy: of farming stock himself, he was at least as generous a democrat as Markham, and at least as good a poet. But

---

* Incidentally, I do not believe that social satire was the intention of Millet himself. His picture was meant to be pure realism, with the touch of sordid ugliness which, at that time, was considered almost indispensable.

as a biologist, he was apt to think strictly in biological terms.

Lord Bryce liked to quote the epigram: "Senators are rich; some are Senators because they are rich; some are rich because they are Senators." The debate between Markham and Jordan might be stated in similar terms: "Peasants are dull-witted: are they dull because they are peasants, or peasants because they are dull?" I am not a biologist, and hardly dare to express an opinion. But, for once, I am inclined to side against Dr. Jordan. The case is not clear: it is difficult to distinguish between irremediable stupidity, and atrophy due to unfavorable circumstances. The political personnel of the Third French Republic compares favorably with that of other leading countries; yet, if we look at the picture of a French Cabinet, we realize that some of those men are barely two generations removed from "the man with the hoe." I have had among my American students promising young men who could have posed for that tragic figure. A breed may seem dull, because it is primitive and inarticulate; yet virgin soil is more fruitful than asphalt, and unrefined ore more valuable than tinsel. But we need not take sides in the debate. The purely agricultural state—a village economy such as still prevails in remote parts of Africa, without any higher organization—would be a total blank on our literary map.

The commercial state offers a much more congenial atmosphere. The most perfect masters of art and literature, the ancient Greeks, and, among the Greeks, the Athenians, were essentially traders. The one important city that scorned commerce, Sparta, also turned its back upon art. Even under Roman supremacy, the Greeks retained their leadership in commerce and culture alike. To be sure, the Phœnicians, more thoroughly commercial than even the Greeks, have left us little art and no literature, while we still read, for their beauty as well as for their spiritual significance, the writings of a noncommercial people, the ancient Hebrews. It might seem flippant to retort that, at any rate, the Phœnicians taught us our letters—writing is a by-product of business; and if the Jews were not commercial-minded in Biblical times, they have gloriously made up for it in the last two thousand years.

In the middle ages, we still find commerce and culture going hand in hand. The Court of Champagne, for instance, shone with particular brilliancy in the thirteenth century. It was the means of introducing the Southern lyric into Northern France, and became the center of those great Romances of Chivalry which provided, at the same time, entertainment and a code of refined breeding. Now the wealth and power of the Counts of Champagne rested upon the great fairs, of international importance, which were held in that province. When the fairs were ruined by the Hundred Years' War, the culture of Champagne went down. Medieval England was mainly agricultural: but the England represented by Chaucer was decidedly commercial. No single city since Athens stood so high in culture as Florence: and Florence was above all a commercial community. The political factions were identified with the trades; and, finally, a dynasty of Bankers, the Medici, became Princes, gave a Pope to Rome and Queens to France. The reigns of Francis I and that of Elizabeth were marked by intense economic activity as well as by artistic splendor.

Objections, naturally, flock to our mind. The two communities in which commerce was frankly paramount, Venice and the Netherlands, have produced great art, but no great poetry. Is it impossible for the lyricist to sing, unless he turns his eyes to the hills? Louis XIV apparently scorned trade; he certainly despised the Dutch, who balked and finally defeated him. But the glory of Louis XIV is inseparable from his magnificence, which would have been impossible without Colbert. When the country was ruined by the King's extravagance, French culture suffered an eclipse. Louis XV might be too kingly to "haggle about peace like a merchant", and a nobleman lost caste if he engaged in trade: but French commerce was expanding all the same, and the financiers played an extremely active part in the society of the Enlightenment.

In the eighteenth and nineteenth centuries, England was supreme in commerce even more than in manufacture. Socially, she might be ruled by the rural gentry: intellectually, London's preëminence was beyond challenge. English art, although creditable, did not lead the world; but English thought and English letters undoubtedly did. New York is not America's political center, nor the historical seat of culture, nor the home of the purest aristocracy, nor is it the heart of a manufacturing region. Its literary leadership, which is unquestioned and almost tyrannical, is based on trade, and on the chief instrument, the ultimate refinement of trade, banking.

The individual artist may and probably should spurn riches — *Pecunia tua tecum sit!* — and riches, even unspurned, may pass him by. Yet it is riches that make art as a whole possible. This is not quite so mercenary as it sounds. We bow before the inevitable, we do not worship it: the purest idealist has to recognize the necessity of food without becoming a glutton or even a gourmand. Commerce, creator of riches, is the essence of our civilization. The city, as soon as it is more than a place of refuge perched on a hill, is essentially a market. Commerce means communication, intercourse, exchange: thoughts are bartered as well as wares, and literature is a commerce of the spirit. Commerce means variety of experience; it brings together town and countryside, and cities which are remote and strange. Commerce means the caravan and the ship, which open a trail of longings and dreams. Commerce is a matching of wits: while the immemorial contention with the ground and the seasons makes the ploughman a part of inanimate nature.

Then the commercial community implies a modicum of freedom. Under barbarism or tyranny, commerce is hampered. As Napoleon grew more despotic, he interfered more heavily with trade. The age in which the commercial ideal was most clearly predominant, the eighteenth century, was also the one that evolved a "liberal" economy and an individualistic philosophy. And it is usually conceded—we shall, however, debate the point in its proper place—that liberty is a favorable condition for literature. Civil and economic liberty, at any rate.

Finally, commerce is linked up with prosperity and

peace. Without commerce, even a fertile agricultural country could not rise above mediocrity. And prosperity, although it may become gross, insolent and deadening, is essential to the elaborate arts. The shepherd may play his pipe in the shade: but a symphony, an edifice, a drama, a romance, imply generous leisure, both for creation and for enjoyment, with the plenty and the security that make that leisure possible.

We have heard so much of the Industrial Revolution, which we date back to the days of James Watt, that we unhesitatingly call our culture that of the Industrial Age. This, in our opinion, is at least premature. The world has never yet lived under a pure industrial state: we are barely entering upon it at present.

By the term *business,* we understand as a rule both industry and commerce; but there is a great difference in method and spirit between the two. In the commercial community, distribution operates on a more elaborate scale than production, and brings larger rewards. The merchant is the true prince. He gathers the labor of the agriculturist or small manufacturer, advertises it to the world, and brings it to market. In the industrial community, production is paramount, marketing is secondary: distribution can be effected without commerce. The point of view is different, and the atmosphere will not be equally favorable to literature in both cases.

Industry in the modern sense, *i.e.,* mechanical mass production, was born only yesterday. Until the end of the nineteenth century, America was still overwhelmingly agricultural and commercial; men who are not yet tottering to their grave may remember the days when our industries were referred to as "infants", in great need of protection. Although France, under Louis XVI, had a faint foreshadowing of modern industry, although she made a conscious start under Napoleon III, she is only at present in process of industrialization, and her spiritual leaders are still protesting against the change. The definite industrialization of Germany does not go back beyond the seventies.

England, of course, has a much longer record. But it is surprising how little the Machine Age affected English thought and English institutions for nearly a century and a half. The Industrial Revolution was not clearly focussed in the public mind until it was named by Arnold Toynbee in 1883. For the greater part of the nineteenth century, the landed aristocracy and the squirarchy wrestled for predominance against the merchants rather than against the manufacturers. The working classes voted for the Manchesterian Liberals, a mercantile class, unless, swayed by Jingoism, they turned to the Tories. When foreign observers thought of England's economic supremacy, it was the City, the Bank, the Exchange, Lloyd's, that first came to their minds: the Black Country afforded only a dim fuliginous background. English civilization was extraordinarily complex —nominally feudal and agrarian at the top, essentially colonial, maritime and financial, and all but unconsciously manufacturing. The novel of industrial life was an exception in the nineteenth century, and remains an exception to-day. Walpole, Galsworthy, Priestly, are still Victorian in this respect. H. G. Well's great romance of modern business life, *Tono-Bungay,* depicts the promoter, the advertiser, the merchandiser, not the manufacturer.

Industry was an ugly, ill-kempt infant. It littered the country with incredible squalor. It brought grime and stench, the tenement instead of the cottage, the *pub* instead of the jolly old inn. No wonder poets and prophets united in cursing the new Horror. The craving for storied Yesterday and glamorous Elsewhere, a legacy of Romanticism, intensified the abhorrence of the artistic mind for the hideous present.

The worst of this reaction is over. We are now able to see the elements of power, and therefore of beauty, that industry has to offer. The most disagreeable infantile ailments have been overcome. Dirt, clatter, discomfort, are not necessarily linked with industrialism. They are wasteful and inefficient. Industry is increasingly clean, sanitary, comfortable. As the superficial, temporary objections are disappearing, the lineaments of the full grown industrial state are becoming discernible.

Commerce, so far, has implied liberty, competition, individualism. Industry, even though her "Captains" may do lip service to the gospel of Adam Smith, — industry is profoundly *collectivistic*. It frowns upon competition, which is waste; and upon individualism, which is incompatible with the best use of the machine. Will standardized efficiency provide a favorable atmosphere for literature?

Industrial conditions present such undeniable advantages that it is idle to deplore them: we are not going to smash our machines, like the Erewhonians. On the other hand, these same conditions are the result of human efforts and can be altered by human efforts: there is no cause for meek or craven acquiescence. Certain it is that the Machine Age, when it is in undisputed sway, will change our environment and affect all our values.

Again, we must not forget that we are still in the transition period. English culture, after a hundred and fifty years, has not been fully industrialized. American culture is traveling faster in that direction, but is very far from having reached the goal. France is hesitant, Italy is facing both ways. Russia alone, all adverse traditions swept aside, is rushing headlong into the full Industrial Age. But rushing is not the same thing as living: Russia's crisis does not give even an inkling of what her art might be under normal Industrialism. All images are blurred in the whirlpool. For a *petit bourgeois* Liberal like Georges Duhamel, America offers "scenes of life in the future" from which he recoils. For the average American hybrid, whose mind is partly rural, partly commercial, rather than industrial, Russia is a hideous menace. The industrial community is still in the making: we dare not mix observation and prophecy. For the literature with which we are familiar, the Commercial State is undoubtedly best. Literature under the industrial dispensation may be no less great, but it will be different.

Chapter 5

THE POLITICAL ENVIRONMENT

Man is a political animal, and the organization of the City can not fail to affect his mode of thinking. Among the circumstances that create "environment" and thus influence literature, Taine naturally included political conditions. He contrasted "the two Italian civilizations", that of ancient Rome, and that of the Renaissance. The land was substantially unchanged; the people, in spite of innumerable migrations, had retained their ancient vigor and many of their physical traits—the artist can still find all the "old Romans" he needs in the poorer districts of modern Rome. But the structure of the state and its international position were radically different.

A first glance will convince us that literature has bloomed under all possible régimes: Greek democracy, Roman Cæsarism, the turbulent municipal aristocracy of medieval Italy, feudal France, the national autocracies of Francis I, Elizabeth, Louis XIV, the acephalous bureaucratic government of Louis XV, the landlord and merchant oligarchy of nineteenth century England. Just as climate kills literature only in extreme cases—the absolute desert of sand or ice—a political régime has decisive action only when it assumes the most exaggerated form—absolute anarchy or absolute despotism. But such cases are exceptional, and can not be permanent.

So, whatever our own preferences may be, it is safe, so far as literature is concerned, to disregard mere political forms. In many cases, the differences between them are merely questions of vocabulary. The French writers of the seventeenth century, reasonable and upright men, spoke of the King in terms which, to us, sound fulsome, absurd and degrading. But, to them, the King was a living flag, the symbol of unity at home, and national greatness. Their "royalism" was not abject servility: it was exactly what we would call to-day good citizenship and patriotism. In the nineteenth century, a poet like Victor Hugo could accommodate himself to several successive régimes: he was not a turncoat or a Vicar of Bray: he served a permanent reality under changing symbols.

The distinction between Monarchy and Republic is among the loosest. A constitutional monarchy of the English or Belgian type is evidently a crowned Republic; a dictator like Porfirio Diaz is a monarch except in name. Ancient Poland, with an elective King, was frequently referred to as a Republic. *Protector,* like Cromwell, *Stadtholder,* like William of Orange, *Regent,* like Horthy, are ambiguous titles. Napoleon was until 1807, on his coinage, the *Emperor* of the French *Republic,* a confusion imitated from Augustus himself. Italy offers the uneasy shadow of an hereditary constitutional monarchy, all but obliterated by a vigorous dictatorship.

The words *democracy* and *aristocracy,* in political parlance, are even vaguer. American Democrats are aristocratic in the South, demagogic in the North. There may be political democracy combined with social aristocracy: such was for a long time the case in certain South American countries. The constitutions gave all power to the people: in reality, it never left the hands of·a few privileged families. In Spain, on the contrary, under the forms of a monarchy, absolute or constitutional, and with the most elaborate aristocratic *étiquette,* there prevailed a spirit of genuine democracy: hidalgo and mendigo are brothers. The terms are vague in their political meaning: but, in culture, they stand for two very definite tendencies. There is a "democratic ideal", an art of the people, for the people, and even perhaps by the people, represented by Dickens, Victor Hugo, Tolstoy; and there is an "aristocratic ideal", an art reserved for the élite, the erudite, the sophisticated—Milton *vs.* John Bunyan. The conflict between them is all important in our subject: but it is a social and spiritual problem rather than a political one.

The essential difference, for our purpose, is that between the *autocratic* and the *liberal* states. (*Authoritarian* would be a more accurate term than *autocratic* and *totalitarian* is now in fashion: but both are so ugly that they can appear only under the veil of a parenthesis.) Autocracy, *i.e.,* irresponsible authority, may be exercised by one man—tyrant, despot, absolute monarch, dictator; by a group, lay or clerical—the jealously closed and all-powerful aristocracy of Venice, the Jesuits in eighteenth century Paraguay; by a party—the French Jacobins, the Bolshevists, the Fascists, the Nazis. In all cases, rigid conformity is enforced: in externals, which is easy enough, but also, as searchingly as possible, in the secret of men's thought. The ideal of the Inquisitorial State is to detect and stifle an incipient heresy before it has come to light: prevent the most minute spark, and there will be no conflagration.

A freethinker under Philip II of Spain, a monarchist and Catholic under the French Terror, a determined *bourgeois* in Moscow, a Communist in Los Angeles, are equally under suspicion that they are "about to think criminally." We borrowed three of our four examples from countries supposedly under popular rule: the Liberal State, on the contrary, may exist under a monarchy, even a nominally absolute one, like that of Louis XVI; under an aristocratic or a *bourgeois* régime; and even under a democracy. The *mores* of a country matter far more than its statute book. "I care not who makes our laws, so long as we are free to write our own songs."

We can hardly escape from the hypothesis that the Inquisitorial State creates a spiritual vacuum in which literature languishes and dies. But, according to our rule, we must allow no hypothesis to pass unchecked.

The first objection that comes to mind is the brilliancy of the Augustan Age. Vergil did not simply happen to be the contemporary of Augustus, and his friend: it was the majestic peace of the Empire that made Vergil possible. His gentle silver voice might not have been heard but for the great hush and repose that came upon the Latin world: "A god himself provided this leisure." The case is not decisive. Obviously order, even at the cost of liberty, is more favorable to certain kinds of achievement than the tumult of civil strife. But the autocracy of Augustus was not complete; it was carefully veiled under the traditional forms of the Republic. The spirit of the vigorous old oligarchy had not been fully emasculated; it survived for several generations. Then the writers of the Augustan Age had received their formation under the preceding era: only by its own fruit, that is to say by a second and third generation, can a régime be adequately tested.

The case of Louis XIV, the French Augustus, is strikingly parallel. Here also, we have undoubted autocracy: "What the King wishes is the law"; "For such is the King's pleasure." Louis XIV had no need to say: "I am the State": no one dared to doubt it aloud, very few doubted it even *in petto*. With that formal autocracy came the most perfect flowering of the French genius, the age of Bossuet, Boileau, La Fontaine, Molière, Racine.

On closer inspection, Louis XIV appears somewhat different from the pure autocrat of popular histories. He had no Parliament in the English sense of the term, and the courts of justice that went by that name did not oppose him as they had opposed Mazarin and were to oppose Louis XVI. He had tamed the unruly nobility, and he rode roughshod over any velleity of popular protest. But, a naturally reasonable, moderate, almost timid man, he did not suppress the privileges that limited his own prerogative. Monarchical France was in fact, if not in theory, a complicated system of traditional checks. The Clergy, with its enormous wealth and influence, was to a large extent a self-governing body. The aristocracy, the judiciary, the provinces, the cities, the guilds and crafts, still clung to their ancient rights, which were not to disappear until the Revolution. France had no written constitution, but she had a jungle of "customs" and charters. Modern Royalist historians may choose to exaggerate this aspect: but they are not wholly wrong. The French king appears as the hereditary Protector of innumerable self-governing associations, rather than as the omnipotent despot.

Then, as in the case of Augustus, we must remember that all the great minds that flourished between 1660 and 1685 had reached maturity before absolutism became unquestioned. The Fronde was still a quivering memory: the young King compelled hastily to flee from his capital, the greatest in the land allied with Spain against their lawful sovereign, the royal cause identified with Mazarin, a despised foreign adventurer. The generation which grew up under the first twenty-five years of the autocracy was of far smaller stature: in fact, the period 1685–1715 may be considered as the decadence of pure classicism. Literature bloomed again in the eighteenth century, under a régime which, theoretically autocratic, had the saving grace of being ineffective, and was liberal at least by fits and starts.

The French Revolution had but one poet, André Chénier, and sent him to the guillotine. It is hardly fair, however, to consider a life-and-death crisis as though it were a permanent régime. Even in America, the war years and the post-war hysteria revealed a great deal of the Inquisitorial spirit, which fortunately melted away when "normalcy" was restored. For the same reason, we can hardly judge of the effect that either Bolshevism or Fascism may have on literature.

Napoleon, a third Augustus, restored internal peace, order, prosperity. He desired to foster art and literature; he reorganized the Institute of France, he offered prizes: all in vain. The genuinely great writers under his reign, Madame de Staël, Joseph de Maistre, Chateaubriand, were his determined opponents, one and all. His official poets sank into depths of inanity hitherto unplumbed: it is an era of tenuous ghosts.

French Republican tradition speaks of the Second Empire in the same terms as of the first: while tyranny prevailed, literature, with Victor Hugo, remained in exile. This is a farcical exaggeration. Quite a number of authors did not leave France; many of them—About, Augier, Taine, Renan, Flaubert, Sainte-Beuve, even George Sand, lived on friendly terms, if not with the Tyrant, at least with his cousins, Prince Napoleon and Princess Mathilde. The Tyrant was a gentle Utopian socialist at heart, and France was spiritually so divided that she had never been so free.

Both Alexander I and Nicholas II of Russia had some of the qualities of Napoleon III, although the second Bonaparte, in our own opinion, was immeasurably superior to either. But, during the greater part of the nineteenth century, under Nicholas I, Alexander II, Alexander III, Tsarism was a genuine autocracy. Yet Russian literature, under these despots, took its place among the noblest in the world. Gogol, however, born in 1809, had been influenced by the liberalism with which Alexander I had toyed; he was ultimately an unconscious victim of the increasing vacuum, and never finished his *Dead Souls*. Dostojewski was sentenced to death for plotting against the régime: if he was later converted to "Holy Russia", at any rate his genius was not rooted in conformity. Turgeniev was by temperament and experience an Occidental, a cosmopolite; he was more at home in the Western capitals than in Moscow. Tolstoy's family had preserved the memory of the Dekabrists; the Count himself turned into a Christian anarchist. Not one of the giants was in any sense a product of the autocracy; their presence only registers the failure of the autocracy to suppress dissent.

It is a curious fact that the scientific mind can accommodate itself to tyranny far better than the literary mind. The tyrant is not hostile to the scientist: except when he enters into conflict with religious dogma, the scientist is harmless. His work is frequently esoteric, inaccessible both to the masses and to the governing class: the power of the despot expires at the door of the laboratory. The literary man on the contrary expresses himself in terms that are "understanded of the people"; and express himself he must. Art is individualism, science seeks the subjection of the individual to absolute laws. The philosophers of the Enlightenment, like Voltaire and Diderot, in so far as they were scientifically minded, had for their ideal a beneficent despot rather than a liberal régime. They had been on friendly terms with Frederick II and Catherine II: their successors rallied to Napoleon. Monge, Berthollet, Lacépède, Lagrange, Chaptal, Cuvier, were among the great personages of the Empire (but not Lamarck, too daring in thought to be *persona grata*).

Napoleon himself liked to pose as one of them, a member of the Scientific Section of the Institute. Renan was torn between his literary and his scientific propensities. When the poet in him had the upper hand, he was a liberal; when the scientist prevailed, he dreamed of a dictatorship exercised by the Academy of Sciences, by means of elaborate methods of torture. The very intelligent group that supported Porfirio Diaz called themselves the *Científicos*.

Perhaps the most favorable conditions are found in the Oppressive State that fails to oppress. Complete liberty may degenerate into license and vulgarity: a man has to shout in order to be heard. Ineffective despotism is an ideal environment for culture. It breeds at least a moderate amount of discontent, thus providing an incentive to criticism and therefore to thought. In America, we were until recently so perfectly satisfied with the general principles of our Constitution that our political thought had become atrophied: politics had become a battleground for second-rate personalities and ephemeral issues. We were all so free to think that we did not care to think at all: Abbé Dimnet's charming little book on *The Art of Thinking* came to us with the freshness of a revelation. If we had a "tyrant", he would give us something to think about.

Opposition to despotism creates in us a sense of daring, adventure, heroism. This is particularly welcome to the literary mind, which thrives on exaltation and loves attitudinizing. Victor Hugo never was so well pleased with himself as when he penned the defiant line:

Et s'il n'en reste qu'un, je serai celui-là! *

* And if only one remains (irreconcilable), I shall be that one!

81

Then "oppression" compels us to use finer tactics and keener weapons, the rapier of allusive irony rather than the bludgeon of blatant assertiveness. This sharpens the wit of author and public alike: the reader watches intently for veiled epigrams, and, in his eagerness, supplies them if they are wanting. Controversy was carried on a very dignified plane under the Second Empire. At the top, there was a very gentle Tyrant; under him, a vast and rather stupid police. Thought was not stifled: but direct insults were barred out. Either the writer had to be satisfied with the discussion of general principles, or he had to use subtler methods than vituperation. France learned a great deal in those days about "Tiberius"; Soulouque, Emperor of Hayti, attracted a disproportionate amount of notice. In the last few months of the régime, the ban was lifted, and vulgarity rushed in like a turbid flood. There were still traces of urbanity in Rochefort's weekly pamphlet, *La Lanterne,* under the Tyranny; there was none in his shrieking *Marseillaise.* Clemenceau, a ruthless censor while he was waging war, had, unconsciously, a refining influence upon journalistic style. I remember a delightful article in a Socialist paper denouncing the oppressive methods of "Lenin": every reader mentally substituted "Clemenceau" and chuckled. Perhaps the Tiger himself grinned. We should thank the Power that compels us to whisper instead of shouting. It is excellent training.

From this somewhat paradoxical point of view, the most favorable age was that of Louis XV. Then ineffectual oppression fostered both true liberty and delicate wit. The great men of the time were alternately petted, admired, feared, imprisoned. When they heard a carriage stop at their door, they never knew whether it was to take them to the Bastille, or to a supper party with the highest in the land. Voltaire, Diderot, Rousseau, knew such exhilarating alternatives. The *Encyclopaedia,* officially confiscated and destroyed, was safely stored against a better day by the very authorities that were supposed to suppress it; it was enjoyed privately by the King in whose name it had been condemned. *Philosophy* had to be supplied through ingenious bootlegging methods, which whetted the natural craving of mankind. In our own country, censorship has repeatedly played the part of the ineffective despot, thus sharpening our taste for literature that is not primitive. But for a providential censor, the general public might never have heard of James Branch Cabell. Now that it can be sold openly, *Ulysses,* an enormous and difficult book, is not likely to have such earnest readers as in the golden days of its outlawry. Boston, in condemning *Candide,* restored freshness to a masterpiece, a task that no professor and very few critics could have achieved.

Inefficient tyranny, better than sheer anarchy, is also far better than a *reasonable* régime: for reasonableness means the dictatorship of the dull. But it must be inefficient, and unfortunately such is not always the case. To say that the spirit invariably triumphs is unwarranted optimism. Even the cautious qualification "in the long run" will not make the assertion quite safe. We know, as a matter of record, that a number of masterpieces have survived persecution: we have no means of knowing how many potential masterpieces have been silently strangled in the dark. The Middle Ages as a whole, Italy after the Renaissance, Spain after the *Siglo de Oro,* Russia and America in the nineteenth century, the English stage from Queen Anne to its very recent revival, all give us a feeling of frustration. The elements of greatness were there in abundance: they should have yielded a richer crop. A blight was at work: spiritual oppression, under various forms, had gone beyond the point where it could be stimulating.

The tyranny of one man, or of a small group, is seldom crushing for any length of time. Except during brief crises, it is rather bracing. The tyranny of the many is far deadlier. You can dodge a sword, if you are nimble enough: you can not escape the invisible, ubiquitous, insidious censorship of Mrs. Grundy. This is a mere restatement of our previous position: *mores* matter more than statute book, social conditions more than political forms.

Chapter 6

THE SOCIAL ENVIRONMENT

I

THE only examples of "social conditions" given by Taine are two religious movements, Christianity and Buddhism: evidently the word "social" covers a multitude of virtues. We shall take it in the more usual sense, which implies the division and relations between classes. But, out of respect for our guide, and not merely on that account, we must devote some attention to religion as a part of the social environment.

In many cases, the religious factor takes precedence over all the rest. When we evoke the Middle Ages, we think of them as Christian first of all, not as feudal. Spain, in our mind, is Catholic, rather than Iberian (whatever that may mean), or peninsular, or semi-African, or imperial. And many interpretations of American culture have been offered, with reverence or derision, in terms of the Puritan spirit.

We have therefore no desire to belittle the religious element. But, as in the case of politics, we find that it does not depend upon any particular form. Just as all kinds of poetry may thrive under King or President, all kinds flourish also under priest or presbyter. Any collection of world classics will contain the works of Pagans, Jews, Catholics, Protestants and Free Thinkers. Prophet and Psalmist, Homer, Plato and Lucretius, the Norse Sagas, Dante and Pascal, Milton and Wordsworth, Blake and Shelley, Rabelais and Rousseau, down to H. L. Mencken and G. K. Chesterton, all have their niche, great or small, in our Pantheon. Nor would it be easy, in many cases, to classify authors according to their religious affiliation.

It is a sobering thought to consider how little our culture has been affected by our nominal faith. The Western world was conquered by a religion which condemned violence and spurned riches: but after nineteen hundred years, it shows little willingness to renounce either. Theoretically, a fatalistic creed should benumb and demoralize those who profess it. But the Calvinism of the Huguenots, the Jansenism of Pascal, the scientific determinism of Taine himself, led to a renewed austerity of life and a more intense vigor of purpose. There seems to be no stronger will than the will which denies its own freedom.

Madame de Staël claimed that Romanticism and Protestantism went together, since both exalted the individual at the expense of established authority; Classicism and Catholicism, on the other hand, were both founded on formal discipline and reverence for the past. There is some truth in that contention. Yet Romanticism was marked by a great revival of Catholic fervor, not only in France, but in Germany. No one could have more of the Romantic quality—the lone venture of an intrepid soul—

than the Catholic mystics, such as Santa Teresa. No one could be more meekly submissive to a traditional orthodoxy and a definite ritual than many conservative Protestants.

So far as culture is concerned, the same difference exists in religion as in politics between the Inquisitorial and the Liberal State. However lofty the faith, if rigidly imposed, it will have a deteriorative influence. It is not Islam that has paralyzed the Arabic world, nor Greek orthodoxy that has hampered Russia, nor Catholicism that has blighted Spain, nor Protestantism that has benumbed large classes in America. It is, in all cases, *l'Infâme,* Intolerance, against which Voltaire waged his lifelong crusade. No religion, not even the weirdest sect in Southern California, can kill art and literature; fanaticism, if unchecked, would do it. Atheistic fanaticism, of course, is no whit better than the rest.

The great centers and the great eras of culture were those in which no single faith wielded exclusive power. In England, the Establishment has never been able to destroy either Catholicism or Dissent; in the eighteenth century came the Deists; in the nineteenth, scientific agnosticism. America started her national life in the free spirit of the Enlightenment. In spite of the clamor of a few fanatics, the Protestant majority shows no desire to disfranchise heretics. France is known as a Catholic country: but, since the Renaissance, four religious traditions have been contending, the Gallican, the Ultramontane, the Protestant, and the free Naturistic faith of Rabelais, Molière, Hugo, Zola—a spiritual family not to be despised. The varieties of religious experience are even more numerous than the sects; and they do not coincide with the sects.

With these words of caution, we are free to admit that the religious atmosphere is of commanding importance for the student of literature. Favorably or adversely, it affects every author who has a soul, even one, like Théophile Gautier, for whom only the external world exists. Every one follows a guidance, wrestles with an angel, or is pursued by the nemesis of a faith. Taine himself was tragically torn. French Rationalism, German Idealism, English Empiricism, the historical spirit that urged the acceptance of Christianity, the experimental method which suggested the agnostic attitude, all strove for his allegiance. He never was able to harmonize Descartes, Hegel, Bacon, Bossuet, Darwin; and, after giving offence to all parties, he sought refuge in the compromise of a Protestant burial.

It is a question whether the religious factor has ever been quite so potent as the national. Every religious war in modern times had a political background. It was not Catholicism that was defeated with the Armada, it was Spain. It was not Popery that was driven from the throne in 1688, but absolutism; it was not Rome and Calvin that fought in sixteenth century France, but aristocratic factions, the Guises, the Colignys, the Bourbons, the Condés. His Most Christian Majesty Francis I allied himself with Turks and Protestants against the leader of European Catholicism, Charles V; Richelieu and Mazarin, princes of the Church, pursued the same policy. If willing martyrdom be the test of faith, then Patriotism in the modern world has millions of martyrs to Christi-

88

anity's hundreds. When the two rival creeds come to an open clash, as in the question of taking the sword, conscientious objectors (not all of them on Christian grounds) are in a pitiful minority. Mankind is still worshipping tribal gods. And those gods are athirst.

II

As a rule, the words *social conditions* evoke the idea of *classes*. When we speak of a man's social environment, we think of the circles in which he moves familiarly, of the class to which he belongs. The social environment for literature in general means the structure of society, its formal or loose division into classes.

There have been many different social systems in human experience; and there seem to be no fewer in the animal world. At one extreme, we find a régime of rigid classes, with impassable barriers between them. Rigidity can not be complete without hereditary distinctions, and the classes thus hardened from generation to generation are called *castes*. At the other end, we find Shelley's ideal:

> The loathsome mask has fallen, the man remains
> Sceptreless, free, uncircumscribed, but man
> Equal, unclassed, tribeless and nationless,
> Exempt from awe, worship, degree, the king
> Over himself. . .

A beautiful dream, when expressed in Shelley's words; in the eyes of most, a dream; in the eyes of some, not even beautiful. Between these two poles, endless variety prevails. The classes may be so fluid that their very existence may be questioned, as in *White* America; or they may commingle with such difficulty that they almost amount to castes, as in pre-war Prussia. There may be an unchallenged hierarchy of classes, as in nineteenth century England, where every one, thank God, *knew his place;* or there may be open conflict. There may exist a division and balance of power between the classes, or one element may definitely predominate—the aristocracy in old Hungary, the middle class in France, the proletariat in Soviet Russia.

Social conditions are easily confused with political conditions. Many of the words in—*cracy,* aristocracy, mesocracy, democracy, offer that ambiguity.* Ideally, the social and the political régimes should be in such close harmony that they might be considered one and the same. Practically, such harmony has hardly ever prevailed. On the eve of the French Revolution, the State was officially an autocracy, with a theocratic foundation and an aristocratic coloring; in fact, it was a *bourgeois* bureaucracy, with the nobles as splendid parasites, and the king as an impressive, heavily gilded figurehead. Society, at the same time, was formally dominated by the aristocracy: but its vital power was found in the rich middle class. The most enlightened protectors of the arts, the friends of the *Philosophes,* were financiers. The Marquis de Marigny, whose delicate and generous taste had such an influence on that exquisite period, was a Marquis by the grace of his sister, the Marquise de Pompadour, *née* Poisson, a *bourgeoise.* Madame Geoffrin could not have been presented at Court; but she had her own social realm of the

---

* However, autocracy, theocracy, technocracy, necrocracy, have no social implications.

Rue Saint-Honoré; artists, poets, philosophers, flocked to her gatherings; foreign princes fondly called her *Maman,* and, returning to their thrones, felt themselves in exile. In a word, the political régime was an absurdity in terms of the social régime; and both were absurd from the point of view of the prevailing doctrines: for the gospel preached by Jean-Jacques Rousseau, and eagerly accepted by the liberal *bourgeoisie,* was undiluted democracy. Confusion could hardly be worse confounded.

It *did* get worse confounded, however, when the word *social* became chiefly connected with the nature of property; when, by the *social* question, men understood the conflict between capitalism and some form of communism. The Social Democrats are not necessarily more socially inclined than other parties; in *The Social Register* and *The Social Revolution,* the word is obviously used in radically different meanings. Until Socialism became the most vital of our problems, class distinctions had very little to do with the various conceptions of property. Although there were survivals of feudalism in France as late as 1789 and in other parts of Europe for several decades longer, all classes accepted individual ownership as a natural and sacred right. The peasant in his field, the artisan in his little workshop, the merchant great or small, the industrialist, the aristocratic landowner, were all of one mind on that point. No difference in wealth, culture, birth or graces, could alter that fundamental unanimity, which, even to-day, is barely shaken in America. Many plebeians, rich or poor, could not be more passionately attached to a régime of private ownership if they belonged to the most ancient aristocracy;

and, among socialist leaders, there are men who came from the upper middle class and even from the nobility. It can hardly be disputed that a proletarian régime would seriously influence our culture. Leon Trotsky has devoted to the problem of *Literature and Revolution* a singularly able and no less singularly inconclusive book. But the new class division, capitalist *versus* proletarian, by no means coincide with the familiar hierarchy, aristocracy, middle class, manual laborers.

Finally, to make confusion absolutely inextricable, class names are frequently used to denote differences in taste. *Aristocratic* stands for *refined; bourgeois,* for *commonplace* and *mediocre; popular,* for *cheap* and *vulgar.* This is not merely insulting: it is woefully inaccurate. The art patronized by the aristocracy may very well be coarse or insipid. As Matthew Arnold noted, the nobles, as long as they retained their separate existence, remained to a large extent Barbarians. There is no proof that the fox-hunting squire, or the Prussian Junker, were particularly urbane and delicate in their æsthetic appreciation. The *popular,* whether springing from the people like the old ballads, or appealing to the people like *Les Misérables,* is not necessarily low. And, throughout the centuries, the middle class has provided the most enlightened element in society.

This triple confusion is best exemplified by the various acceptations of the word *bourgeois.** From its original sense of *city dweller,* the term came to mean *middle class citizen,* as opposed to the non-urban elements, the aristoc-

---

* For a fuller discussion of this term, *cf. Beyond Hatred: Mesocracy in France.*

racy and the peasants. The *bourgeoisie,* not the nobility, was ever since the Middle Ages the mainstay of the French state, and the center of literary activity. But its political supremacy was not officially recognized until 1830, with Louis-Philippe, the Citizen King. With political triumph came spiritual loss of caste: the Romanticists, most of them *bourgeois* themselves, made the word a substitute for Philistine. *Epater le bourgeois*—to flabbergast the Babbitt—was the first duty of every self-respecting artist. The hosier and the grocer were singled out as particularly offensive. Yet William Blake, the perfect incarnation of extreme Romanticism, was the son of a hosier. No one could be more aristocratically disdainful of the Beotian than Ernest Renan: and his mother kept a village grocery store.

Then Marxism made *bourgeois* synonymous with capitalist. For the Marxian, a duke and a wealthy artist are both *bourgeois.* For the artist, King Louis-Philippe and Prince Albert, of the most aristocratic blood in Europe, were hopeless *bourgeois.* I have had a few glimpses of orthodox socialist households, and they were most *bourgeois* of all. There is no case in which it is more indispensable to define our terms.

The classic example of the caste system is furnished by India. Once again, to our shame and regret, we must be satisfied with a question mark. We are not sufficiently familiar, even at second-hand, with the literature of that country to trace any connection between its social structure and its cultural achievements; and we know that our *a priori* sympathies are not to be trusted. A caste system has been repeatedly advocated by men who were great artists: Plato, of course, in his *Republic,* and, a long way behind, Fénelon in his *Telemachus.* Oddly enough, Plato, it will be remembered, banished poets from his orderly state; and there is no promise that the Salentum of Fénelon would produce any great art or great poetry. Aldous Huxley, in his *Brave New World,* gives a Swiftian satire of a scientific commonwealth, biologically divided into castes. Such an environment, in his opinion, would be deadly to all æsthetic values. These literary examples prove very little. On the whole, the sentiment seems to prevail that castes are unfavorable to art; but that sentiment has not hardened into firm belief.

Such an opinion, if it were adopted, could easily be supported by theoretical arguments. A caste-bound world is an immovable world, and therefore likely to be a stupid one: if your chief desire is to prevent change, you must first of all prevent thought. Hard and fast divisions create either sullen resentment or stolid resignation below, inane pride and sloth above: in either case, they are hardly conducive to achievement. The case would be strong, if theories by themselves could carry conviction.

Slavery is one form of the caste system. Antiquity had slaves, and produced art and literature that we still revere. But antiquity preserved a paradoxical kind of cultural democracy: a slave could be a teacher, a philosopher, a poet.

America, both British and Iberian, offered that aggravated form of caste in which social differences are emphasized by race, and indelibly marked by color. Yet culture did not perish among the slave-owners. It is difficult, however, to consider the instance as decisive.

Slavery, as an essential factor in the life of the Southern States, prevailed for barely a hundred years: the attitude of the Revolutionary Fathers on that question was far less bigoted than that of the cotton planters on the eve of Secession. A century is a brief moment in human history.

It can hardly be denied that the effect of slavery on the Negro mind was detrimental: it is highly to the credit of the race that the prolonged ordeal did not wholly destroy its spirit. The subordination, even when it was no longer called slavery, of the Indian element in Mexico and South America, coming after ages of a native caste system, has benumbed the Indian soul: its restoration to normal activity is almost a desperate venture. The whites in both continents are faced with the same problem as Tolstoy's hero in *Resurrection*.

The effect on the dominant caste had certainly not been wholly good. We have repeatedly expressed our affectionate admiration for the Southerners, among whom we spent many happy years; and we have valued friends among South Americans of pure Iberian descent. It always seemed to us that they had not done themselves full justice. They came from the best stock in Europe; they had excellent traditions of culture; they had leisure and wealth; their own contribution, exquisite at times, has been somewhat meager. And we must add that the South remained in close intellectual contact both with England and with the North; Iberian America remained linked both with Spain and with France. Whatever degree of civilization they maintained was not wholly autonomous.

In modern Europe, the caste system has never fully

prevailed. Society in the Middle Ages was stiffly hier-archized: but, just as philosophy in the ancient world could transcend even the spirit of slavery, Christianity in our era was able to override or at least to qualify serfdom and feudalism. The first order in the land was not the hereditary nobility, but the clergy, recruited from all classes. If there was a constant tendency to reserve the highest ecclesiastical dignities to the well-born, that tendency was never accepted in theory, nor did it entirely prevail in practice. A commoner could become Abbot or Bishop; a swineherd, according to popular tradition, was one of the greatest Popes. The essentially democratic character of Christianity, Ebionism, the Gospel preached to the poor, was never wholly forgotten. Bossuet gave before an aristocratic congregation a sermon on "the eminent dignity of the poor."

Although no one will insist more than an Englishman on "good blood" and the hereditary principle, the British aristocracy never was a closed caste. The younger sons of younger sons would by slow degrees merge with the gentry and even relapse into the common people; at all times, energetic commoners could rise in the social scale, and ultimately reach the peerage. This process was greatly accelerated by the economic triumph of the commercial element in the eighteenth and early nineteenth centuries. To-day, the descendants of belted earls sit at Westminster on the same benches as bankers, brewers, and newspaper barons.

In France, society had a tendency to stiffen on the eve of the Revolution, and that very stiffening was one of the direct causes of the great upheaval. Under Louis XVI, it would have been difficult for Bossuet to receive a bishopric, or Vauban a Field Marshal's baton. But, for hundreds of years previously, much greater fluidity had prevailed. The King's service was the stair by which *bourgeois,* in a few generations, could ascend to the highest nobility. The whole Colbert connection tried to forget the linendraper of Rheims, their forefather, and were granted magnificent titles. Many functions and distinctions carried noble rank with them; aristocratic privileges could actually be bought; and *mésalliances,* although frowned upon, were not unheard of, even in princely families. In the nineteenth century, the exclusive character of the nobility belongs to the realm of polite fiction. All that can be said is that titles still command a premium on the matrimonial market: the aristocratic son-in-law is a stock character in light comedy.

What about the classless world prophesied by Shelley? It has not come to pass even in Russia: else the "class war" would be over, and the "dictatorship of the proletariat" an absurdity. Has it been realized in America? In theory, no doubt: all immigrants are requested to leave their titles behind as they pass through Ellis Island. In practice, the class fluidity which exists in England and in France is even greater in America. But the class ideal, attenuated, half-ashamed of itself, still survives. We need not refer to its most virulent manifestation, color prejudice: we firmly believe that this deplorable feeling is social, not racial, in its origin. But it is found also within the ranks of our White, Nordic and Protestant rulers. There are local centers of resistance to unqualified democracy: many spots in the old South, the First Families of Virginia, the

Daughters of the American Revolution, the Back Bay dynasties of Boston, and, only yesterday, the ghosts of Washington Square, evoked by Mrs. Wharton. Plutocracy is not absolutely irresistible; there are a few strongholds of "Society", beleaguered, indomitable, that can not be forced by any million-dollar artillery.

Until the Post-War Era, when the floodgates that guarded higher education burst open, a degree from a dozen privileged institutions was still vaguely equivalent to a patent of gentlemanliness. Not a few people subject their children to Latin, and, themselves, feign unlimited enthusiasm for golf, because both are examples of conspicuous waste, and appurtenances of the leisure class. During our great Crusade for Democracy, temporary gentlemen by act of Congress were taught to behave offensively to their subordinates: all social intercourse was prohibited between officers and privates, although the example of the French army proved that snobbishness was not essential to discipline. It is openly acknowledged that certain religious denominations enjoy greater social prestige than others. There is profound significance in the folklore saga of Mr. and Mrs. Jiggs: American womanhood is dedicated to the great task of re-creating social distinctions in Lincoln's Republic. The belief that "a man is a man for a' that" is not ingrained in the American mind. We are far less ready to acknowledge social superiorities than are the British or even the French. No true-born American will freely proclaim: "I belong to the lower *bourgeoisie*." But when it comes to asserting our own social superiorities, we challenge the field.

We are intimately persuaded that the spirit of social

distinction is one of the strongest factors in civilization, and, less directly, in culture. In another part of this book, we shall attempt to discuss in some detail the influence of that spirit upon literary production. But we do not believe that spirit to be ineradicable. Certainly the old castes have almost entirely vanished, and the old classes are losing ground. Constant efforts are made to revivify them through an injection of alleged science: but there are serious chances that we shall escape the *Brave New World* with which Aldous Huxley is impishly threatening us.

Even in the interpretation of the past, we are far from claiming that the *class* idea provides a magic key. There are some forms of literature that bear unmistakably the imprint of one class: but even they have been appreciated by the other classes as well. It is most probable that *bourgeois* and common people, in the Middle Ages, enjoyed the fighting epics and the love lyrics that mirrored the life of their *betters*. Conversely, there is every reason to believe that the feudal baron chuckled over the merry tale, or roared at the broad farce of strictly popular origin. Molière made sport of the courtiers while some were sitting, not merely among the spectators, but on the very stage. The aristocracy applauded furiously *Figaro's Wedding,* a brilliant attack against their own privileges. Bunyan has been read in castle halls, and Milton in the backshop. There is a thorough democracy of the nursery tale; even the "sophisticates" are drawn from all ranks; while supreme greatness ignores the barriers of caste.

Chapter 7

THE MOMENT (TIME AND TRADITION)

RACE, according to Taine's conception, is practically independent of time. Elaborated through "myriads of centuries", it remains unaffected by mere historical periods. Climate, by which we mean all the data of physical geography, does alter indeed, but only with geologic slowness. All the other factors in environment change very perceptibly with time. The desert can be made to blossom like the rose, forests can be cleared, marshes drained, lakes created, rivers diverted, in a single generation. Empires melt away, religions lose their hold, social classes are subjected to violent transformations, in the course of a few decades. If we want to define a people's civilization, it is not sufficient to find out what their blood is, and what land they inhabit, but also at what *time* they live. "Truth on the hither side of the Pyrenees," said Pascal, "error beyond." Even more obviously could we assert: "Truth yesterday, error to-day." So the third factor in Taine's formula is *le moment,* which is usually translated by *time*.

But time is an ambiguous word, and does not render

accurately what Taine had in mind. *Time* adds nothing real to *environment:* for environment exists only in time. If you describe the time of Samuel Johnson, you describe his environment, and *vice versa.*

In order to establish a distinction between the two, we might restrict *environment* to the personal circumstances of the writer, and reserve *time* for those more general factors which affect whole groups of contemporaries. Environment would be treated anecdotally, time historically. We may consider the facts of Samuel Johnson's experience, his birth at Lichfield, his education, his life in London, as his environment; eighteenth century England as his time. But the distinction soon breaks down. The central character and the background are part of the same picture.

Boswell was not an unconscious forerunner of Taine: he told us all that he knew about Dr. Johnson simply because he was deeply interested in Dr. Johnson. He did not fail to describe Johnson's earliest environment; and he himself calls our attention upon the fact that the environment depends upon the time:

> His (Johnson's) father is there (on the parish register) styled *Gentleman,* a circumstance of which an ignorant panegyrist has praised him for not being proud; when the truth is, that the appellation of gentleman, though now lost in the indiscriminate assumption of *Esquire,* was commonly taken by those who could not boast of gentility.

At the *time* of Johnson's birth, the word gentleman had a wider meaning than at the *time* when Boswell was writing. Again:

His mother was Sarah Ford, descended of an ancient race of substantial yeomanry in Warwickshire.

What was the connotation of yeomanry in those days? We can not understand the social status of the Johnson family unless we know the social structure of eighteenth century England.

Mr. and Mrs. Thrale, Garrick, Goldsmith, Reynolds, Boswell himself were members of the inner circle; but there were many concentric rings, with no hard and fast division between them. A larger one would take in Chesterfield; George III himself would have to be included. Where does *environment* give place to *time?*

It has been suggested that the economic and social conditions constitute *environment,* the political conditions constitute *time.* Johnson's England was still dominated by the squirarchy but saw the rapid development of the commercial classes and the rise of industry: that is *environment.* Under the nominal rule of the Hanoverian line, it was governed by such men as Walpole, Chatham, North: that is *time.* This distinction seems to us to repose on two antiquated ideas.

The first is that, in history, social and political elements can be separated. Nothing of the kind: not exclusively dynasties, ministries, battles, treaties, belong to history, but economic and intellectual transformations as well. Voltaire was aware of this nearly two hundred years ago, and it were well if the "New Historians" would learn the lesson.

The second delusion is to a large extent the result of the first. Because, for many centuries, political changes were recorded while social changes were not, we are still under the impression that social conditions are quasi-permanent (environment), and political conditions in a constant flux (moment or time). The facts tell a different story. No doubt a nation may scrap its constitution twelve times in three generations, like France between 1789 and 1875, while its economic and social life is not correspondingly modified. But it is perfectly possible also for the social régime to evolve far more rapidly than the political. The forms of English Parliamentary government are substantially the same to-day as in the eighteenth century: but in the meantime, England has gone through a couple of *social* revolutions or rather renovations. The American Constitution is nearly a hundred and fifty years old: our present social-economic régime—the definite subordination of agriculture, mass production in industry, world leadership in finance, the passing of anarchical individualism, the waning of the Puritanical ascendancy, —came to full consciousness only in this generation. This will become increasingly apparent, as we take the habit of considering a masterpiece, a scientific discovery, the invention of a new process, the opening of a market, as no less worthy of a place in history than the Hayes-Tilden or the Harding-Cox contests.

The literal translation *moment* would hardly be more satisfactory. For the usual meaning of *moment* is the instant, the mere flash of time. "A historical moment" would be a snapshot, a still picture, the characters standing immobile on a motionless background. On the contrary, with *time,* Taine wanted to introduce the sense of motion, of change. The same factors, taken statically, form the environment; taken dynamically, they constitute time. We may call this, with the Hegelians, the concept of *becoming;* we may call it *evolution;* more plainly, *history*.

This implies, not merely the fact of change, but change as the result of a force moving in a definite direction. This force Taine calls "acquired velocity": literally *momentum*. If we may use an Einsteinian expression with which the readers of Sunday papers are all familiar, we exist in a space-time continuum. We are not time-less or instantaneous: duration is as indispensable to our existence as dimensions. We can not be thought of without air to breathe or soil upon which to rest our feet: neither can we be thought of without our yesterdays. Shall we add: and without our to-morrows?

It is tempting to assume, as we all do without reflection, that time flows evenly and for all things alike. But this is true only of *conventional time,* as measured by our watches, or by those cosmic chronometers, the revolutions of the heavenly bodies. If we were all carried by the stream of time at the same rate, we would not be conscious of change. Nothing in my room gives me the sense that I am hurled through space at an incredible speed: all the familiar objects remain placidly at their wonted place. It is the unevenness of motion alone that makes motion perceptible. Similarly, time exists for us only because things move at a different tempo. If a whole generation grew old evenly, homogeneously, all keeping the same pace, without contact with a new generation, it would never know it is growing old. If, in a civilization, institutions and beliefs evolved in absolute harmony, preserved exactly the same relation to one another, they would appear to be eternal. But creeds, laws, manners, techniques, wax and wane each in its own fashion. They combine into patterns that are incessantly altering. It is this endless series of dissolving views that we call history, and that gives us the sense of time.

This sense of time is the very essence of *human* culture. Science, in a way, is unhuman. It thinks in light-years, in geological ages, in countless generations. Its time-scale is so enormous, so different from the minute time-scale of human experience, that there is hardly any common measure between them: science seems to be dealing with the eternal. In the eyes of science, two thousand years lend no authority to an error, like the Ptolemaic system: it is but a discarded hypothesis. In art and literature, two thousand years constitute a triumphant "test of time", and amount to immortality.

There is therefore a kind of radicalism inherent in scientific thought. Whatever science believes to be true must be true *in itself,* in terms of to-day as well as of yesterday. Culture is historical: the present exists only in its relation with the past. Science can evolve at any moment a new code of symbols: culture can only alter, but never wholly discard, its inherited modes of expression. Even James Joyce, in his *Work in Progress,* must keep in contact, at least intermittently, with the traditions of the English language.

Tradition!: we have uttered the key-word, perhaps the shibboleth, of all culture: "the best that has been thought and said. . ." always a *has been*. Education consists in preserving and transmitting that heritage; good taste, in conforming to its norm. A *gentleman* is a man with a past: the immediate past of good schooling and favorable home influences; the remoter past of a good ancestry; and the whole past of the race at his command, under the name of culture. The plebeian, the vulgarian, is, as in Rome, *homo novus,* a *new* man.

It would seem like irony if we were to defend the advantages of traditional culture: so plain are they—to every *cultured* mind. It is evidently a benefit to the world that Homer, Plato, Vergil, Dante, have not been allowed to die. The language of every educated man is an unconscious mosaic of allusions; even his random thoughts are laden with the wisdom of the ages. This gives to *literature* worthy of the name a depth of resonance, a richness of harmonics, that plain speech does not possess: imagine Milton or Anatole France without the majestic perspective of their background.

Tradition does not merely preserve masterpieces, isolated and entire, or absorbed into the general thought: it nourishes and enriches the masterpieces themselves. Great works grow after their author's death. Meaning is poured into them; new illustrations are brought forth; their obscurities are elucidated, in ways that the writer may never have dreamed of; every imitation, every quotation from them, every allusion to them, establishes a new contact and brings in new life. The Bible as literature becomes broader and deeper with the centuries: Milton, Blake, Carlyle, Kipling, have created new overtones; even the shrill pipe of Voltaire or Cabell adds an unexpected and subtle note to the magnificence of the concert.

Shakespeare, if he were to take a Shakespeare course in one of our colleges, would be astounded at the profundity of his own *Hamlet;* or rather *Hamlet* is no longer his own: it belongs to innumerable scholars, poets, philosophers, the greatest of whom is Goethe. Similarly, Unamuno's *Don Quijote* shows how much the Knight of the Dismal Countenance has grown in spiritual stature since the days of Cervantes. Molière's *Tartuffe* and his *Misanthrope* have acquired a multitudinous life. The best example of such enrichment is Mona Lisa. Her smile is the symbol of mysteries to which Walter Pater has devoted one of the most elaborate pages in the golden book of English prose. But the mysteries need not have been in Leonardo's mind. They are the sum total of the dreams of ten generations—an increment not entirely earned. In probing the painter's intentions, we have multiplied them a hundredfold. Such is the *momentum* of culture.*

This may become even plainer if we try the counter test, if we examine those books which have failed to grow. A crucial example is offered by the French Bible. In England, the Bible has become a standard for the vernacular; it has generously given of its treasures to all comers, but it has received much in return. When we read the Bible, an innumerable accompaniment of dimly recollected poems, hymns, prayers, sermons, phrases, even homely anecdotes and family happenings, turn the Book into a symphony as rich as life. In France, the Bible has not become rooted in the literary soil; it has remained, for believers, a sacred book; for non-believers, an exotic book.

---

* "On a somewhat lower social plane, she might be a rapacious landlady at the seaside, hopeful of making a favourable impression upon her prospective lodger but quite determined that she shall get decidedly the better of the bargain." Clifford Bax, *Leonardo,* p. 122.

Its grandest imagery appears strange, excessive, Oriental in character. A few great writers, Bossuet, Racine in his last two tragedies, Lamennais, Victor Hugo, were steeped in the Bible. But the inexhaustible lore of Biblical allusions, reverent or familiar, even frankly humorous at times, which is part of the English heritage, is sealed to the French. The French Bible has not *grown*.

Another example from the religious literature of France. The Huguenots had two great poets, Du Bartas and Agrippa d'Aubigné. Both wrote on an ambitious scale, with deep earnestness, and with no lack of spirit. At present, Du Bartas's epic, *The Week,* is mentioned merely as an oddity of literature; and, although belated justice has been done to d'Aubigné's magnificent poem, *The Tragics,* it has not taken its place among living masterpieces. Every child knows those uninspired rhymesters, Malherbe and Boileau: only a student looks into d'Aubigné. Why? Because both the sect to which these writers belonged, and the literary school they represented, went down in defeat at the end of the sixteenth century. The Huguenots, after Henry IV's abjuration, were doomed to remain a hopeless, isolated, distrusted minority; the style of the Renaissance, daring, extravagant, but gorgeously alive, was sacrificed to the clearness, logic and taste of neo-classicism. Those two poets were debarred from founding a tradition: so with every decade their language became more antiquated, their obscurities more obscure, their oddities more shocking. Goethe recognized in Du Bartas a great poet: French critics consider this judgment as a lapse of taste: "Even a Goethe," they say, "is no competent judge of a literature not his own."

Both opinions are defensible. Du Bartas was *potentially* a great poet: but circumstances killed those potentialities. His fame did not acquire momentum.

It may be more profitable to insist upon the dangers of tradition than upon its benefits. More profitable, but no whit more original: for the iconoclastic tradition itself is a hoary one. The iconoclastic path, however, is evidently the more perilous, and should be traveled upon with greater care.

If tradition keeps masterpieces alive, it also cumbers the ground with fossils. Not for all time: but for too long a time. Tradition becomes a *necrocracy,* a graveyard government; it makes for a purely retrospective culture, a museum civilization. In its veneration for the antique, it imparts artificial dignity to the antiquated.

In my childhood, I was a constant visitor in the Louvre Museum (I confess I ran through the picture galleries as fast as the slippery floors would allow, in order to reach my real goal, the Naval Collection). Many decades later, back from the Wild West, I was suddenly struck with the dinginess, the pomposity, the commonplaceness of three "old masters" out of four; and I began to see a gleam of sense in Courbet's sally (was it Courbet's?) that the Louvre ought to be burned down. Tradition too sedulously cultivated leads to decadence. We must constantly make an effort to break loose from the necropolis, the library, the museum, and rediscover the world for ourselves.

Momentum, the constant enrichment of the human mind, is a blessed fact in a healthy civilization; but that fact is far wider than what usually goes by the name of tradition. A man who is conscious of momentum is historically minded; he treasures the gifts of the past. But he is likewise a modernist: he believes that the present also is capable of spontaneous activity. The historical spirit is the recognition and acceptance of change. Tradition may be exactly the reverse: the refusal to change. The historical spirit notes facts, but imposes no duty. It is aware that human sacrifices, slavery, tyranny, once existed; that war, certain forms of monarchy and ecclesiasticism, are still with us. But such acknowledgement implies no reverence. These things *were,* or *are:* this does not prove that they *should be.* Tradition, on the contrary, insists that relics of the past must be honored and maintained. The historical spirit is all-inclusive. Everything that exists to-day is the result of yesterday. Radicalism, Bolshevism, Futurism, are historical products just as much as Toryism. Tradition is selective: only certain elements are picked out as deserving to be preserved. Tradition is not only a limited part of life to-day: it is also a limited part of history.

Man would be paralyzed if his memory were too retentive; his mind would be warped, if what he is allowed to remember were too narrowly prescribed. There is only a difference in dignity between *custom* and *tradition;* there is no essential difference between tradition, superstition and prejudice. This seems a hard saying: but tradition is the last defense of the indefensible. A permanent need, manifested afresh every day, is not a custom, a superstition, a prejudice, a tradition. We must have sleep and food, even as our ancestors had them, but not *because* our ancestors had them. We must have religion, but not because St. Paul said so; and government, even if Washington had never lived. Neither an experimental nor a logical truth needs the force of custom: it is not a "tradition" that water is composed of oxygen and hydrogen. Tradition is dragged in as an argument only to bolster up absurdity.

Thus "a dull classic" ought to be a contradiction in terms. If he has become dull, he should no longer be a classic. Shakespeare is a fact, not a tradition.

The worst feature in tradition-worship is its pharisaism. We beg leave to quote a characteristic passage from Aldous Huxley's *Music at Night:*

> Culture, as Emmanuel Berl has pointed out in one of his brilliantly entertaining pamphlets, is like the sum of special knowledge that accumulates in any large united family and is the common property of all its members. "Do you remember Aunt Agatha's ear trumpet? And how Willie made the parrot drunk with sops in wine? And that picnic on Loch Etive, when the boat upset and Uncle Bob was nearly drowned? Do you remember?" And we all do, and we laugh delightedly; and the unfortunate stranger who happens to have called feels utterly out of it. Well, that (in its social aspect) is Culture. When we of the great Culture Family meet, we exchange reminiscences about Grandfather Homer, and that awful old Dr. Johnson, and Aunt Sappho, and poor Johnny Keats. "And do you remember that absolutely priceless thing Uncle Virgil said? You know: *Timeo Danaos. . . .* Priceless: I shall never forget it." No, we shall never forget it; and what's more, we shall take good care that those horrid people who have had the impertinence to call on us, those wretched outsiders who never knew dear mellow

Uncle V, shall never forget it either. We'll keep them constantly reminded of their outsideness.*

But those wretched outsiders will strive hard to learn the shibboleth. If the tradition itself is beyond purchase, its external effects may be imitated to perfection. The nemesis of tradition is spurious culture. Sir Edmund Gosse's father believed that God had created the world six thousand years ago, all complete, with its geological strata and their fossils, *as if* it had existed for millions of years. Similarly, the eighteenth century landscape gardener erected ruins in a new park, so as to give it a synthetic flavor of antiquity. Molière's *Would-Be Gentleman* ordered from the best dealers in such wares what the French call "a varnish of culture." *Parvenus* in all countries procure for themselves an ancestral home and ancestral portraits. An American College, Oxford's infant brother, announces: "There is a tradition in this College that Freshmen are not allowed to walk diagonally across the green. This tradition goes into effect next Monday at 8 A. M." Traditional culture which aims at importing fashionable prejudices reminds us of the ingenious processes whereby parchment or ivory may be *aged* with coffee or tobacco-juice; worm holes in furniture faked by firing fine shot; and cobwebs quickly grown to make bottles look venerable. There is nothing finer than the gentleman of the old school—a classical scholar, loyal to his Church and to his King, fond of gentlemanly sports and addicted to gentlemanly tippling. But the institution that turns a modern lad into

* *On the charms of history and the future of the past.*

such a bewigged family portrait is an efficient cobweb factory.

In his eloquent *Prayer for Teachers,* Glenn Frank confesses: "We have been content to be merchants of dead yesterdays, when we should have been guides into unborn to-morrows." Bravely said; but Glenn Frank was challenged to outline a course of literary studies based on his principles, and found it more discreet to refrain: the University President is not strictly accountable for every word of the columnist. There are *yesterdays* that should not die, and *to-morrows* that should never be born—to wit, the next war. The present writer has reached the age when it no longer seems the height of wisdom to kill off the old. But he firmly believes that literary culture need not be identified with tradition worship. The example of science, and of some of the arts, is encouraging in this respect.

We have emphasized the "radicalism" of science; we are aware, however, that the difference between the scientific attitude and the historical is not absolute. The new symbols of science must be integrated with the old; the most revolutionary thought, in order to be intelligible at all, must have some point of contact with traditional thought. And science, not so very long ago, was no less tradition-bound than literature. The *Ipse Dixit* of Aristotle was law in natural philosophy as well as in poetics. The Medical Faculty of Paris fought against Harvey's circulation of the blood, because it had not been taught by "Hippocrates and Galen." The willingness of science to cast aside time-worn hypotheses is a conquest of yesterday.

On the other hand, literature and the arts are attempting to escape from the thraldom of the past. This was one of the ideals of Romanticism: "Who shall deliver us from the Greeks and the Romans?" But the Romantic revolt was neither complete nor consistent. It sought emancipation from certain ancient models: but it was eagerly looking for precedents in other realms: Shakespeare, the Middle Ages, the ballad, the primitive epic. It was a shift from one past to another past—and a more self-conscious one. Perhaps architecture will provide the clearest indication of possible change. Toward the end of the eighteenth century, architecture had become such a slave to classical tradition that "purity of style" was its highest aim; orthodoxy according to Vitruvius led to the most lifeless pastiches. The Romantic nineteenth century widened the field of imitation, but remained scrupulously imitative. When an architect was commissioned to build a railroad station, he had first to consider whether it would be Doric, like the portico to Euston, or Gothic like St. Pancras, or Romanesque, or Renaissance. To-day such antiquarian preoccupations strike us as positively ludicrous. We are creating the art of to-day with the materials of to-day and for the needs of to-day.

This does not imply that we must destroy ancient works of beauty, or relegate them to the position of museum pieces. We still worship in the old Gothic churches; nay, it is legitimate for us to build new Gothic cathedrals like St. John the Divine, if we feel ourselves the spiritual contemporaries of St. Thomas Aquinas rather than of Clarence Darrow and Aimée Semple

McPherson. And if we happen to like Doric columns, we should not scruple at using a few in our skyscraper or railway terminal: provided we express thereby our own delight in the form, and not merely reverence for ancient canons. We must free ourselves from prejudices, including the futuristic prejudice.

The same spirit may prevail some day in literature. To discard tradition does not mean to destroy the past. To know Shakespeare is a privilege, not a duty; to be guided by his standard in our own work would be manifest foolishness.* Shakespeare's aim was frankly to provide entertainment, not to write school texts. The test of a classic is the power to survive. In so far as he is alive, he needs no elaborate explanation. If he is dead, he is no classic. We insult the great writers of the past when we insist that they have to be imposed upon the new generations. So long as we genuinely and fondly remember "Uncle Virgil", he is a delight; if his "priceless things" have to be drilled into us, he becomes an old bore.

Tradition-worship is a survival of the days when human learning was precarious, a small flickering flame to be tended with religious care. We need no altar to the sacred fire, now that any one can buy a box of matches for one penny. Culture is so ubiquitous that one particular book might fall into oblivion without any danger of loss for its essential message. The thought would pass into "floating literature", that is all.

* Sir Hall Caine, expressing his æsthetic and scholarly disapproval of spelling reform, said: "Shakespeare's spelling is good enough for me." A "dear old soul", urged to take a trip in an aëroplane, answered: "None of your new-fangled inventions: I prefer to stick to the railroads as God created them." Two perfect examples of the traditionalist fallacy.

Aye, but is there not power in definite knowledge, and charm in conscious allusiveness? You may repeat:

> Laugh, and the world laughs with you,
> Weep, and you weep alone. . . .

but will you enjoy these words of wisdom quite as much, if you do not remember whether they were written by Martin Tupper or by Ella Wheeler Wilcox? Is it possible to be *cultured* without knowing "the best that has been thought and said"? But, for one thing, is there an infallible canon of the "best", are there "books that every child should know"? From the Chinese point of view, our ripest scholar is a barbarian; from ours, their most learned mandarin is an ignoramus. When H. G. Wells, some quarter of a century ago, visited a girls' college in the Eastern States, he was asked: "Doesn't it remind you of *The Princess?*", and replied ingenuously: "What princess?" They put him down at once as a vulgarian: as though familiarity with a very pretty mid-Victorian poem were a valid test of culture!

No doubt such writers as Milton and Anatole France would lose heavily if we failed to catch all the happy reminiscences of the Culture Family—the trick of phrase borrowed from Uncle Virgil, the naughty twinkle learned from Cousin Voltaire. Apart from the element of snobbishness denounced by Huxley, is the allusive game worth the candle? The phrase must be good, to begin with: if it is not, I care little whether Vergil used it first. True: not quite true. There *is* virtue in allusiveness. It enables us to use condensed formulæ instead of heavy explanations. If, in speaking of the joys of poetry, I mention "Xanadu" or "a peak in Darien", I convey far more than twenty words of mine could express.

But this undeniable advantage is not without drawbacks. The first is that your audience becomes more narrowly circumscribed. To many, your language will appear recondite, or even cryptic. "We accept the risk: we would rather appeal intensely to the qualified few than superficially to the undiscriminating many." A worthy sentiment: but it is by no means certain that the people you include in your magic circle are worth your while and that those whom you leave out are not. In the old days, all forms of superiority were fairly in harmony. Everybody who was anybody was familiar with the vocabulary of the tribe, and with its fund of reminiscences. To-day, this can no longer be taken for granted. The esoteric is no less a danger than the commonplace; most objectionable of all is the commonplace that deems itself esoteric.

The second danger is that conscious allusiveness may detract from a beautiful thought at least as much as it adds. Do we not often wish that we did not remember so much, so that we could come upon simple and great things with the quivering delight of discovery? Why can we not climb our own peaks in Darien? Instead, when we come across:

Our birth is but a sleep and a forgetting . . .

we nod blandly, a little wearily, as to an old acquaintance in whose company we no longer find any zest. O for a course in un-reading, that would blot out all the classics from our minds, and give us a fresh start!

If we abandon, if even we minimize historical culture, shall we not be reduced to the awful simplicity, the functional starkness, the *Sachlichkeit* affected by certain forms of contemporary architecture? It might not be such an unmixed evil. But it need not have any such result at all. The depth and richness of the mind is not measured by historical book learning. If the author be powerful or subtle, scholarliness *may* add to his strength or to his grace; but, if he be commonplace, classical ornaments will be sheer pedantry. Many a don could quote as abundantly as Montaigne or Sir Thomas Browne: but the result would not be literature.

Overtones need not all come from the past. The antique shop is not the only one that is well stored. A *rich* mind is a well-informed, highly organized, sensitive mind. Take, among our contemporaries, those who give us, not the impression of crude power, but that of abundant and varied wealth, easily available, generous without ostentation. At random, we might name André Gide, Stefan Zweig, Aldous Huxley, Ortega y Gasset, Salvador de Madariaga, among these exemplars of modern culture. They allude to the past without hesitation: it is not pedantry in them, but natural familiarity. Yet their outlook is not retrospective: rather circumspective. They live and think in the present. One thought calls for an illustration from politics, another for one from travel. A literary phenomenon evokes a similar scientific phenomenon. Verbal felicities are not limited to classical allusions. Good literature does not feed on literature.

We shall be accused of cultural bolshevism: if this be

treason to humane letters, make the most of it. Our
warning against tradition means no irreverence toward
the past, no sacrifice of the living past. Hold fast to that
which is great and good in terms of the present—the religious truths that are still true, the political doctrines
that are still workable, the masterpieces that we still
enjoy. For the rest, let the dead bury their dead.

Chapter 8

NATIONALITY AND LITERATURE

IF we follow the convenient groove, we shall take it for granted that, between nationality and literature, there exists an intimate and inevitable connection. Each literature is sharply separated from every other by the high fence of language; each language belongs primarily to some nation.

Exceptions, in their wonted way, will flock to our minds. We are aware that several of them enjoy a paradoxically vigorous life. Few countries have a stronger national feeling than tetraglot Switzerland; and there seems to be no ardent desire, on either side of the water, for the English-speaking world to be reunited. Still, roughly speaking, literature, language, nationality, go together. In the study of an author, the nation is the natural background. Race, environment and time concur in its formation. The perfect nation is one in which men of the same blood and of the same speech dwell close together in the same homeland, cherish the same traditions, are organized under the same laws. In his *History of English Literature,* Taine had constantly in mind the formation of the English nation; his disciple Jusserand made their common ideal plainer when he called his great work *A Literary History of the English People*. The temptation is almost irresistible to turn this approximate truth into a law, and the law into an ideal: literature is, and should be, national. It is the purpose of this work to defy irresistible temptations.

Of the three great factors which we have examined, the one which is most essential in creating and shaping a nation is that of *time*. The most casual observation will convince us that men who live under the same flag are not all of the same breed. America and France, certainly not less nationalistic than other countries, are racially the most heterogeneous of all. It is no less evident that national unity is not the fruit of physical environment. Our four corners, Washington and Florida, California and Maine, differ widely among themselves, and differ at least as much from Iowa or Missouri. In France, the Alps and Brittany, the Pyrenees and Flanders, Alsace and Corsica, are strikingly varied. On the other hand, both sides of a political frontier usually belong to the same physical world: the two banks of the Rio Grande, of the Saint Lawrence, of Lake Leman, of the Rhine, may not be of the same color on our school maps: but nature ignores our conventions. Not even small islands are marked out as forming homogeneous nationalities: there are three definitely conscious peoples in Great Britain, and two in Ireland. The Danube basin, which should form one vast unit, is split up into half a dozen hostile states—hostile even when some of them were living under the same King and

Emperor. All we can affirm of geography is that in certain cases it hinders, in others it favors unity: it never creates it.

A nation is a historical product, a tradition. It is the habit of living together: but it is a habit deepened into consciousness, consent, willingness, *will*. Five centuries of Turkish rule, the immemorial dynasty of the Habsburgs, failed alike to create nations. A nation is a constant act of faith; Poland survived in the hearts of her sons; the United States *is*, because we believe in the United States. A nation is a perpetual plebiscite: but one in which the dead also have a vote. The long-established custom of living together creates a *momentum* which a single generation finds it hard to overcome. Had that faith, obscurely preserved, not been rekindled; had that momentum completely lost its force, Grant's victory would have been in vain, and secession would have been inevitable.

We must cleanse our minds of superstitious awe when we think of the national spirit. Its origin may be obscure, but it is not mysterious; venerable with age, but not sacred. It had to assert its right to existence against the spirit of a larger whole: the countries of Europe are fragments of the Roman, the Carolingian, the Austrian, the Russian Empires; the countries of America had to tear themselves from England or Spain. It had to establish its supremacy over the spirit of smaller units— tribes, provinces, minor states,—themselves struggling for separate life, like Ireland, Catalonia, Porto Rico under our eyes. Neither secession nor annexation is a crime in itself: the stronger will, the longer will, is law.

Had Ireland weakened, Home Rule, and *a fortiori* independence, would have been treason.

Is this desire to form a self-contained unit, this *territorial will,* the very center of human culture? On the face of it, no. Man's basic needs—food, shelter, sex—are no less keenly felt when the boundary line is shifted and the design of the flag altered. The more profound yearnings, the higher achievements, religion, philosophy, science, are independent of frontiers. Neither for the starving man nor for Spinoza does the national state exist. Nationality occupies a middle ground, vast enough, but hard to define, for it is constantly expanding and contracting. And in a similar position, although not absolutely the same, do we find also literature.

The literary tradition and the national tradition merge at many points: but they do not quite coincide. The illiterate may be patriotic, like Joan of Arc; the leaders of literature may be cosmopolitan, like Jean-Jacques Rousseau. Any forcible assimilation between the two traditions would be ludicrous; still worse, any attempt to measure both by the same scale of values. But their close alliance can not be denied. It is often said that European literatures, at the end of the eighteenth century, were renovated through the national spirit. The converse seems to us even truer: the growth of national consciousness is a form of the Romantic revolt. This problem will be examined in its place. But, whichever side we take, we must admit the interaction of the two factors.

The national-political and the national-literary ideals are both *myths:* they are compounded of memories and dreams, far more than of direct experiences. But myths are not delusions or lies; and they have power over the hardest of facts. The national *type,* which plays such a leading part in politics and in literature, has no absolute existence. There is no Platonic "Idea of the Englishman", of which all actual Englishmen are but the distorted shadows. On the other hand, the English type is no mere fiction, no stock character that can be impersonated by any fairly competent actor. England's brilliant success in the last two centuries has spread to the four corners of the earth the Anglomaniac cult, not seldom oddly mingled with Anglophobia. There have been innumerable "English gentlemen", self-made, in Hamburg or Bordeaux, in Buenos Aires and Bombay, and even in Kansas City. But the spurious can soon be detected from the genuine.

The *type* is not a carnival costume: all its elements are in the man himself. But it is not the whole man: it represents a selection among potentialities. All tendencies are latent in all men: the notion of *type* makes it easier, without and within, to capitulate to some inclinations that we might have resisted, to cultivate others that we might have neglected. I witnessed in the South the tragedy of a fine Negro family gradually giving up the fight, stooping to the standards that were expected of them, almost imposed upon them. Treat a man like a "nigger", make him feel he is a "nigger", and he will act like a "nigger." The *type* incites us both to laziness and to heroism. An Englishman is as proud of his refusal to think logically, as of his punctiliousness in wearing formal dress for dinner. *Un-English,* it has been said, is a perfect fallacy in one word. But there are few truths as potent as such a fallacy.

We are inclined to think that the *type* idea is a dangerous one. It sanctions weaknesses far more than it fosters strenuous endeavor. The positive virtues are not national. With some slight shift of emphasis, it is right in all countries to be brave, truthful and kind. In essentials, there is no need to remind ourselves: *"Noblesse oblige:* we are from Lichtenstein and must keep up the great Lichtenstein tradition." The notion of type is a tempter at our elbow, encouraging self-indulgence. I may dream of being a great musician: what is the use? I do not belong to a musical race—and I resign myself to slipshod conformities. It is not our strongest points, but our pet failings, that are exalted into national traits, and thus made amiable, lovable, almost admirable. So one country will give prestige to muddleheadedness or snobbishness; another to pedantry or brutality; a third will smile complacently at its loose sexual code; a fourth will take pride in tippling, superstition, race prejudice.

The superficiality of the national type has been proved over and again. We might easily throw out of court any striking exception—a Scottish Sardanapalus, a Neapolitan Calvin, an Alabama Hegel, if such were found. But the commonly accepted national ideal may change in a generation, and even in a few years. No faster, however, than the physical type. Cartoonists still cling to a lanky Uncle Sam and a beefy John Bull, whereas the "typical" American is now heavily built, and the "typical" Britisher is slender. We were so sure that the muzhik worshipped his Little Father the Tsar, and would do so for ever, that some Americans are still shaking their heads incredulously at the Russian Revolution: these people are not playing the game, they are not true to type. Thirty years ago, every hardware salesman in Brummagem was persuaded that he had naval sense in his blood, whereas the Germans were hopeless landlubbers: he may have learned better by this time. Easygoing Italy finds herself suddenly stern and efficient, and seems to like it. Most *types* are as antiquated as the imperial goatee of the stage Parisian.

The type is a Jekyll-Hyde affair. Not merely because we never see ourselves as others see us (*we,* whoever we may be, are invariably good-natured and naïvely trustful, so we are invariably duped by the relentless, scheming, unscrupulous foreigner—whoever *he* may be). But even in our own eyes, we assume widely different aspects. Every nation has its heroic and its cynical moods. Uncle Sam is by turns generous to a fault, the crusader of democracy, pouring his wealth out in the service of "the common cause"; and, almost overnight, he is the suspicious, hard-headed, close-fisted business man, with nothing but scorn for his past generosity. Germany may to-day feel herself Beethoven, to-morrow Frederick II. England is chivalrous and mercantile, proverbially "perfidious" and scrupulously honorable, pitiless and tender. Ireland is lost in a reverie filled with mystic longings and sadness: but a man who attended a New York Police ball reported: "Celtic dreaminess and melancholy have been greatly exaggerated." France, "eternal France", "logical France", perhaps because I know her best, seems to me most bewildering of all—

generous and sordid, mystic and sceptical, invincibly per-
severing and easily discouraged, (madly adventurous and
prosaically prudent, Don Quijote and Sancho Panza.)
National psychology is not a chaos: but it is a kaleido-
scope, and the pattern may be changed at any moment.
Or again, the national *character* is not Proteus: but it
possesses a richer wardrobe than a Hollywood star, or
William II in all his glory.

All this holds true of the national-literary type. A
tradition is a capricious and weak-minded tyrant. It
hampers you at every turn with its irrational "Thou
shalt" and "Thou shalt not." But it yields flabbily to
determined rebellion: yesterday's bandit receives his
badge as to-morrow's *gendarme*. It is un-French to be
ponderous, un-German to be flippant, un-English to be
analytical . . . until the right man appears.

Let us take as an example the "Gallic" tradition of
irony in French literature. Handed down from the
early Middle Ages, it affected writers who, in other
climes, might have scorned it altogether. Montaigne
was nourished on the mighty classics of Greece and
Rome; he had before his eyes the tragic conflict between
Catholics and Hugenots: but the Gallic tradition made
it possible for him to smile. Pascal is the most profound,
the most ardent, the most tortured of mystics, and a
great mathematician withal: yet he wielded irony with
masterly grace. Voltaire was a philosopher, a scientist,
an historian, a reformer—so earnest that he burnt with
fever at the thought of injustice: yet all we remember
of him is the deadly precision of his wit. Renan was a
strange hybrid of scholarliness and religiosity: had he

lived either at Oxford or Tübingen, he would never have indulged in the voluptuous dilettantism and the urbane raillery of his latter years. Anatole France had the antiquarian tastes of a Benedictine monk, with an Anglo-Saxon propensity to sentiment. *The Crime of Sylvester Bonnard* and *The Book of My Friend* appeal to pure and gentle souls who enjoy a smile half-blurred with tears. Had he been a subject of Queen Victoria, he might have rejected the temptation of writing *The Rôtisserie*. The Gallic smile is found on lips of every shape. In the history of literatures as in the history of nations, a tradition is a very real personage—far more real than most characters of flesh and blood. The Monroe Doctrine counts for much more than President Monroe; the Puritanical Spirit has more substance than Jonathan Edwards.

True: but tradition, as we have seen, is but a small part of the truth, as far as the past is concerned; and it gives no safe indication of any truth to come. Literary tradition has exactly the same value as very incomplete statistics. We agree that there is a "Gallic tradition"; there is a better chance to find it among French theologians than among their German or American colleagues. But some of the greatest French writers—Racine, Montesquieu, Balzac—were affected by it only in their minor works; some others—Corneille, Bossuet, Rousseau, Buffon, Hugo, Zola—show no trace of it at all. At one time, the best representative of Gallic wit was Heinrich Heine, a German Jew; to-day, it might well be Aldous Huxley.

Literary tradition, like political tradition, is as arbitrary in its exclusions as in its inclusions. In three successive centuries, the official leaders of French literature had thought it incumbent upon them to give their country a national epic. They all failed: Ronsard with his *Franciade,* Chapelain with his *Pucelle,* Voltaire with his *Henriade.* Hence the *law: "Les Français n'ont pas la tête épique":* the French have no genius for the epic. It was not realized that the failure was due to the lifeless pastiching of a miraculous *pastiche,* Vergil's *Æneid.* Then the enormous and vigorous body of the French medieval epic was rediscovered; Agrippa d'Aubigné was brought to light; Victor Hugo wrote his uneven but magnificent *Legend of the Centuries;* the epic quality was manifest even in Zola; and the bogus "law" had to slink away.

The unreserved exaltation of Nationalism, both in politics and in literature, is a recent phenomenon. In the Middle Ages, "nations" were but local sections of the Catholic International. In Neo-Classical times, the dynasty, not the nation, was the historical unit: with the Habsburg Empire, this conception survived as late as 1918. Alsace became almost at once a loyal possession of the French crown; only at the time of the Revolution did it grow into an integral part of the French nation. The keenest minds of the eighteenth century owed allegiance to the Enlightenment rather than to the territorial state. Not only did poets and philosophers cheerfully serve a foreign king; but soldiers and financiers felt free to move from land to land. Most influential in French history were the Scot, John Law, the German, Marshal Maurice de Saxe, the Swiss, Necker. When democracy took over the heritage of the dynasties, when Romanticism substituted sentiment for reason, nationalism became supreme.*

Literature offers a parallel evolution. The great themes common to all medieval Europe—the religious works in Latin, the miracles and moralities, the farces and tales, the Carolingian and Arthurian epic cycles, *Reynard the Fox* and the *Romance of the Rose*—give the period a cultural unity far deeper than national differences. Humanism, Neo-Classicism, the Enlightenment, were Pan-European phenomena. A thorough Frenchman like Boileau ignored the purely French writers of the Middle Ages, but had at his finger tips his Greek, Latin and Italian classics. Samuel Johnson was a sturdy, insular Briton: yet he was more familiar with antiquity, with Boileau, Racine, Molière, Rousseau, than with Anglo-Saxon poetry. Goethe was as cosmopolitan as Frederick the Great himself. Even after the Revolution, the French Romanticists were not national: they rebelled against their own classics, and followed with enthusiasm Shakespeare, Ossian, Walter Scott, Byron.

This international spirit did not die a hundred years ago; nor is it, in our own days, limited to a few "men without a country." Cosmopolitanism begins in the nursery, with Æsop, Brer Rabbit, the Grimm Brothers, Andersen, *Pinocchio;* it continues through adolescence, with Jules Verne and Alexander Dumas; it reaches the masses, with the Bible and *Les Misérables;* it tops the best-sellers list, with *All Quiet on the Western Front* or

---

* *Cf.* Albert Guérard: "Herder's Spiritual Heritage: Nationalism, Romanticism, Democracy", in *Annals of the American Academy of Political and Social Science,* July, 1934.

Grand Hotel; it appeals to the educated, with Dostojewski, Ibsen, Nietzsche; it is the rule with the sophisticates, with Baudelaire, d'Annunzio, Valle Inclán, André Gide.

Nationalism is a fact: historically, a recent one; occording to all indications, transitory; in our opinion, dangerous rather than beneficial, an "aberration" rather than a virtue. But, fortunately, it is not so potent a fact in literature as in politics. All the nationalism of Messrs. W. R. Hearst, William Thompson, and other apostles of American Sinn Fein will not efface *English* literature from our tradition. Even those English writers who have attained greatness after our Declaration of Independence are ours by rights. To this day, we refuse to consider Kipling and Shaw as aliens: their rudeness is of the kind which we allow within the family. No Bismarckian policy could drive Grillparzer or Hebbel out of the German Confederacy; no Italian power can veto the *Anschluss* of Schnitzler, Wassermann, Keyserling, Gottfried Keller, Carl Spitteler, to the spiritual *Reich*. Rousseau never was a true Frenchman in any sense of the term: but the history of French literature can not be written with his name left out.

Some prophets of Nationalism are preaching that the first duty of the American artist is to picture *the American scene*. The Pulitzer prizes were founded to encourage this tendency, although one was awarded to Pearl Buck's epic of Chinese life, *The Good Earth*. If our ideal of literature be phonographic and photographic realism, no doubt we should note those things only which we have actually heard and seen: this condemns equally James Branch Cabell's Poictesme and Thornton

Wilder's Peru. But even this rather partisan conception of art would not make for one hundred per cent Americanism. If an American happens to be better acquainted with the boulevards of Paris than with the superhighways of Detroit, with the beauties of Tahiti than with those of Muncie, Mattoon or Milpitas, by all means let him write *realistically* of that which he knows best. There is no "American scene": there are "American scenes", so varied that no man can master them all or reduce them to a natural unity. And wherever an American artist casts his American eyes upon land or people, he annexes the scene to cultural America. No artist should despise his own folk; none should strive to be exotic and pose as an expatriate in his own country; but no artist either should consider wilful parochialism as his highest duty.

If by "Americanism" those critics mean, not the American scene, but the American ideal, we have a right to ask: "Which?" Whatever may be your criterion, you will find yourself aligned with foreigners against some of your fellow Americans. What is "the American ideal"? Is it Liberty and the Pursuit of Happiness, or is it stern Puritanism? Is it the pioneer's life, the vast open spaces, the ready pistol, the Western romance—or is it high efficiency and mass production, with their inevitable concomitants, intricate organization and mechanical conformity? Is it the Nordic and Protestant tradition, or Jeffersonian free thought? Is it Boston culture, or is it Will Rogers? In all cases, you will banish from your spiritual commonwealth millions of legal voters. Is your horror of the League of Nations to be the supreme test? Then excommunicate the spirit of Woodrow Wilson, Taft, Lowell, Herbert Hoover, Franklin Roosevelt and not a few others. Will you keep your patriotism pure by keeping it undefined? Then you will be most truly international: for "My country, right or wrong!" can be said in all languages, and emotional response to flag waving is very much the same, whatever may be the color of the flag.

Of course it would be pernicious nonsense to believe that Major Henry Bordeaux, because he is a member of the French Academy, stands on a higher level of culture than Sherwood Anderson; but would it be less pernicious to maintain that the Reverend Harold Bell Wright, because he is a true-born American, chock-full of American *mores,* writing an honest-to-God American vernacular, and depicting the wholesome American scene, should mean more to us than Thomas Mann? No, literary nationalism will not do. It is not even an honest prejudice: it is a cult for ultra-sophisticates who, since everybody has discovered Montparnasse, find it smart to rediscover Middletown.

Chapter 9

THE PROPER FIELD OF THE SOCIOLOGICAL METHOD

It has been a favourite pastime with students of literature to demolish Taine's method; but it pulls itself together again, and bobs up, every decade or so, as "scientific criticism", "sociological criticism", and even—God
save the mark!—as "the newer criticism." According
to our pragmatic principle, such popularity must be
deserved. The foregoing study may have seemed entirely destructive. Our intention, however, was to ad-
just rather than to disprove. The workman hammering
at a block of marble looks as though he were destroying
the block: under the sculptor's direction, he is revealing
the statue.

The sociological method explains everything *about*
literature, but not literature itself. It works as well for
the mediocrity as for the man of genius: the worst writer
in the language can boast: "I too have Race, Environment and Time!" Its cocksure determinism stumbles at
every step upon the unexplainable. Taine provided us
with a standard example. He devoted a stimulating and
entertaining book to *La Fontaine and His Fables*. Race,

environment and time made La Fontaine a "fable-tree", which bore fables as inevitably as a pear tree brings forth pears. But La Fontaine and Racine were both born in Champagne, within a few leagues and within a few years of each other, in exactly the same social stratum. The one wrote mocking and cynical fables, the other tragedies of fatal passion. And of the thousands of Champenois whose "race, environment and time" were the same as theirs, not one can compare with either of them.

We shall not embark upon a sophomoric discussion of determinism. Determinism may be true in the abstract: this is no concern of ours. In the most rigid sciences, such as celestial mechanics, a problem of such complexity may arise, that the human mind has to admit a temporary check. A literary problem is not merely one with three unknown quantities: it is one with an unknown number of unknown quantities. The scientific definiteness of Taine and his successors is a delusion. We felt from the beginning that there was "something" to race, environment and time. After this survey, we still feel that there is "something" to them: how much, we do not know. The terms are loosely defined; the relative value of the three factors is undetermined; and there are other factors in reserve, vaguely called *genius* and *chance,* which may be more powerful still. Taine's *Introduction* is bristling with "laws": but his hard-and-fast critical system reminds us of Alice's croquet party in Wonderland. The arches "Race" walk away; the balls "Environment" uncoil themselves and scurry off; the mallet "Time" stares at you with a puzzled, reproachful expression. The game is all the more delightful for being instinct with life: but the outcome is beyond scientific computation.

Of the three fatidical factors, Environment is at the same time the most obvious and the least certain. Human culture, a product of tradition and will, defies environment with surprising success. At least, this holds good within the brief limits of cultural history—a few hundred years, at most a few thousand. The songs of misty Scotland are enjoyed in arid Australia; the sonnets of the aristocratic Elizabethan Age still serve as patterns in democratic America. There are "world classics" which are treasured in common by all men of European origin, under all climates and all régimes.

Heredity is an undeniable fact: but race, in literature, is a wild hypothesis. We have no right to apply the principles of heredity, with any degree of minuteness and with any hope for accuracy, to the vast, arbitrary groups we call *races*. Even if we had fully established the physical characteristics of the race, we should still be a long way from a scientific connection between the physical and the mental.

There are blonds and brunettes: but blond *vs.* brunette literature is nonsense. Tradition, on the contrary, is a matter of record. We may dislike it, we may fight against it, but it is there. Supposing a mysterious disease should kill off all the blonds: so far as we can foresee, the main course of our civilization would not be altered. There would be plenty of dark-haired scholars to expound Shakespeare, and no lack of dark-haired poets inditing sonnets to their dark-haired ladies. Whether that course would be deflected and its momentum slowed down, is a matter of fanciful surmise. If, on the contrary, all the blonds were taken *at birth* and transported to a continent of their own, without the slightest connection with their history, it is certain that they would not reconstitute, out of their natural gift of blondness, the legacy of our culture, the masterpieces of Homer, Dante, Shakespeare; it is probable that they would not reach an equivalent stage for thousands of years. Culture is tradition, or if you prefer momentum, not race.

When blond Barbarians finally disrupted the decadent Roman world, the result was not a sudden rush of progress, but a relapse into barbarism which lasted for five hundred years. And it would have lasted longer, if so much of the old culture had not survived. So much for the coming upon the scene of a new, and supposedly superior, race.

Let us reverse the terms: in Hayti and Liberia, the accession to power of an "inferior" race has apparently led to a stagnation or regression of culture. But the social aspect of the question is more evident than the racial. If Hayti had been populated with ignorant *white* serfs, and if the mob had killed off or driven away all the elements which had a monopoly of traditional culture, the result would have been a similar set-back. This was not the case with the French Revolution, because, in proportion, the victims were far fewer; and because, among the Revolutionists, a good many were better educated than the aristocracy. The social shift did imply some loss in culture (we have not fully reached again the eighteenth century level), but no catastrophic destruction. There are at present as charming and as cultured people at Port-au-Prince as could be found in a French provincial town of the same size. And it is not proven that a few thousand *white* proletarians, if they had been practically abandoned in the marshes of the West African coast, would have done a much better job than the Liberians. Civilization is not *in the blood*: it is a tradition. And let us hope that its "acquired velocity" is increasing.

This conception is frankly opposed to the fatalism of the Racialists. There is no abyss between man and man. Whatever is *humanly* right can be taught to all men; whatever a nation lacks, it may acquire. There is no French logic and American logic, no English honesty and German honesty, any more than there are Italian triangles and Turkish triangles.

But this view, far from committing us to radicalism, acts as a warning against it. Civilization is a vast collective tradition, far more complex than any mind, far larger than any group; it has momentum; it can not be altered suddenly. An individual child may be easily transplanted; an isolated adult, if he be willing, can be assimilated, although never to perfection; a compact group, even a single family, offers much greater resistance; a whole social class, an entire nationality, can not jump from one civilization to another. Class and nation have a civilization of their own, which permeates their being, and has become second nature. The change of a few words or forms will not alter these deep-rooted facts. It is admitted that the Negroes, at the close of the Civil War, were not ready for wholesale admission to full citizenship. It is now confessed that we can not turn Filipinos into standard Americans. Japan changed its costume at the time of the Meiji, but remained the most tradition-loving of great nations. The Russian Revolution has been surprisingly successful: but only because the discarded civilization was itself a recent importation from the West.

Never and *At Once* are both misleading. But it is possible, through a cautious hybridization of cultures, to strengthen their common elements and minimize their differences until they cease to be a cause of strife. We do not want abruptly to renounce everything American in favor of a cosmopolitan culture which is still woefully vague; still less should we throw our whole tradition overboard, and replace it with some alien nationalism, after the fashion of certain expatriates. But it would be no less foolish to deny ourselves enrichment that is ours for the asking. There is nothing "un-American" about *Homo Sum*. Whatsoever is good throughout the world is ours, and should be incorporated in our tradition. The only result of Cultural Protectionism would be to stunt our growth.

The *Racialists* claim that the *Humanists* (in the widest, Terentian sense of the term) think in lifeless abstractions; that they know *Man,* an idea, as in the eighteenth century, not the flesh and blood realities, the Englishman, the Italian, the American. But the Humanist is not committed to the myth that all men are equal; still less to the absurdity that all men are identical; he professes, on the contrary, that all men are different. It is the Racialist who is creating general types, Platonic ideas, which have no concrete existence: *the* Negro, *the* Jew, *the* Russian, *the* German. In a quarter of a century of

American life, I have met thousands of Americans, but never *the* American, a purely statistical creature, who is five feet nine inches tall, earns $1242.18 a year, owns one sixth of a car, and possesses two and five eighths children.

The application of this discussion to literature is two-fold.

If we are interested in an author, we shall want to know all about him; conversely, knowledge fosters and deepens interest. We are tempted to read the books of the people we have met, and to meet the people whose books we have enjoyed. In that quest for information, "Race, Environment and Time" provide a good general programme. If we go through with it, we shall have no hard-and-fast law, no rule of criticism, no explanation: but we shall have gathered a quantity of facts, conveniently classified, which will enrich our enjoyment. Remove all the scientific claims from Taine's method, and what remains is excellent.

Our second conclusion is that the proper field of literature is *literature,* not nationality, not even language. It is far more important, at every stage of our development, to read good books than to read American books. Washington Irving is a charming minor essayist: but it is better for us to know Goethe than to know Washington Irving. As our opportunities are limited, we should go straight to essentials. In the grammar school as well as in the university, those world masterpieces which have become part and parcel of our own heritage should take precedence of national second-raters. Not only would this bring art into line with religion and science, which are already supra-national; but it would also bring the *study* of literature into line with the actual *facts* of literature. From the kindergarten to the grave, man seeks the best. If the best is grown in our own parish, we must not despise it; but, should it come from the antipodes, it is still the best.

Part II

Homo Scriptor
The Author as a Social Type

Chapter 10

THE LITERARY TYPE

THE reader must be fully persuaded by this time that we have no faith in the objective existence of *types*. Types are abstractions, stiff bloodless creatures of the logical mind. You never can prophesy, with any certainty, whether the member of a given group will act "true to type." Types, however, are not sheer delusion. Their existence is partly statistical, partly mythical. As statistical abstracts, they have some basis in reality; as myths, they have power to inhibit and to encourage.

The "literary type"—the quintessence of innumerable "literary types"—is among the most puzzling of all. None has enjoyed a more prolonged and distinct existence: Plato, Aristotle, Horace, already spoke of poets as a *genus*. None is so self-conscious, and none possesses a stronger formative influence: men strive laboriously to look, dress, talk, drink, love, like poets. On the other hand, the very nature of poetry is individualism. The first article in the code of priest or soldier is: "Thou shalt obey"; in the code of the gentleman: "Thou shalt conform"; in the code of the poet: "Thou shalt be different." As a result, the soldier type is plain, clear-cut, permanent; the poet type is myriad-shaped and elusive.

We are using the word *poet* instead of the more general one *author*. We have no thought of limiting ourselves to the writers of uneven lines; but we do want to limit ourselves to those men in whom the creative, the personal element predominates: and that element is essentially the artistic or poetic.

We shall therefore leave out of our survey, at this stage, all those for whom artistic creation is secondary, even though they may hold an important place in the history of literature. For instance, we shall eliminate from our consideration the *Bookman* in his different varieties—the scholar, the antiquarian, the critic, the professor. He is emphatically a man of letters: on the face of it, far more so than men of fashion like Byron. He may be a master of style. But he is not on the battle line; his activity is in the auxiliary services. This exclusion connotes no lack of respect or affection. We find much more pleasure in good criticism than in poor lyric. The "ripe", "mellow", "fruity" scholar, such as Sir Edmund Gosse or Professor George Saintsbury, is a delightful character indeed: we deeply regret that, west of Boston (or should we say west of Cape Race?) he should be such an exotic. We need scarcely add that the bookman and the artist may blend. There are scholarly poets like Milton, and critics who raise their craft to the creative level like Sainte-Beuve. Walter Pater's thought was too vital, his art was too exquisite, for us to place him among the "mere" bookmen. Creators, on the other hand, may affect the bookish attitude. Anatole France's favorite impersonations, Sylvester Bonnard, Jerome Coignard, Lucien Bergeret, are denizens of Bibliopolis, and smile, not without vanity, at their own pedantry; Cabell added a new involution to his irony through his fanciful and recondite learning.

We love to linger in this twilight zone: but we know that the "typical poet" is not to be found there. The antiquarian might be interested in medals rather than in manuscripts; the collector might be gathering postage stamps or match boxes instead of first editions; the professor might be teaching political history instead of literature, and their psychology, like their mode of life, would remain very much the same.

We must also exclude, under the same rule, those men who use literature only as a vehicle: the statesman, the reformer, the preacher, the philosopher, the historian. Here the distinction is far more delicate. "Pure" poetry, absolutely divorced from thought or purpose, is a will o' the wisp. The most detached artist is preaching; in the name of Art for Art's Sake, he advocates either beauty-worship, or a philosophy of futility. We hope to examine this puzzling problem in a companion volume.

There are, however a number of clear-cut cases. Many leading statesmen in Europe and in America have written books, not invariably poor, and not invariably on political subject. But their most devoted admirers would hardly claim a place in literature for Presidents Hoover and Coolidge, or even for Presidents Wilson and Theodore Roosevelt. In France, Clemenceau the writer was but one of the minor aspects of Clemenceau the man of action. In England, the fairly voluminous *Works* of

Gladstone are a curiosity, and a dusty one at that. The cases of Bryce and Morley would be worth arguing; those of Burke and Macaulay even more so. With Napoleon and Disraeli, we reach genuine artists, poets if you please, that is to say creators: but for them, however, the literary medium was a secondary one. There is no doubt that Rousseau and Carlyle belong to literature, although they preached unceasingly; and that Tolstoy did not lose his literary standing when he wrote *The Kreutzer Sonata, Resurrection,* or even *What is Art?*

We shall not seek the type either among those for whom literature is first of all a gainful occupation: the hackwriter, the author of potboilers, and, in most cases, the journalist. They live by their pen, blunt or sharp; they reap their reward, pitiful or splendid; and they are to be judged by the exacting standard of the commercial world. If they deliver on time the standard article at the standard price, they deserve credit—according to Dun and Bradstreet's. There is nothing more dishonorable about writing readable stories than about manufacturing the chewing gum advertised on the other side of the page.

In this case also, no absolute rule can be laid down. The priest who lives of the altar is not guilty of simony; an author may lose amateur standing without losing his talent. David Starr Jordan defined success as "doing the thing you like and getting paid for it." Shakespeare and Molière were very frankly "in the business." De Foe and Diderot had their years of Grub Street. Alexander Dumas was an *entrepreneur* on a large scale, gathering and marketing the work of Auguste Maquet and a host of others. Balzac's feverish production was a neck-to-neck race with the sheriff. The mighty *Misérables* was deliberately planned and advertised to be a best-seller. Few authors are absolutely free from the mercenary motive—especially if you include social advancement and prestige under material rewards. "No man but a blockhead," said Samuel Johnson, "ever wrote except for money."

I was once taught the useful difference between mushrooms and toadstools; the ones offer a ring which is lacking in the others. But, in many cases, the genuine ring may be so faint as to become invisible; in others, a spurious ring will appear, hard to distinguish from the real one. I decided to leave the matter to experts. In literature, there are works that remain genuine art, although they were frankly made to sell; and commercial articles that closely imitate the artistic. To tell them apart, a delicate touchstone is required.

Finally, we must separate the artistic type from its wilful caricature the Bohemian: "dwellers on the coast of Bohemia" and Philistines at heart, so well depicted by W. D. Howells and Margaret Kennedy; *bona fide* Bohemians also, if they have no claim to art or literature except their bohemianism. Unclipped locks, absinthe and a pack of creditors do not make a poet, if no poems are forthcoming; they only make what Spengler would call a case of *pseudomorphism:* in the vernacular, a faker.

Supposing we had isolated *the typical poet:* what would be the use? A purely negative one perhaps: but negative is not the same as negligible. It will give us no key to the baffling problem of greatness: but it will help us define the problem. If we subtract from both poets the elements common to Campbell and Coleridge, we shall be better prepared to feel the differences.

But this belongs to a criticism of values, with which this book is not concerned. In the study of literature and society, the action of the literary type is of definite importance. Literature, as we have said, is a distorting mirror. Each individual author has his personal equation, his aberration, which must be taken into account. But there are elements common to most writers, and not common to all their contemporaries. These elements define *Homo Scriptor:* it would be a source of error to identify them either with the single writer under study, or with the whole period and nation.

There are, for instance, in certain medieval works as well as in certain grotesque carvings, traces of an irreverent, almost irreligious spirit, which seems incompatible with the "pure" and "ardent" faith of the age. These are found quite early: in the *Pilgrimage of Charlemagne,* which is approximately as old as the *Song of Roland.* The *naïveté* of the time offers a convenient explanation: our ancestors were untaught children, and knew no better. We have our suspicions: the *naïveté* might be found chiefly among the Romanticists, who gave us such a conventional picture of the times "when Knighthood was in flower." The Middle Ages were as frankly anti-clerical as they were superstitious: superstition and anti-clericalism form a loose aggregate, which allows doubt to filter in. The people who made such broad fun of their monks can not have believed every word that the monks told them. Still, we do not want to turn a medieval market or pilgrimage crowd into a Voltairian audience. There was no lack of yokels, and burgesses, and clerics too, who could not tell the difference between an authentic miracle and a miracle of irony: in our own days, they would vote *Thais* an edifying tale. Those who knew enough to laugh in their sleeves were, in all likelihood, very few; but, among those few were, first of all, *the poets themselves.*

Their profession attracted men who were clever rather than submissive; who had received the rudiments of an education, but who, like Villon, were ill-adapted to discipline; quite possibly dissolute, and all the more disposed to scoff, as openly as they dared, at all authorities. Ironical freethought, which peers at us so strangely through the veil of naïve orthodoxy, is certainly not representative of the public as a whole, and it is not purely accidental: it is part of one literary type.

We have selected this rather remote and controversial example, because it is not so trite as others. It is plain, for instance, that Romanticism never truly represented the masses or even the classes. It was a fashion among the artists and poets, and is to be explained in terms of artistic or literary psychology. England in the first decades of the nineteenth century, France a few years later, were not in the least romantic, although the vogue prevailing among artists was bound to spread—very thinly—to *bourgeois* drawing rooms and backshop parlors. Under the Second Empire, literature was tinged with pessimism: there is no sign that the French people, from the Imperial Court down to the peasantry, were similarly affected. With all its glitter and corruption, the régime brought solid prosperity, which was honestly enjoyed. The disease known as *Decadence* preyed upon the *literati* in the closing years of the nineteenth century, but spared the nations. This discrepancy was more evident in London than in Paris: the French had some cause for national discouragement; but the England of Victoria's two Jubilees had not deserved Aubrey Beardsley and Oscar Wilde. The sophistication and cynicism that followed the Great War—more accurately, the fruit of America's *gran rifiuto*—betray the state of mind of a very small group. We may have been in the mood for *This Side of Paradise* and *The Sun Also Rises:* but you, and I, and President Coolidge, were not really sophisticated and cynical.

All this simply reasserts the fact that, within the general framework of a society, literature enjoys a large measure of autonomy. In order to understand a writer, it is not sufficient to know the "race, environment and time" factors, which apply equally to author and public. By the fact of becoming an author a man joins a group which, even without any material organization, has an existence, an atmosphere, a code of its own. This group is based first of all on natural selection: few men are forced into successful authorship against their secret inclination. That fundamental element is strengthened by tradition. Obviously, all authors are not alike, any more than all Americans are alike. Obviously also, they are at least ninety-nine per cent human and barely one per cent literary. But that one per cent does influence their literature.

Chapter 11

PHYSIOLOGY OF THE AUTHOR TYPE

Is there a physical type of the author? The reader will remember that, according to Taine, certain "marked differences" in bodily structure corresponded with certain "innate dispositions." Some varieties of men are "capable of superior conceptions and creations, others are limited to rudimentary ideas and inventions, just as there are certain breeds of dogs better fitted for racing, others for fighting, others for hunting, and others still for keeping watch over house or herd." This opens entrancing vistas. If we were able to follow up Taine's suggestions, we might some day pick out our poets and our generals with the same certainty as we get a spaniel or a bulldog.

But we are not even within sight of the goal. I am tolerably familiar with the iconography of authorship, and I find it impossible to visualize the composite picture of "the author." When we can tell, by looking at a portrait, that it represents a poet, it is on account of some artificial detail: the wind-tossed mane and the hygienic loose collar of the Shelleyans, the flowing beard,

like that of a river god, of the ancient philosophers, restored to favor by the poets of the eighteen-sixties, Tennyson, Hugo, Longfellow; the rapt, *Excelsior!* gaze. All
this is pardonable, but histrionic.

Many of our effigies of great writers are thus conven-
tionalized, turned into symbols of the work rather than
likenesses of the man. Rodin gave us a haunting vision
of the Dantesque spirit that conceived the *Human
Comedy:* monstrous, formidable, with unfathomable all-
fathoming eyes, a mouth like a gash tortured into a leer,
the folded arms of defiance, the recoil of fascinated horror. But Monsieur de Balzac in the flesh was short,
podgy, greasy, rubicund, loud and hilarious. Tennyson's
description of Victor Hugo remains strikingly beautiful:

> *Weird Titan,*
> *Cloud-weaver of phantasmal hopes and fears . . .*

But the Weird Titan was small, neat, and rather too
punctilious in his old-fashioned courtesy. Shakespeare's
picture is the only strong argument in favor of the Bacon-
ian hypothesis. It would be ungenerous to dwell on the
regrettable features of certain authoresses, from Madame
de Staël to a modern American poetess. The advent of
photography, and especially of the "candid camera" in
contemporary journalism, has destroyed the myth of the
literary type. We are persuaded that, on their passports,
our most aërial songsters, like the rest of us, resemble
escaped convicts.

Our impressions, although not vague, are, we must
confess, very loose. But, if a conscientious research worker
were to tell us that the average poet is auburn haired,

grayish-blue eyed, and weighs 159 pounds stripped, the natural answer would be: "What of it?" or, for genuine Americans: "Oh, yeah?"

There is one fairly definite notion, however, that bears investigation: poets are sensitive, fragile; their souls wear out their bodies; beloved of the gods, they die young. It is within the reach of any one to work out the vital statistics of the Immortals. Without any effort, innumerable names flow from our fountain pen: Sophocles, Lope de Vega, Calderon, Goethe, Arndt, Paul Heyse, Tolstoy, Metastasio, Goldoni, Carlo Gozzi, Manzoni, Voltaire, Chateaubriand, Lamartine, Mistral, Anatole France, Paul Bourget, Wordsworth, Landor, Samuel Rogers, Carlyle, Tennyson, Browning, Ruskin, Thomas Hardy, Robert Bridges . . . all well beyond the scriptural three score and ten. In terms of life insurance, poets are good risks, and entitled to preferential rates. In only one class do we find greater longevity: among our Southern Negroes. But the imagination of colored folks ranks far higher than their accuracy.

Marlowe, Shelley, Byron, died young; but Marlowe's death, and Shelley's, were due to accidents; Byron's, to very abnormal causes: the three men were vigorous, and even athletic. Chatterton committed suicide. Keats remains the one striking example of a supreme poet cut off in his prime. It is true that we can not take into account all the geniuses that perished before the world had heard their names. It is true also that a long life affords better opportunities for notable performance, and that a very long life will give a good writer rather excessive prominence. The years, as they accumulate, may crush you, or raise you far above the crowd: it depends partly on your skill, and far more on your luck, whether you remain on top of the pile. *Peccavimus:* we made too much of Anatole France, on the strength of his nearing eighty; we accorded him the European primacy once held by Voltaire, Goethe, Hugo and Tolstoy, and made him look absurdly small on the massive pedestal of his fame. We have ranked Thomas Hardy a little too high, simply because he happened to be the last of the Victorians. We are in danger of spoiling G. B. Shaw: the majesty of a living classic does not fit well with his cap and 'bauble. We may therefore assume that in literature, many writers failed to impress the world simply because time was not granted them; while others rose high partly because they happened to live long. But this is true of all professions. Keats, Poe, Heine, and, in our own days, Katherine Mansfield and D. H. Lawrence, show what can be done in spite of an ailing body; but great achievements, as a rule, are facilitated by physical vigor.

The longevity of the man is not the same as the longevity of the author. Sainte-Beuve claimed that we all carry in our hearts a poet who died young; the writer of verse may not be aware that the poet in him is dead. Many living worthies are statues on their own monuments. Few men have done their best work after sixty. Hardy, whose epic drama *The Dynasts* is held by many to outrank his novels, is one of the exceptions. But, while not supreme, the writings of old men may stand very high. Goethe and Hugo, after seventy, preserved powers that justified their primacy. There are beautiful notes in the swan songs of Landor, Tennyson, Browning. An old writer, quite apart from the inevitable weakening of his faculties, labors under an unjust disadvantage. If he perseveres in the accustomed way, he will be accused of repeating himself. His formula will have lost its freshness; a whole generation of imitators will have made it commonplace. If he wanders into unwonted paths, he is "falling off from his standard", he is "losing himself." When, under Napoleon, the Parisians heard the familiar boom of the cannon of the Invalides heralding some new victory, they shrugged their shoulders with indifference: the public has been less than fair to the latterday books of Rudyard Kipling. Paul Bourget, well over eighty, is still turning out at least one volume of fiction every year. It sells, it is respectfully and frigidly noticed by the press, but no one pays any serious attention to it. Yet there is no evidence that the new book is noticeably worse than his work half a century ago. This remark, it is true, might cut both ways. Mr. Cabell, at fifty, decided that *James Branch Cabell* was played out; but he at once started a fresh career as *Branch Cabell*. We may live to see *Branch Cabell* exhaust himself by the time he is seventy-five: then *Cabell* will take up the wondrous tale.

Longevity naturally evokes the corresponding term, precocity. When does authorship begin? There are few infant prodigies in literature. The case of Opal Whiteley, which created quite a stir a few years ago, is not authenticated beyond cavil. Her diary was a curiosity rather than a masterpiece: remove the extraneous elements, the age of the authoress, the alleged mystery of her origin, the quaint French names she gave to animals and trees, and very little remains. Her gifts, which can not be denied, have not borne later fruit. We are willing to believe that Daisy Ashford's *The Young Visiters* was not written by J. M. Barrie. Conscious or not, it was a delightful satire: delightful, but extremely slight, and, after all, only a happy accident.

Indeed it seems as though the only art in which children could excel were music. An eight-year-old pianist or violinist, strangely enough, is not a musical box in human shape. He expresses feelings for which he has no words; he may develop, not merely into a great virtuoso, but even into a genuine master. Mozart was such a *Wunderkind*. What is the difference? The actual technique of literature, beyond the elementary knowledge of language, is not so elaborate as that of piano or violin. Does music, in spite of ambitious intellectual *programmes,* express only those rudimentary moods which are common to all ages, and which perhaps reach below the human level as well as above? I have seen *music* looking out of a dog's eyes: but music without words.

The poetic urge comes with adolescence: in this, as in so many other respects, it is strangely akin to love and religion. Poetry marks the early dawn of puberty, the moment when youth falls in love with love. When love dreams assume human form, the poetic impulse loses its perfect clearness.

How is it, then, that masterpieces are written by men in their late twenties, rather than by boys and girls in their teens? But we must distinguish the mental (or better the sentimental) age from the chronological. The true poet is, intermittently at least, the eternal adolescent. Even Goethe at sixty, the glorious head of a great national literature, the dean of European letters, philosopher, scientist, man of the world, Olympian—Goethe could actually fall in love with a child.

Then we must remember that "masterpieces"—the thought will constantly recur throughout this book—are stamped as such by their public; and the influential public, the public that buys books, controls magazines, writes reviews, fills professorships, awards prizes, elects to Academies, is a grown-up public, contemptuous of callow sentiment. Adolescent poets are easily repressed by the irony of their elders, and even more by that of their contemporaries. As a rule, they have not found their proper medium. They can only imitate or rebel: two effective manners of not being themselves. Perhaps the safest hypothesis is that poetry can never be "pure" poetry, sheer music; thought and experience do count, and these deepen with age. All this may explain a certain lag between the poetic impulse, which comes with early puberty, the first poems worthy of notice, which rather belong to the eighteenth or twentieth year, and those revealing full mastery, which have to age in the wood quite a while longer.

If we accept the view that poetry belongs to adolescence, it will be difficult to admit that the poetical gift might manifest itself, *for the first time,* in middle age. Poets are born about sixteen, not about forty. There have been many cases of poets revealing themselves to the public in their late maturity, like Agrippa d'Aubigné, the Huguenot captain, and Thomas Hardy, the realis-

tic novelist. But both of them had written, in privacy
if not in secret, for many years. It is not inconceivable that
the gift may lie dormant, almost unconscious. Edmund
About relates the queer case of Monsieur Guérin, who
carried unawares an undeveloped twin in his body; suddenly, the twin began to grow, and had to be obstetri-
cally removed, to the infinite embarrassment of Monsieur
Guérin. Such a freak may occur in the literary world.
As a rule, whoever did not feel the poetic fire at sixteen
will never feel it at all. Potential poets are as numerous
as potential lovers or potential Christians; *great* poets, no
rarer than great lovers or true Christians. The paucity of
genuine poets need not imply that Nature is parsimoni-
ous: it may mean that *self-poeticide* is a widely prevalent
form of murder.

The author's *temperament,* although it manifestly has
a physiological basis, will more naturally be considered
under psychology. If we had hundreds of monographs
such as the one that Dr. Toulouse devoted to Emile Zola,
we *might* discover the physical concomitants that denote
literary superiority. So far, there is not even a self-respecting hypothesis in that direction. Phrenology is in
disrepute; it may come back—there have been stranger
turns of the wheel. The cephalic index, as we have seen,
is hardly safer: Mrs. Atherton is an angel who rushed
where scientists fear to tread.

There remains one biological factor which might be
of capital importance in the study of literature: *heredity.*
While *race* is far too hazy a concept to be of serious value,
ancestry is much more definite. Literary gifts, although
they may be revealed and perfected through training,

are pretty evidently inborn. The best teaching may enable a man to write correctly, and even to write *well*: it will not turn him into a writer. Ancient experience is in accord with modern science. "Poets are born, not made"; and Boileau, much as he believed in the virtue of Reason, rules, and hard work, opened his *Art Poétique* with the warning: "In vain will a rash author attempt to scale the heights of Parnassus, if he does not feel the secret influence of heaven, if his star, at his birth, has not made him a poet."

As heredity is a patent fact in so many fields, as its laws in simple cases have been defined with remarkable accuracy, we are tempted, with the hasty logic which so often gets the better of scientific caution, to assert that heredity *must* operate in *all* cases. There is no marked ability that is not the sign of an inborn tendency; there is no inborn tendency that could not be traced, if the facts were known, to some ancestor. Sir Francis Galton, in his *Hereditary Genius,* did not fail to include a chapter on *Literary Genius*. As the school of Galton is still lustily alive, as his name is still one to swear by, we urgently recommend the reading of that chapter. In our opinion, it is extraordinarily convincing—in disproof of Galton's thesis.

We start with a fundamental ambiguity. Genius! What is Genius? We shall have to devote a whole chapter to the discussion of that essential term. In common parlance, it denotes a gift so extraordinary that it may well seem mysterious. For Galton and his school, it means simply marked superiority of any kind, established by wide recognition. He includes among his instances many names that no literary critic would ever dream to consider as geniuses. Now this ought to make a marked difference. Mere *superiority* may often be explained in terms of environment: education and opportunities. There are dynasties among professional men, among craftsmen, even among artists, which require no other hypothesis. If a child is decently intelligent, his education in a particular line will begin unconsciously at his father's table, with chance questions answered off-hand by an expert. The child will *play* at his father's craft; later on, his father will be his teacher and his guide, or, at any rate, will be able to pick out for him the best teachers and guides. Tools or books will be available; the boy will have valuable sympathies and connections at the very outset of his career: he is born in the purple. A Huxley, connected on every side, for three or four generations, with science and literature, would be inexcusable if he did not show some brilliancy. In order to catch up with the young aristocrat or plutocrat of culture, the child of the farm or the slum will have to reveal overwhelming powers.

So it is not safe to judge by the men who have done creditable work in their father's line. Their success proves that they were not fools: it does not prove that they were geniuses. With a trifle more luck—greater commanders in the field, an abler assistant at his elbow, a demoralized opponent—the younger Moltke might have been quoted as an outstanding example of military genius running in certain families. He came within an ace of success: and we know that his military gifts were not of the highest order. He was aware of it, and begged the Kaiser not to impose upon him a crushing responsibility. His *apparent* superiority, which fate might have left unchallenged, was entirely due to opportunities. His rise to the supreme position in the German army was not an instance of hereditary genius, but only one of nepotism.

In order to establish Galton's thesis, it would be necessary to discriminate experimentally between inborn gifts and a favorable environment. To that end, we should have to shift the children around—to entrust the heir of the successful man to the petty shopkeeper or the hard-struggling mechanic, and *vice versa*. This would have to be done on a sufficiently large scale; and there is no sign that many families are ready for such a sacrifice in the interests of science. Moreover, the children would have to be unconscious of the change; *and the parents also:* else the essential conditions would not be comparable. We can not sufficiently repeat that it is impossible to experiment with human beings as freely as with rats, guinea pigs, and Mendel's sweet peas.

This quantitative method failing us, we should restrict ourselves to *genius* in its more unquestioned and most striking form, genius such as it appears, in each nation, not more than a dozen times in a hundred years. Within these limits, the theory breaks down altogether. In many cases, we know neither the ancestors of our geniuses nor their progeny; when we do know them, they are not geniuses themselves. There has been no Dante Junior, no Shakespeare the Son, no Voltaire Fils, no Goethe the Younger. The three authentic sons of Napoleon, the Duke of Reichstadt, Count Walewski and Count Léon, revealed no transcendant gifts. Rousseau "experimented" with his children by sending them all to a foundling's hospital: all have disappeared without a trace.

Galton's chapter is so weak that it raises the contrary question: why is it that there is no true "literary peerage", why is there so little transmitted superiority? We must reassure the sons of great writers in the same way as Reverend Clarence Macartney found it necessary to reassure the sons of ministers: favorable instances are numerous enough to prove that there is no inescapable blight. Beyond this it is difficult to go.

Many explanations have been offered for this paradoxical phenomenon. The first is that men of literary genius, when they are parents at all, are not invariably the best of parents. In fact, they are frequently the reverse. The intimate biographies of writers are not always edifying. Irregularities, quarrels, nervousness, despair, often poison the home atmosphere, and would make the growing boy vow that he will get as far away from literature as he can. Unfortunately for this ingenious explanation, it is not confirmed by the facts. Those writers whose lives were unimpeachable, like Tennyson, were not more successful than the others in transmitting their genius. On the other hand, the clearest case of heredity is perhaps that of the two Dumas. The father, with all his absurdities and his commercialism, had indomitable verve and a matchless narrative gift. The son, absurdly depreciated to-day because of his excessive cleverness, perfected the problem play before Ibsen, and the long, brilliant preface on social problems before Bernard Shaw. Now, old Dumas was a flamboyant example of the prodigal father, and took his parental responsibilities with incredible lightheartedness.

Perhaps, in many cases, superiority in the father was the result of a struggle; the son reaches too easily a stage which should be conquered. To win the right of meeting the great on a footing of social equality is in itself a challenge and an education; to take that right for granted, as your father's son, weakens the virtue of the experience. In literature, as in politics or in business, the heir is seldom equal to the founder of the line. Yet his gifts may not be inferior: only they fail to grow, for lack of a sufficient incentive. The romance of success can hardly be repeated generation after generation.

Sonship is therefore a dangerous position in literature. To follow in your father's footsteps condemns you to mere *pastiche;* and so you may well feel discouraged in advance. To depart from his methods and standards carries with it a suspicion of disloyalty. The superficial encouragement of a literary home turns into a very real inhibition.

While the sons of writers are thus hampered from within, they find no' predisposition in their favor among the public. Their inferiority is taken for granted. Victor Hugo's sons, Charles and François, had no lack of ability. It is hard to tell how far they would have gone, if in everybody's eyes and in their own, their father's glory had not reduced them to insignificance. His grandson, Georges, was admirably gifted. But the poem of which he and his sister Jeanne were the heroes, or rather the victims, *The Art of Being a Grandfather,* hung like a millstone round his neck. He was The National Infant: France never admitted that he could grow out of his swaddling clothes. He had to be an artist almost surreptitiously. Maurice Rostand wrote the tragedy of his own fate: his father's fame imprisons him as in a "Crystal Tomb."

It is absurd to talk of literary genius as though it could be measured in scientific terms. Ability is inextricably mingled with success, and success with opportunity. Napoleon fifty years earlier or later would not have been the Napoleon we worship. Rousseau's unknown children may have had all their father's *genius:* but that genius was inseparable from a preëxisting movement, of which Rousseau became the symbol even more than the guide.

The history of literature is not that of individual achievements, but that of public taste. This makes the study of hereditary genius practically hopeless: gifts may be transmitted, but not the chance of revealing them. As a concession to Galton, we are willing to admit that great work can hardly be expected from the descendants of unmitigated morons. Even then, we are reluctant to give up the saving clause: "The wind bloweth where it listeth."

Chapter 12

SOCIOLOGY OF THE AUTHOR TYPE

UNDER the wilfully formidable heading *Sociology,* we propose to examine two different problems. The first, and by far the simpler, is: from what class in society do authors principally come? The second, much more puzzling: what is the place of authors *as such* in organized society? Do they naturally aggregate themselves to one of the existing groups, or do they form a group of their own?

I

We note without surprise that, until the nineteenth century, very few writers came directly from the common people. The masses, for one thing, were illiterate; the literature which was fully recognized required a classical education. A young peasant who managed, under such unpromising circumstances, to show some promise, might be steered into the Church and the Universities. If he left those havens of safety, he was seldom heard of again. Villon's posthumous luck was a miracle; he might, however, have preferred a living to a legend. Religious literature, more democratic in certain respects than her profane sister, gave us John Bunyan the tinker; "philosophy" had Diderot, the cutler's son; the lyric offers Bobbie Burns, the Ayrshire peasant.

The nineteenth century gradually removed one disability by offering education more generously, and another by weakening social prejudices. So the sons of working men who made their mark in literature become more numerous as we approach our own times. However, even at present, the proletarians are not represented in the literary field in proportion to their numbers. The parvenu of letters is rarer than the financial parvenu. This does not establish that the poorer classes are, intellectually, the lower classes. It rather indicates that refined, traditional literature is a luxury that the people can not well afford. The first desire of the working man is to turn his son into a *bourgeois,* not into an artist. There is snobbishness no doubt in such a consciousness of the social hierarchy; but there is also a more definite feeling. The poor suffer from insecurity even more than from physical discomfort: what they dream of is an established position. Authorship is a gamble; the fame and emolument that it brings are precarious.

The conditions we have just sketched belong to a passing order. Increasingly, education is placed within the reach of all; increasingly, literature throws off the thrall of certain social conventions. The time may not be far off when a knowledge of literary tradition will be a heavy handicap. The Proletarian State is fostering literature: according to Stuart Chase, an author in Russia may receive the largest income allowed in that country. But the conditions adverse to the literary expression of the working classes had prevailed, almost without a challenge, until a hundred years ago; and, even in America, these conditions have left traces which can not be ignored.

The titled aristocracy, at the other end of the scale, is infinitely more fertile for literature than the masses. If, however, we consider, not their respective numbers, but their respective opportunities, the difference is no longer so striking. In the Middle Ages, the noblemen were fighters, and took pride in their lordly ignorance; but from the dawn of the Renaissance at any rate—earlier in Southern France and Italy—it was no longer ungentlemanly to be literate. The aristocracy had education, leisure, social refinement, prestige: what did they do with all these advantages? No doubt there were great writers among them, and even on the throne: of the two French poets that stand out in the murky welter of the fifteenth century, one was a vagabond, Villon, the other a prince of the royal blood, Charles of Orleans. But the *Debrett's Peerage,* the *Almanach de Gotha* of Literature, remain slim. After all, why should the well-born exert themselves in writing? Their existence, which can be filled with vigorous activity as well as exquisite enjoyment, is their daily masterpiece. Sports, the hunt, the army, diplomacy, court intrigues, court functions, love affairs, are freely open to them. Let others indite: *they* have only to live.

Although we are told that Romanticism and Democracy are both the spawn of Rousseau, Romanticism, at one stage of its development, had an aristocratic tinge (Shelley and Byron were well born), or affected an aristocratic pose. The Baroness de Staël, the Viscount de Chateaubriand, Count Joseph de Maistre, Alphonse de Lamartine,

Alfred de Vigny, Alfred de Musset, Honoré de Balzac, gave French literature—for the unwary—the prestige of a Social Register. And we must not forget that George Sand, although she turned socialist, was Baroness Dudevant and a descendant of Marshal de Saxe, while Victor Hugo was a Spanish Count.

Most of this is an amusing Romantic delusion. The magic *de* is no patent of nobility, even when it is not gratuitously assumed as it was by Balzac. Chateaubriand, Lamartine, Vigny, belonged to the lesser provincial nobility; but Hugo's title, conferred on his father by King Joseph, had never been recognized either in France or in Spain. As for Mesdames de Staël and Dudevant, the titles belonged to their husbands, who were decidedly husbands *in partibus infidelium.*

In modern English literature, we find great pleasure in some of the work by Lord Dunsany, and, in a semi-literary field, we admire those undoubted aristocrats, Rosebery and Balfour; but no English lord has reached the summit of fame since Byron. Literature has contributed far more to the peerage (Macaulay, Lytton, Disraeli, Tennyson, Morley, Bryce) than the peerage to literature.

It seems as though, in our semi-democratic days, a handle to one's name were a serious handicap. Guarding ourselves against our own unconfessed snobbishness, we refuse to take a literary lord seriously. Alfred de Vigny bragged that he had "stuck on the gilded crest of the nobleman *an iron quill* which was not without beauty." This ludicrous image, ready for the hand of the cartoonist, is perhaps the best symbol of popular opinion on the subject. A belted earl should not be a quill driver: it does not belong to the type.

This leaves us with the middle class as the favored breeding ground of literature. It sounds paradoxical: we are accustomed to consider middle class and Philistinism as equivalent terms, and the *bourgeois* as the very antipodes of the artist. If an artist can not be an aristo-crat, he will go straight to the people. The French Romanticists who, about 1824, were all Knights of the Throne and the Altar, by 1830 had cast in their lot with democracy. To-day, a self-respecting poet may be flaming red or lily white, a bolshevist or a royalist: for the middle class, he has the haughtiest scorn.

This attitude, snobbish at times, not seldom generous, must be accepted as a fact. But it does not dispose of the previous fact, that most writers have their origin in the *bourgeoisie*. The two extreme classes are hampered in their cultural development: the lower, by lack of educa-tional facilities, by lack of leisure, by social prejudices that press upon them from without, by an inferiority complex which inhibits them from within; the upper, by the sloth and vanity which come with unearned distinction: like Lord Melbourne, they prize most highly those honors about which "there is no damn'd nonsense of merit." A social curse, a social privilege, are equally benumbing. The *bourgeois* alone has both the incentive and the op-portunity.

The middle class reaches indefinitely above and below. In a country like America, it is so freely open to "the people" that the distinction between them is blurred— blurred, but, as we have seen, none the less real. In France, the passage from the one to the other takes at least one generation. On the other hand, there is an upper middle class that mixes freely and actually merges with the gentry. The *bourgeoisie,* in fact, is not a class at all, but the substance of our *bourgeois* world. The aristocracy and the "lower orders" are both survivals. England preserves her Lords as she keeps up the Beefeaters and the Lord Mayor's Show; and I heard, ages ago, Bernard Shaw open a debate at Toynbee Hall on the very sensible proposition "that the working classes are useless, dangerous, and ought to be abolished."

In that enormous middle class, some strata are more favorable than others to the breeding of literary men. The best of all seems to be the professional world: lawyers, doctors, ministers, professors, military and naval officers, civil servants. There we find education, discipline, comfort without display, and a sense that there are obligations superior to material rewards. *"Noblesse oblige"* is far truer of this group than it is of the peerage itself. In classical France, for two centuries, the majority of writers came from that element, especially from minor state officials, and from those legal dynasties which had founded "a nobility of the gown" rivaling, in wealth and influence, the "nobility of the sword."

Most writers, then, are *bourgeois* by birth and education. But they are *bourgeois* out of sympathy with their class. There is a fine indifference to paltry economies and petty conventions among the aristocrats and among the proletarians. The great lord can afford to be careless; the pauper is without care because he is without hope. The *bourgeois,* in between, must scheme, save, keep up all the decencies: admirable virtues, but plodding, lack-luster, almost stodgy, in which there is no romance.

It is natural, therefore, that the artist, on entering upon his career, should leave the *bourgeois* world behind. Not merely the thoroughbred artist: but every young *bourgeois* who has a touch of the poet in him—and there is enough poetry in the very fact of youth to make the experience almost universal. So the son of Respectability has his fling of rebellion; he affects Bohemianism and the latest iconoclastic fad; he flocks to Greenwich Village or Montparnasse. After this generous sowing of wild oats, he returns meekly to his tame *bourgeois* world. Jean Richepin, who posed as a super-tramp and circus athlete—an anticipation of our Jim Tully—ended in the sedate uniform of an Academician, a favorite lecturer to the little white geese and the dowagers of conservative Society. But the Prodigal Son returns with a wistfulness that may find its expression in genuine literature. And, once in a while, he never returns at all.

II

It has been admitted throughout the ages that authors formed among themselves a brotherhood which obliterated social distinction. In the ancient world, the slave as well as the Emperor could be a philosopher and could be a poet. Charles IX, who loved poetry and dabbled in it, was expressing a commonplace of literature when he wrote to Ronsard: "Both of us wear crowns." This principle—at any rate this convention—has been respected in the French Academy ever since its foundation: prince,

173

prelate, poet, meet on equal terms. What place should this Ancient Order of Bards occupy in society?

According to Plato, none whatever: the world is still smiling at this ostracism of poetry by the greatest of metaphysical poets, the father of a noble brood. At the other extreme, possibly no less absurd, we meet the conception of the Poet as prophet, and shepherd of nations. Above our pettifogging parliaments, blind leaders of the blind, we need a House of Seers. In between, we find all possible positions, with two more definite than the rest: the writer as a *parasite*—honored retainer or mere buffoon; the author as *business man*. There are as wide differences among lawyers or among ministers as there are among writers. But we know pretty definitely where the lawyer and the minister, as such, stand in the community. The writer, on the contrary, has not yet found his normal level.

The easiest solution is for the writer to be financially independent. "He inherited a small competence which enabled him to devote himself to literature": such statements abound in biographies. There have always been "gentlemen-writers", and would-be gentlemen as well. Congreve affected to despise his prominence as a playwright; Byron still kept up the pretence that he would receive no payment for his work. (It is true that he allowed his publisher to slip him a check when he was not looking, and grumbled when the check was not handsome enough.) For centuries, English magistrates and members of Parliament went unpaid. Fine disinterestedness on their part, wise economy for the State? As a matter of fact, the practice proved one of the worst fences for the preservation of class monopoly. In the same way, the principle that writers should not be paid would bar out of literature all those who are still under Adam's curse, and have to earn their bread. Besides, if commercialism is a peril to the integrity of literature, so is amateurishness.

There have always been professional authors: in exchanging ballads for bread, Vachel Lindsay was consciously reviving a tradition as old as Homer himself. But the earnings of the profession, until the eighteenth century, were small and precarious. For the solid world, the wandering minstrel is hard to distinguish from the beggar. The famishing poet is a stock character in satire, drama and romance. Victor Hugo made use of Pierre Gringoire as comic relief in the tragic gloom of his *Notre Dame de Paris:* a sketch in light, sure touches, which reveals more humor and delicacy than the Weird Titan is usually given credit for. Rostand followed the same approved line in the second act of his *Cyrano de Bergerac.* At times the smug contempt of the safely established *bourgeois,* like Boileau, for his down-at-heels colleagues, is little short of nauseating.

"Poets must live,"—although the substantial Philistine might very well retort: "I don't see why." So they had to seek the protection of the powerful and the wealthy. The *Patron* is an institution in art and literature. It is one of the painful sides of our study to read the fulsome dedications of great writers to noble lords, and even to obscure plutocrats. Corneille, as proud in his verse as an old Roman or a Spanish hidalgo, discovered extraordinary virtues in a certain M. de Montauron: a recognized manner of holding out his hand. In its most objectionable form, patronage was discarded by Pope, and withered under the scorn of Johnson. But it had survived until Johnson's time. Read again that scathing letter to Lord Chesterfield. It is not a repudiation of patronage: it merely asserts that the noble lord was seeking honor and gratitude for benefits he had not conferred.

Patronage need not always be degrading. Maecenas could be open-hearted as well as free-handed. The most acceptable form of patronage is that which comes from the Sovereign himself. The King's bounty is not an alms, but a national reward. The most independent writers could accept it without a qualm. The list of pensions awarded by Louis XIV honored both the Grand Monarch and the recipients, among whom were found even subjects of enemy countries. Samuel Johnson, with his bristling pride, found no incongruity in being granted a pension: it is true that his rather wicked definition of the term could not be expunged from the mighty *Dictionary*, and caused him some embarrassment. The practice was continued well into the nineteenth century: Victor Hugo, hardly more than a "marvelous boy", was thus rewarded by Charles X, and, as late as 1883, Matthew Arnold was given a pension of two hundred and fifty pounds for his services to literature. Tennyson confessed: "Something in that word 'pension' sticks in my gizzard." That was in 1845. The wound to his gizzard did not prove mortal: he lived forty-seven years longer.

But this frank method is going down with the prestige of monarchy. Writers would feel squeamish at receiving support from politicians; democratic voters, even in the most Athenian of Republics, would grumble at squandering the people's money on loose and idle rhymesters. If the blessings of the party system, log rolling and the pork barrel were introduced into literature, we might have a body of subsidized Pindars that would worthily match the subsidizing Solons: *horresco referens.*

Even in royal days, authors were frequently assisted, not by direct grants, but in the form of sinecures. Racine and Boileau, for instance, were Royal Historiographers who prudently refrained from excessive historiographical zeal. (G. P. R. James, so cruelly burlesqued by Thackeray, was the last Historiographer Royal.) One of the most approved forms of reward was through Church preferment: partly in memory of the days when clerics had a monopoly of learning, partly for the more practical reason that the Church was wealthy, and her wealth at the disposal of the sovereign. There are famous, and indeed glaring, examples of this in English literature. Few men could be less Churchly than Jonathan Swift: insanely proud, savagely partisan, foul in thought and word. But his political services coupled with his literary genius marked him for advancement, which never reached the heights he desired. In Sydney Smith we find, on a much reduced scale, the same combination of politics and wit: the result was a good "living." Even in our own times, Dean Inge's ecclesiastical dignity was the fruit of caustic humor and a fine journalistic sense for effect, no less than of Neo-Platonic scholarship, orthodoxy and saintliness. In Sweden, Tegner, the epic poet, became a bishop, although his private life was far from exemplary. In France, there were, throughout the classical age, "commendatory abbots" whose sacred revenues supported decidedly profane lives. Pierre de Ronsard, some of whose erotic poems are almost Italian in their vivacity, was such a semi-ecclesiastic. Bourdeille, who wrote the spicy private chronicles of the time, has survived under his clerical name of Brantôme. In the eighteenth century, Abbé de Bernis won favor with charming verses on Madame de Pompadour's dimples, and ultimately became a Cardinal: oddly enough, a very good one. Miss Tallentyre will have it—on what authority I know not—that Voltaire himself was offered the red hat. Unfortunately for the gayety of nations, the practice has been discontinued: Mr. James Branch Cabell deserves to be at least a Canon, and Mr. George Jean Nathan an Archdeacon.

As a reward for literary merit, lay sinecures survived longer than ecclesiastical benefices. Until a few years ago, in France, it was the rule to appoint literary characters as heads of the great national libraries and curators of the principal museums. Thus the Arsenal Library, in Paris, was twice a poetical center: with Charles Nodier at the dawn of Romanticism, and, at the close of the nineteenth century, with Jose-Maria de Heredia. Leconte de Lisle, Prince of the Parnassian Poets, was the leonine and saturnine Librarian of the Senate; he had under him a rather fractious sub-librarian by the name of Anatole France. At times, the poet may justify his appointment: Pierre de Nolhac was an excellent curator of Versailles. The Departmental Offices and the City Hall in Paris are swarming with literary men: this is said to increase appreciably the consumption of official paper. It requires an effort to visualize Joris Karl Huysmans, and especially Paul Verlaine, as bureaucrats. The method is not totally unknown in our country: Theodore Roosevelt, so eager for the efficiency of the Civil Service, offered a position in the Customs to Edwin Arlington Robinson. Our rare but sharp encounters with custom officers induce us to believe that they all are poets in disguise: *genus irritabile vatum*. . .*

What shall we do with our poets? Alfred de Vigny has devoted to this problem a strange and beautiful book, *Stello.* His survey is not cheering: the aristocratic Ancient Régime allowed Gilbert to starve; the London mercantile plutocracy offered Chatterton a position so menial that he preferred suicide; the democratic French Revolution beheaded André Chénier. It is Vigny's contention that society is *hostile* to poets: it would be more reasonable to say that society does not recognize the poet's right to idleness. Patronage in any form, direct or disguised, from individuals or from communities, offers insuperable difficulties under modern conditions. The Philistine world, *i.e.* the working world, can hardly be expected to take poets at their own valuation, or even at the valuation of a small clique. If writers are recognized by the general public, they need no subsidy.†

There are men of genius who can not sell their wares, or

---

* The United States and the Second Spanish Republic have frequently appointed writers to diplomatic posts.

† A promising way would be for each University to keep a poet, without pedagogical obligation, just as a pet. This, we believe, was tried by Miami University, which, perversely, is not found in Miami, Florida, but in Oxford; and not Oxford, England, but Oxford, Ohio: it seems to play hide-and-seek with the geographer. At least two other cases have reached our notice. The experiment, as far as we know, has not changed the face of the literary world.

who scorn to do so, or who have none to sell: our advice to them would be, not to seek a patron, but to adopt a simple mode of life, work for it, and write in their spare time. We can not recommend Villon's methods of self-support, which included larceny and maybe worse; nor Spinoza's—lens polishing is too close and too sedentary for health and inspiration. An outdoor occupation, not too strenuous, would be ideal. The pastoral tradition might be revived. A forest ranger, a rural mail carrier, have matchless opportunities for poetry. So has a policeman, on a safe beat.

If we reject parasitism, the alternative is to force recognition on your own terms. We have already quoted David Starr Jordan's definition of success: to do the thing you like, and be paid for it. *For it:* not for some make-believe activity. The man of letters *as such* came into his own in the eighteenth century. Alexandre Beljame has shown very convincingly the great difference between the status of Dryden and that of Pope. There was no lack of dignity and sincerity in Dryden: yet, without being mercenary, he was *retained.* De Foe had no standing. Addison and Swift owed theirs partly to political influences. Pope, on the contrary, was The Poet, and nothing else; and Richardson was The Novelist. Henceforth literature could be a wholly independent and respected profession.

Voltaire admired and envied this British sturdiness. He had suffered from the absolute lack of status of the author in France: lionized one day by the most aristocratic society, cudgeled the next without hope of redress. He did more than any one to enhance the prestige of the

Man of Letters: all Europe bowed to King Voltaire in his royal seat at Ferney. But his position was not entirely due to his literary fame. He was a sedulous courtier and a shrewd business man; he would have risen high in any capacity. Rousseau, without such extraneous advantages, achieved even greater success. He raised the power of the Man of Letters in society so high, that he could afford to shun and denounce society. The author as hero or representative man became an acknowledged figure. Goethe conquered a unique place in German life on the sole strength of his writings: at the Court of Weimar, he conferred more honor than he received. Chateaubriand, Lamartine, Hugo, Balzac, Zola, even Anatole France, had the same ambition, which was accepted without a smile: a poet is a Peer of the Realm by right divine, under any régime.

This has never been quite true in America. In the perspective of history, we admit that Villon the outlaw ranks above duke, bishop and king: they are remembered because they were his contemporaries. Shakespeare, in our minds, towers above the aristocracy and the plutocracy of his age. But we are unwilling to recognize, even as a distant possibility, the supremacy of the Man of Letters in our own days. In a list of ten prominent Americans, industrialists, bankers, politicians, movie stars and even gangsters would be far more likely to be included than "mere" writers.

Even with us, the literary profession has risen very high. It has attained prestige: in certain cases, a prestige verging upon absurdity. Its financial rewards are erratic, but occasionally they are great. *Literature* is almost big business:

I remember the announcement that a new book of Mr. Harold Bell Wright (*sic transit!*) was being shipped "by the carload." Yet, with all this prosperity, the standing of the craft remains undefined. For one thing, we all feel that there is no necessary relation between success and merit. We are reasonably certain that a good minister, or a good engineer, or a good lawyer, recognized as such by his peers, will rise in his profession. There can be no such assurance for a good writer. The best critics may praise him, and yet he will fail to catch. Popularity is unaccountable. When it is deliberately sought, it may be purchased too high.

So literature is not a career: it is a gamble. Men excellently endowed for it can not adopt it as a vocation. Much work, and some of the best work, is done on an amateur basis: by men with private means or with other sources of income. Literary men may form national and international associations; if they choose, they may turn themselves into a Union affiliated with the American Federation of Labor. But their organization will only have a loose and superficial relation to the true purpose of literature. Authors do not constitute an "order" in the community, like the medical profession, the bar, or the clergy.

We see no reason to deplore such a situation. "Organization" would make literature the slave of its own past, the tool of a sect, the tool of a particular social system. It would impose upon us "standards", after the desire of the Neo-Humanists. Fortunately, literature remains a living force, never wholly tamed. Official and exclusive possession of the truth makes for legalism, pedantry, pharisaism: whenever that spirit appears in literature, literature turns into a cult, and sickens.

Far from desiring that poets should become a clergy, we would rather see the clergy dissolve into a free company of religious poets. What a magnificent impulse would religion receive, if its ministers were bound by no vows, sworn to no orthodoxy; if they spoke when and where the spirit moved them, and then only; if they were not compelled, in order to earn their stipend, to be "inspired" every Sunday at eleven o'clock! Neither the lyricist nor the mystic can be *retained;* and writing without the lyric note, religion without the mystic flame, are stale and unprofitable.

Chapter 13

PSYCHOLOGY OF THE AUTHOR TYPE

I

In our quest for the *author type,* physiology has been of little avail. A trainer might pick out a likely sprinter or prize fighter; at any rate, he might safely reject the candidates who did not come up to certain specifications. But there is nothing in the physique of a man that marks him out as poetical timber. Sociology leaves our minds in confusion. In the present state of our knowledge, the only definition of *Homo Scriptor* with any claim to validity will have to be a psychological one.

At the outset, we must reiterate the familiar words of caution. Let us not forget that a *type* arbitrarily isolates certain common elements, and gives them what may seem to be excessive prominence. *Homo Scriptor* is first of all *Homo,* presumably *Sapiens.* It must be remembered also that the notion of type takes no account of values. When we seek to define "the author as such", we obtain no clue to the greatness or mediocrity of individual authors. Indeed, the mediocre ones may be "truer to type"; while, in the very greatest, the type becomes a subordinate

184

element. "We were expecting an author," says Pascal, "we find a man": the words apply admirably to Pascal himself. This will explain why our Psychology of the Author may seem disparaging: what we are studying at present is the professional deformation rather than the creative power. The mystery of genius will be reserved for a following chapter.

The fundamental trait in the psychology of authorship is *Conceit*. The word is ugly, and we should like to substitute for it "noble pride", or "consciousness of genius": but remember that we are including in our survey the small as well as the great, and the smaller side of the great. Horace was a man about town, light-hearted, facile, witty: when he remembered he was a poet, he started bragging magnificently, as only poets can: *Exegi monumentum Ære perennius. . . .* This has become an eternally recurrent theme in literature. Poets boast of their immortality, of their power to confer immortality, with unblushing confidence. "Love me," says Ronsard, in all seriousness, to his Helen: "your beauty will pass away, but my words of praise will not pass away." "Marquise," writes Corneille (the provincial Church Elder enmeshed in the toils of a stage coquette), "my gray hair may not appeal to you: but remember I am Corneille; posterity will know of your charms only through my verse."

To all creative writers—poets in the wider sense of the term—might be applied the words of Lanson about Chateaubriand: "He had every form of pride: from the pride which is a virtue, to the pride that is sheer foolishness." Hence the proverbial touchiness of the poet, his enormous appetite for praise, his vanity even in trifling matters. Hence Byron's consciousness of his romantic beauty, hence the dandyism of Bulwer Lytton and Disraeli, the æsthetic refinements of Oscar Wilde. Exceptions? By no means: in the literary quarters of all great capitals, you will meet men who, through some trick of speech or manner, through some oddity of garb, seek to arrest your attention, and proclaim: "Behold! I am a poet."

When the French poets met in Paris, after the death of Léon Dierx, to elect their lawful *Prince,* it is claimed that, on the first ballot, there were three hundred votes and three hundred names proposed; on the second ballot, Paul Fort won with two votes. An unkind legend, in all probability: still it indicates what the world expects of the literary man. Bernard Shaw's colossal conceit is put down by many readers as a rather elementary form of humor. "The greatest dramatist since Shakespeare!—Why *since Shakespeare?*" We rather interpret it as fearless candor. Shaw is in the grand tradition; his defiant self-assertion is far better than the Chinese circumlocutions affected at times by Victor Hugo: "the obscure writer of these insignificant lines."

There is no more outrageous form of conceit than the claim to inspiration; and there is none that is more universal. Literally, it means the assumption of an almost divine character: it is no mere man, but a spirit, a god, who speaks through the poet-prophet, *vates.* In less mystic terms, it implies that the poet's passing fancies possess a value not given to other men's. This is most clearly manifested in the boundless egotism of Rousseau.

He dared to set himself against the world; and ultimately, he forced upon the world a minute account of his own life, omitting no ailment and no turpitude. Evidently, in his opinion, it was of the utmost importance to mankind that these things should be known. Innumerable writers, ever since, have insisted upon "living their private lives in public."

The Ego is hateful was a classical dictum. The Romanticists turned it inside out: The Ego is the very core of literature. And we believe the Romanticists were right. Without some revelation of the author's innermost nature, the finest piece of writing lacks the literary spark. Even Boileau recognized this, with his insistence on "the secret influence of Heaven": it is that gift of the gods, the poet's personality, that makes a poet. Even Zola taught the same doctrine: for him Art was Nature seen through a tempera-ment. Now, any one who, in society, would obtrude his idiosyncrasies upon us would be called insufferably con-ceited. Imagine a stranger buttonholing you: "Listen to the lovely thoughts that came to me when I was jilted by my sweetheart." That is exactly what the poet does. Why should he not? We like it.

You will demur: you probably have known men who stood high in the literary world and who were unaffected, kind, courteous. I could name two or three myself. Yet I do not believe that this invalidates our diagnosis. First of all, let us remember that all "men of letters" are not "poets", *i.e.,* creators. In the critic, the historian, the philosopher, personality does appear indeed; but, except in rare cases like Carlyle and Nietzsche, it is subdued. Then, men of letters may also be men of the world; they need not be crude. Their conceit will reveal itself in subtler fashion than Shaw's cheerful blatancy, or Victor Hugo's preposterous mock-humility. They may even have the half-apologetic modesty of the highborn: "So sorry I am a Duke; awfully uncomfortable for you, I am sure; but I can't help it." There is also the humility of the *Recessional,* the most boastful of all patriotic songs: "O Lord, we are the mightiest of all nations, and the best: help us bear in mind that we are but men." The poet must have his moments of doubt and despair: but even his self-abasement is only inverted pride, just as John Bunyan, more Luciferian than he knew, claimed to be "the chief of sinners." You may have caught him at a time when he despised, not his own work, but his own glory, because it had spread among fools. More simply: the man of genius usually takes no pride in minor things. He will very sincerely defer to your opinion on some practical matter, with a childlike simplicity that will seem to you touching and delightful: even as Louis XIV, who knew himself to be the Lord's anointed and the absolute master of twenty-four million men, could bow down with charming modesty before Boileau's expert knowledge.*

But, just as Louis XIV never forgot that he was the King, the writer, in his heart of hearts, believes that his Ego is all important; that it is right and proper for him to reveal his secret thoughts, and that the world should receive these confidences in awe and wonder. Without

---

* *Louis XIV:* "Who is the greatest writer under my reign?" *Boileau:* "Sire, Molière"—*Louis XIV:* "I did not think so; but you know better about such things than I do."

such a faith, the lyric flame would die; and it is the lyric glow alone that turns even an inchoate mass of dreary naturalism into a thing of beauty.

The writer *must* be conceited, just as the leader of men must have ambition and self-confidence. "Napoleon," says Common Sense, "was a great man, whose only weakness was his ambition." Common Sense may be responsible for the greatest nonsense. Monsieur Joseph Prudhomme, the symbol of the pompous *bourgeoisie,* put the matter much more tersely: "Had Napoleon remained a modest artillery lieutenant, he would still be on his throne." Napoleon was ambition incarnate: remove ambition, you blot out the career, the man himself. Remove conceit from Bernard Shaw: there will not be enough left to make a Sydney Webb.

Conceit is fostered, in the literary man, by the sense that his achievements are strictly personal, not collective, not fortuitous. In this, he is probably mistaken: the public collaborates with him far more than he knows, and luck is no less essential than desert. But the world, so far, agrees with his view; and, if he compares himself with superior men in other fields, he is justified in his belief. Even a Napoleon must feel that his triumphs are due partly to his lieutenants, to his troops, to his armament, to the morale of the country behind him, to the weakness or the blunders of the enemy. The military leader is a bandmaster, the author is a soloist.

The actor, the musical performer, are in closer touch with the public, breathe their incense in thicker clouds; so their vanity is liable to be, in externals, more flagrant than the author's conceit. But it is not so deep-seated. In so far as they are not fools, the performers are compelled to realize that they are mere interpreters; the applause that goes to them must be shared.

The author's conceit does not depend upon success: it antedates and outlives success. It is a faith, the substance of things hoped for, the evidence of things unseen. It remains unshaken, as a faith should, even though mere "works" should fail. If success comes, the writer is idolized by the outside world, worshipped by an inner circle of devotees. When I had the honor of meeting an illustrious Belgian dramatist, the Lady-in-Waiting whispered to me in religious tones: "The MASTER will now receive you." Even a less mystic head would easily reel in such an atmosphere.

But failure only stiffens pride, makes it more defiant. It increases the sense of difference between the Unique and the Many—"mostly fools," growled Carlyle. (Indeed universal applause should have a sobering effect, but pride receives eagerly with both hands.) To be misunderstood becomes the badge of genius.

It is idle therefore to blame an author for his conceit, any more than a conqueror for his ambition, or a revivalist for his fanaticism. In them, such traits are not faults but the essence of their being. Professor Giese's able arraignment of Victor Hugo could be presented in syllogistic form: Victor Hugo was conceited; conceit is the mark of a mean soul; therefore Victor Hugo had a mean soul. No doubt, if Monsieur Dupont, the corner grocery-man, had the conceit of Victor Hugo, he would be a laughable sight. But Victor Hugo was not Monsieur Dupont.

II

The second trait, one upon which everybody seems in agreement, is that the author is, and should be, *temperamental*. He has the right, *ex officio,* to be capricious, unaccountable, irritable: indeed, if he were not, we would begin to question his literary pretensions. As we have seen, the traits that belong to a type, national or social, are artificially exaggerated by the very notion of type. As soon as a man is in military uniform, it becomes more unpardonable for him to be timid, easier to be blunt and even brutal. The would-be man of letters will cherish and over-emphasize whatever modest amount of temperament there is in him, in order to look more perfectly the part. The real man of letters needs no such exertion: but he will indulge more freely in weaknesses which are forgiven in advance, without which, indeed, he would actually disappoint his public.

There is a fancy dress of the Author, therefore, almost as conventional as those of the Italian *commedia dell' arte*. If we disregard the costume and study the man himself, the trait is not so evident. It would seem that the very great writers have exercised wonderful will-power and self-discipline. We limit ourselves to the mightiest: the case is too clear with men like Edward Gibbon or Sir Walter Scott, whose robust talent was evidently assisted by tireless industry. Dante was an excellent scholar, a scientist, a philosopher: all things which require more than temperament. The mere amount of Shakespeare's writings, in addition to his heavy practical responsibilities as an actor-manager, would prove beyond doubt his steadiness as a worker. Voltaire filled nine lives to the brim. One of them was that of a scientist: ahead of the official mathematicians of his country, he understood Newton. Another was that of an historian, and his information was so conscientious, so solid, that for over a hundred years, his *Charles XII,* his *Louis XIV,* were not superseded. In Goethe we find the careful official, the naturalist, the physicist, the scholar, as well as the poet. Victor Hugo wrote down his Apocalyptic visions with the punctuality of a professional scribe. Looseness, irregularity, may not be wholly incompatible with literary gifts; but certainly the *bourgeois* virtues of order and perseverance, far from hindering those gifts, bring about their fullest fruition.

The literary *temperament,* however, is not wholly a fallacy. Undoubtedly there are flashes of unique beauty in the works of the loosest and most irresponsible Bohemians. It is a scandal that Verlaine should be a greater poet than so many unimpeachable professors and ministers addicted to versifying: it is a scandal, but it is a fact. Even in the experience of the greatest, we feel that inspiration is not the evident, inevitable result of hard work. At times, hard work actually seems to hamper it. Fruition comes later, often after giving up in darkest discouragement; it comes without apparent connection with previous effort, as a spontaneous release.

But the preparation, whether they know it or not, was not without avail. The flash may be the delayed reward. Even if it were not, even if it came as a gratuitous gift from above, it makes all the difference whether it be received by a crude, ill-prepared, slothful mind, or by one ready to respond at once, to follow up with immense resources. In a battle, a commander may have a sudden intuition of the vital point, the exact minute when a single effort will be decisive. If he has no reserves, no ammunition; if his staff is so ill-trained that his command will not be transmitted, his intuition will be wasted. The violinist who achieves a miraculous purity of note may be "inspired": but we may be certain he has not been waiting listlessly for inspiration.

The "release" leaves the author physically, nervously exhausted. Under the discipline which he must impose upon himself, he goes through the inevitable cycle: effort-despair-ecstasy-apathy. This secret rhythm, which he himself can not control, is hard to reconcile with formal schedules and social obligations. The words that Goethe applies to the soul in love: *Himmelhoch jauchzend, zum Tode betrübt,* exulting heaven-high, depressed unto death, are true also of the mind in literary travail. Writers are, of necessity, nervous, just as soldiers and sailors have to be vigorous and brave.

Such an experience is not the privilege of the greatest: it is inherent in the very nature of the work. A sophomore feels it, if he takes his English Composition seriously. Literature requires the *swift* passage from depression to exaltation, and *vice versa.* That which we feel clearly, sanely, moderately, equably, does not give us the thrill of wonder, the response so acute, so exquisite that it is akin to pain, the sudden rediscovery of life. If we could register on some instrument the poet's sensitivity, we should obtain a very jagged line. The *range* may be small, if the transition be sharp: a drop of a few feet, if abrupt, will give you more of a shock, and of a thrill, than a gradual descent of a thousand. That is why level sublimity, as in theology or metaphysics, is so frequently uninspiring; that is why a fall may rouse poetry as well as a flight; inspiration comes *de profundis* as well as *de excelsis*.

III

It is commonly accepted that the artistic or poetic temperament does manifest itself in morality also. There is no radical difference between psychology, the key to behavior, and morality, the rule of conduct. The artist or poet does not submit willingly to conventional discipline; or, from a less favorable point of view, he yields without sufficient resistance to all his impulses. When this disposition takes the form of moods and irrepressible gestures, we call it temperament, or simply temper; when it leads to definite action, affecting others, we call it morality, or the breach of it. In both cases, the foundation is the same.

It has long been admitted that the artist is a reprobate, —or a privileged character. Pious provincial communities look askance upon any form of art, because art to them betokens loose living. On the other hand, young people discover for themselves an artistic or poetic vocation, simply as a license to sin magnificently (not unlike the boy who declared himself irresistibly attracted to the sea, and gave as a reason that "a sailor has a wife in every port"). Like most popular opinions, which so easily turn into popular fallacies, this view of the artist's morality is ludicrously distorted—with a basis of truth.

Few writers of note were out and out "bad men." We

have no desire to whitewash Villon, Byron, Poe, Baudelaire, Verlaine, Oscar Wilde. There was perversity in their thought as well as in their lives, and their fame rests, in some small part, on their alleged turpitude. To say that we admire them for their occasional lapses into correctitude would be unconvincing nonsense: it is wicked to tell a lie beyond the limits of credibility. But the fascination of sin is not exclusively due to the reader's diseased curiosity and to his love for scandal: it arises also from the dramatic contrast between aspirations and abjection, the *De Profundis* element so clear in Baudelaire and Wilde, not found in the Marquis de Sade. Paradoxically, these damaged souls bring us closest to the fundamental Christian experience, the conviction of total depravity, the horror and shame of one's self, the desperate appeal to divine mercy. Everything is strangely mingled in these nether poets and in the feelings they stir up in our hearts: mingled, but certainly not wholly base. Whatever interpretation we choose to offer, it must be admitted that this particular circle of Inferno does not fairly represent the literary world. There are enough writers whose lives were blameless to destroy any fancied identity between sin and genius. On the other hand, there have been worse men than Baudelaire among judges, soldiers and priests.

We can not deny that the biographies of many famous authors are not strictly exemplary in the conventional sense. Even Shakespeare—what little we know of him— or surmise—could hardly be held up as a model; nor Lope de Vega, nor Voltaire, nor Goethe, nor Shelley, nor Victor Hugo; least of all Jean-Jacques Rousseau. But does the literary profession stand unique in this respect? The light of publicity always beats more fiercely upon the illustrious than upon the obscure: Frédéric Masson devoted a learned study to every passing affair of Napoleon: no one cares to list the feminine conquests of Colonel So-and-So. But while in other cases, that light is trained from without, in the case of writers it is assisted from within. They glow with indiscretion; they kiss and tell; indeed at times they might be accused of kissing for the sole purpose of telling. That is why alleged literary history so often has the same kind of appeal as the reports of divorce proceedings. We must know for certain with whom Byron misbehaved, and whether there is a suspicion of truth in *Cakes and Ale.* Louis Barthou, a responsible statesman, head of the Reparations Commission, gravely investigated Victor Hugo's good fortunes and misfortunes. Charles Maurras, the profound theorist of a Royalist Restoration, devoted a book to *The Lovers in Venice,* George Sand and Alfred de Musset. No one could swear that stockbrokers are more virtuous than poets: only stockbrokers are not quite so eager to tell of their transgressions; neither are we so eager to know.

It is true that artists are exposed to temptations second only to those of princes and soldiers: the lute, the crown and the sword, far more than the pocket book, act as aphrodisiacs. Mr. Branch Cabell has given us the budget of his average daily mail: it seems mostly made up of violent assaults on his chastity, and of queries about the pronunciation of his patronymic. Mr. George Jean Nathan, in *Monks are Monks,* assures us that the excess of evil brings its own cure, and that every man of literary repute, if the truth were known, deserves to be called Joseph. Mr. Nathan is a shrewd observer, with ample opportunities for gathering reliable information. But he is suspected of a fondness for the paradoxical.*

We may also admit that the artistic temperament is not easily amenable to formal discipline. Especially the Romantic temperament, which may be considered as the most purely artistic of all. The poet must place intensity before conformity: else he is no poet at all. This rejection of rule is frankly immoral, if by morality you mean a conventional code. But such morality we have defined elsewhere as "statistics with a sanctimonious mask." "This thing," says Morality, "is done; that thing is not done." Granted: but why should *I* do the one, and abstain from the other? Heroism and saintliness are not seldom in rebellion against accepted standards. All martyrs were strictly *immoral:* men who defied authority, tradition, convention, majority rule. Socrates was the corrupter of youth. To the present day, we find it difficult to make up our minds about Rousseau. He strove, blundering, to reach the essential moral truth, which is found only in perfect sincerity. He was not a *good* man: yet we must pause before his challenge: "Let any one dare to say: I am better than he!" Shelley did not evolve a workable rule of life, nor did he always act according to the purest light there was in him: yet his morality was infinitely higher than that of the strait-laced and corrupt society that condemned him. There was much looseness,

* "The Editors (of the *American Spectator*) are charmed to learn from Federico Vittore Nordelli's 'L'Uomo Segreto' that Luigi Pirandello was faithful to his wife from January 1894 to January 1918."

and pride, and pose, in Byron, with many twisted prejudices, rather worse than the straight kind: yet his rebellion was fundamentally *righteous*.

In every case, the artist, and particularly the poet, claims to be an exception: he has unique powers and enjoys special privileges. Can we safely draw a line between the *exceptional* and the *abnormal?* Here we are confronted with the ancient problem of the kinship between insanity and genius: the most baffling, the most hotly controverted aspect of the poet's psychology. Although we have sedulously attempted to avoid it, we have repeatedly come across that mysterious term *genius*. With fear and trembling, we shall now attempt to consider it in its bewildering complexity.

Chapter 14

THE ENIGMA OF GENIUS

AFTER the war and the revolution, Berlin took drastic measures to relieve the house shortage. Superfluous rooms were commandeered, and assigned to homeless families. Strangers were thus forcibly brought into unwelcome intimacy. "What did you do then?" we asked some German friends a few years after the crisis. "Oh! we squabbled." There is a house shortage for thoughts; notions that may be of incompatible temper are compelled to dwell together under the roof of a single word. What do we mean by Religion, Love, Socialism, Democracy? Not one single thing in each case; not even varying shades of the same idea; but concepts in sharp conflict. The thoughts that go by the same name are related, no doubt: but they may fight one another with the ferocity inseparable from civil wars and family feuds.

One such divided household is the word *Genius*. We shall attempt to present seven major conceptions of it: seven is a mystic number, and satisfying to the soul. But seven is a strict minimum: a subtler mind could stretch the catalogue to seventy times seven,

I. Intelligence Quotient 140

Athirst for precision, we first apply to the expert. Genius is a quality of the human mind, and therefore pertains to the realm of psychology. Psychology has an answer ready, lacking nothing in definiteness. *A Genius is a person whose Intelligence Quotient (I.Q.) is 140 or over.* It is the uppermost division in the following scale:

I.Q. below	25	idiot
	25– 50	imbecile

(How advisable it would be, by the way, to substitute in polite conversation the scientific equivalent for the vulgar and offensive term! "The policies of Senator X seem to denote an I.Q. well below 25. . . .")

50– 70	moron
70– 80	borderline
80– 90	dull
90–110	average
110–120	superior
120–140	very superior
above 140	genius or near-genius

If you want further particulars, you will find them in the *Genetic Studies of Genius,* published at Stanford by Professor Lewis Terman and his school. I can particularly recommend Volume II: *The Early Mental Traits of Three Hundred Geniuses,* by Catharine Morris Cox. It is a tome of 842 pages, bulging with statistics, tables and graphs; occasionally, an awe-inspiring algebraic formula fills half a page. The seven main tables in which the chief information is condensed provide fascinating reading. We discover, for one thing, that Ali Wedi Zade, "Albanian robber chief", had I.Q. 155, while Napoleon, a robber chief also (Taine's *condottiere*), measured only 145. Marmont, chiefly known for betraying Napoleon, scores 150; Bernadotte, who managed to found the present Swedish dynasty, 140 only. Evidently Dr. Cox is no Napoleon-worshipper. Marat, the crazy fanatic of the Terror, is credited with I.Q. 170; our Emerson with 155. Victor Cousin, the philosophical mountebank and pontiff of the commonplace, has 180; Diderot, the most dynamic mind of the eighteenth century, 165. Alexander Dumas, the cheerful quadroon, who, by methods akin to Ford's, ran such an efficient romance factory, comes up to 170; Swift to 155: Dr. Cox is free from race prejudice. Wolsey must be the type of a super-genius: 200; Jefferson and Richelieu, 160 only; Rousseau 150 (Professor Irving Babbitt would have guessed 50–70: but he was not trained in the latest psychological methods). Altogether a pretty radical *Umwertung!* We turned eagerly to Shakespeare's line: we found a blank: "No score: insufficient data." This is probably the most scientific statement in the whole book.

Amicus Terman, sed magis amica veritas. We do not believe that, by such methods, even with the most impressive apparatus, any genuine precision could be hoped for. The three hundred worthies who serve as a basis for the study were selected according to some loose "common consent", that is to say haphazard. The facts used in determining their I.Q. were borrowed from biographies of very unequal value, some of them thoroughly uncritical. No "coefficient of credibility" can be much more than the roughest guess. The investigators, however alert and conscientious, were not competent to appraise superiority in domains radically different from their own.

But even if we admitted the validity and accuracy of the method, the use of the term "genius" would remain objectionable. Genius here means a high degree of superiority, the difference between a modest I.Q. 139 and a glorious I.Q. 141. The scheme does not recognize any radical change, any quality that pertains uniquely to genius, and lies beyond mere success or talent. It thus defines genius only by denying it.

The Terman school, which has done such admirable work in the measurement of *gifted children,* would gain if it dropped the unfortunate word *Genius.* Other expressions might be adopted: the American language is never at a loss for ultra-superlatives. Psychologists, who have coined such delightful words as *schizophrenic* and *pyknic,* might easily have enriched our vocabulary with one more Greek monstrosity. At the worst, such a classification as "mental heavyweights" might have done. The class above "a very superior person" immediately brought to our mind the late Lord Curzon and the teasing little rhyme about him. The "Curzon-level" should have been good enough for any one.

Dr. Cox is not to be blamed for the pseudo-scientific use of the word *genius:* neither is Dr. Terman. For Dr. Terman borrowed it from no less an authority than Galton himself, the founder of Eugenics. When we look into

Galton's conception of Genius, we are amazed at its vagueness. Genius, for him, is merely eminence. Hence the extraordinary weakness of his chapter on *Literary Genius*. As we have seen, it opens up a very interesting problem, but exactly the reverse of the one Galton thought he had solved: why is it that so few recognized geniuses are the sons of other recognized geniuses? *Superiority,* evidently, runs in certain families; it is transmitted through the joint influences of heredity and environment, in proportions which have to be finely measured. Superiority, yes: but, if genius is not mere superiority, we are just as much in the dark as before.

II. *The Prodigy*

If we see a man accomplish with extraordinary facility a task which, for the rest of us, would be long and painful, we are tempted to exclaim: "There is a genius!" *Prodigy* would be a safer term. Rapidity, ease, even a high degree of material perfection, matter extremely little: the rarity and value of the result should enter into consideration. A lightning calculator like Jacques Inaudi, a chess player meeting, blindfolded, twenty opponents, a painter who can execute at the same time two pictures with his hands and two with his feet, Charles V dictating at once several dispatches in different languages, all are prodigies, marvelous human instruments, but mere instruments. What is the quality of the mind that uses such a matchless tool? Of what worth is the product? Plain words uttered in the vernacular by Jesus or even by Lincoln outweigh all the polyglot dispatches of Charles V.

The word prodigy is chiefly applied to youthful performers. Those among our readers who may deserve the title need not despair: a few prodigies have turned into geniuses. Mozart is a case in point, and, above all, Pascal —Pascal, a genius by any canon we may choose to apply, and who, in his boyhood, severed from his mathematical books, rediscovered Euclid unaided, using a quaint, childish nomenclature of his own. On the whole, however, the story of prodigies is hardly a cheerful one. Where is Winifred Sackville Stoner, who, a babe in arms, corrected the grammar of her grown-up admirers? Where is William James Sidis, who, at fourteen, "astounded"(?) his Harvard professors by his views on the fourth dimension; who could pick up Russian and Church Slavic in a few weeks; who once sent us a long essay in pellucid Esperanto, proving that the Cro-Magnons were of the same race as the ancient Egyptians; that they spoke the Basque language; that, through Atlantis, they colonized Mexico; who, finally, according to his father, Boris Sidis, formulated the *Law of the Reversibility of Time?* The world is not kind to prodigies; its wonderment is never free from malice; "genius" almost becomes a stigma. The best we can hope for our brilliant young friends, in their maturity, is obscurity and peace. Parenthetically, their parents and educators maintained that neither Winifred Stoner nor William Sidis was a "genius": the merits of their achievements should be ascribed, as in the case of Helen Keller, largely to their teachers.

III. Inspiration

For the plain man, a "prodigy" is merely a two-headed calf. But, in a more religious age, a two-headed calf would have been considered a portent, a miracle. In the conception of genius, there frequently enters the notion of direct intervention from above: the genius is the confidant and the messenger of the gods. The very term genius implies the supernatural, or, if you prefer, the superhuman. It is no mere man who is speaking or working, but, through that man, a *Spirit*. Inspiration explains the apparent ease with which wonders are performed; it also explains the inequality, the unaccountability, of genius. "The wind bloweth where it listeth": the peasant girl, Joan of Arc, the vagabond, Villon, Verlaine, are transfigured for a moment. When inspiration ceases, mere man remains—and how weak, sinful and vain he may be!

This mystic consecration is claimed, not merely for the founders of religions, but for the founders of dynasties as well. Napoleon III elaborated the theory of "Providential Men" as a justification for Bonapartism, imparting to the imperial house a "divine right" more immediate than that of the Bourbons; and it is the sin against the Holy Ghost, in Italy, to doubt the "inspiration" of Mussolini. Poets also boldly assume this prophetic, this Messianic authority: Victor Hugo, in his *William Shakespeare,* drew the portraits of the major geniuses, all stirred by a breath from Beyond, all weird and terrible, all bearing a strange family resemblance to Victor Hugo himself.

All this is poetry—or perhaps mere eloquence. In a sober discussion, this exalted doctrine has no standing. Mysticism and sense have their distinct domains. We do not deny the supernatural claims of genius: we have no means of discussing them. As a rule, when we are using the word genius in a mystic sense, we are merely con-

fessing our own impotence. Whatever we can not understand, whatever we can not explain, even through the
agency of "chance", we ascribe to "genius." It is one of
those residuary and purely negative conceptions, like the
Infinite, or Eternity, which stand for no intelligible reality. Reason in despair seeks refuge in Sublimity. The
word *genius,* in the case of individuals, serves the same
purpose as *Providence* for the world at large. Commynes,
Napoleon, and innumerable others, ascribed their successes to their own foresight and efforts, their failures to
the Inscrutable Will of God. To translate "the will of
God" into terms of puny human experience is nothing but
blasphemous nonsense. A contractor sought release from
an agreement on the plea that the torrential rains which
had hampered the work were "an act of God"; and the
judge in his wisdom decided that "they were not bad
enough for that." Whatever can be apprehended by
human reason is credited neither to Providence nor to
Genius. Such words mark the provisional boundaries of
knowledge.

Although few people nowadays are ready to accept at
its full value the mystic conception of genius, it still imparts to the word a peculiar aura. Genius is a mystery,
and the sacred word must be uttered with bated breath.
For no other reason do we reject and even resent the
Galton-Terman-Cox definition, which fails to recognize
a difference between superiority and genius.

IV. *Infinite Pains*

For the same reason, the definition of genius as mere
hard work is not likely to prove popular. We take it for

granted that "genius" comes in flashes, and that plodding care is a confession of dullness. Yet the "laborious" theory does not lack support. It was Buffon who wrote: "Genius is but inexhaustible patience." And he lived his law. In a classical age, when men believed that unchangeable truth had been attained and could be taught, application was the sole requisite for success. Even Lessing, although a forerunner of the Romantic revolt, still maintained that any one could write perfect tragedies, if only he would follow closely enough the precepts of Aristotle. In the next century, Carlyle, himself a type of the Prophetic Genius, hurling thunderbolts from his stormy crags, defined Genius as an infinite capacity for taking pains. Edison, a wizard not merely in the eyes of the multitude, but also in those of a literary mystic like Villiers de l'Isle-Adam, originated the homely phrase: "Genius is one per cent inspiration, and ninety-nine per cent perspiration."

We have already seen that, obviously, genius is not incompatible with hard work; in many cases, it would not reveal itself without hard work. Men of the facile and flashy type seldom reach the heights: genius requires either labor or travail, and usually both. A descent into the Nether World was a commonplace of classical epic and medieval poetry: what is most *Divine* in Dante's *Comedy* is not its inspiration, but its faultless art, the indomitable wrestling with a hard material (Gautier's recipe for great poetry), that fearful symmetry, that rigid concatenation of rhyme, which make the hundred Cantos a formidable polished block without a fissure. Du Bartas wrote an epic on Creation, *The Week,* which can boast of more "flashes" than Milton's *Paradise Lost;* Strada elaborated an *Epic of Humanity* in twenty volumes, with more "sublimities" than in Dante's; but their fabrics were loose, and they crumbled. The idea of evolution had been evolving ever since the middle of the eighteenth century; under the name of "the historical spirit", it had become almost a commonplace; as applied to the natural sciences, it was formulated at the same time by Wallace and Spencer as well as by Darwin. Why then does Darwin remain the "genius" whose name is attached to the theory? Because of his inexhaustible patience. Relativity goes back to the Greeks; daring speculations about space and time were vented by H. G. Wells thirty years ago, not only in *The Time Machine,* but in a scientific paper read before a learned society; the "genius" of Einstein is not the intuition of Einstein, but the hard work of Einstein. And, in supporting the "laborious" theory, Edison spoke with good authority. His chosen field was not the free realm of imagination, where a daring adventurer may at any moment stumble upon a discovery: his field was the *laboratory:* he was first of all a worker. The versatile Bohemian Léon Cros invented the gramophone, and Sumner Tainter perfected it; to Moses Gerrish Farmer we owe the incandescent lamp. Yet Edison alone is remembered, and without injustice: for he provided the ninety-nine per cent perspiration.

V. Abnormality, Disease, Insanity

The conception of Genius as balance, health, magnificent sanity, would admirably fit Goethe. George Bernard Shaw, who had a unique opportunity to study the subject by introspection, upheld "the sanity of true genius." Yet he himself flirted with the conception that there was a pathological element in genius. The priest in *John Bull's Other Island,* a figure of matchless appeal among the creations of G.B.S., is a poet with a touch of madness. In *Candida,* the sane, jolly, vigorous parson Morell is contrasted with Marchbanks, a bundle of uncontrolled nerves; and the degenerate poet is preferred to the healthy Philistine.

The idea that genius is connected with mental or physical disease goes back to antiquity. The manifestations of epilepsy and hysteria bear a striking resemblance to those of ecstasy and inspiration. Soothsayers and sybils, St. Paul and Mahomet, could be diagnosed as epileptoids. There were facts enough and to spare in history to supply Lombroso with arguments. Especially as Lombroso considered every harmless eccentricity in the family of a genius as the evidence of a taint, while all men whose sanity could not be impugned were denied the title of genius. Q.E.D.

Both Plato and Aristotle admitted the kinship between genius and insanity. The tradition has been preserved in literature throughout the ages: all great poets claim "rapture", a "fine frenzy", which, by all tests, would indicate abnormality. So well established is this doctrine that the most eminently sane poets are ashamed of their sanity, and fake the ravings that Nature denied them. Boileau, common sense incarnate, when he wrote an *Ode* (and what an Ode!) *on the Siege of Namur,* had to feign "holy intoxication"; but, classical even in his assumed madness, he called it "learned" as well as "holy":

Quelle docte et sainte ivresse....

Longfellow, preaching idealism, chooses a lunatic for his standard-bearer: for no sane person will carry "mid snow and ice a banner with the strange device, *Excelsior!*" Yes, the poets are mad; they know it, they proclaim it, they glory in it. An ancient Greek fallacy here raises its head: if they are truly mad, can we take their word for it?

Lombroso's theory has been refuted times out of number, to the evident satisfaction of the refuters. Still, the association between genius and insanity is of such long standing in the public mind that it can not be dismissed with a shrug. Undoubtedly, we are apt to think of sanity in terms of conservatism, conformity, the average. If such be the case, genius, by common consent, is not sane. So much the worse for sanity, you will say. Granted: but, if we depart from sanity, what will be our guide? Do insanity and genius always diverge from the norm in opposite directions? Or may they not travel at least part of the way together?

The irremediably sane man, the one who, for seven dreary years, "kept cool with Coolidge", sees no vision and dreams no dreams: he is an absolute non-conductor of that mysterious fluid called genius. The sensible man endowed with a higher degree of imagination may toy with visions and dreams. But he never takes them too seriously: his faculty is too weak, or his critical brakes are too efficient. He may be a discriminating reader, a teacher, a cultured dilettante, even a stylist, a skilled rhymester: he will never be a genuine poet. Between his dreams and his practical life, he has established an impassable barrier. The mystic, the prophet, the inventor, the true artist, vaults over the barrier of sense. He believes that his ventures are not without bearing upon practical life; the connection between trance and waking is never completely severed; his visions have a prophetic or symbolical value. He brings them back triumphantly to the world of men: the genius goes "behind the Beyond" with a return ticket. Just one step further: there is the man who sees visions, and is unable to distinguish them from reality: the vision becomes hallucination, genius turns into insanity.

Or, if we want to borrow Coleridge's phraseology: good sense never surrenders "disbelief", *i.e.,* a critical attitude, and thus kills in advance anything beyond its own limits. A half-hearted "suspension of disbelief" may lead to the appreciation, but not to the discovery, of strange, unstandardized values. The "willing suspension of disbelief" is the very atmosphere of poetry and genius. The "total suspension of disbelief" is madness. If Shelley had accepted as literal truth his own *Triumph of Life,* or Coleridge his *Kubla Khan,* the only possible verdict would be "mental derangement."

VI. *Eminence or Recognition*

By what token, then, shall we distinguish between Genius and Insanity? Many eccentrics are geniuses in their own conceit; while Max Nordau, who was no fool, branded as psychopathic, in his *Degeneration,* many works which the world has proudly preserved. Aye: there is the key: *the world* passes judgment. Of genius, intrinsically, we know practically nothing. What we do know is the world's opinion.

The three hundred Geniuses of Catharine Cox represent simply Cattell's list of eminence, with Napoleon, of course, at the head, and Voltaire close upon his heels. That list is about as good as any. Like all other such attempts, it is bound to appear capricious and even absurd in certain cases. For instance, Robespierre, with all the earmarks of mediocrity ranks 28, ahead of Pascal (35), of Leonardo da Vinci (52), of Wagner (188).

Now it is obvious that all eminent men are not counted geniuses; it is hardly less obvious that many geniuses were despised and rejected of men. Indeed, apparent failure seems one of the tests of genius. Some people might entertain favorable doubts as to the "genius" of Edmond Rostand if *Cyrano de Bergerac* had not been performed almost as many times as *Abie's Irish Rose*. Cleon, Balfour and Clemenceau were all credited with the remark, when they were interrupted by unexpected applause: "Did I say something foolish?"

But if immediate success with the crowd is a valid presumption against genius, some kind of response there must be: else genius disappears without a trace. Our Jefferson Aloysius Kegelbahn may be a transcendant poet, and he may know it. But you do not, and there the matter ends for our mute inglorious Milton: mute indeed is he whose words fall on deaf ears. If Alberta Christina's father parades the streets of London as "Sargon, King of Kings", followed by a handful of loafers, we merely smile; let one thousand walk in his steps, we shall take notice; one hundred thousand, he will be a portent, like the founders of certain American sects; one million, and he becomes a major character in history, a genius. Socrates and Jesus had disciples, however few. On a different plane, so had Mallarmé. Without such a chosen band, their names would have perished. If the small company of the faithful had not won larger circles, the founders might have remained oddities in world history rather than geniuses. Paradoxically, genius is a palm conferred by the common man.

VII. *Mutation*

Most men recognize a difference even among the élite of the eminent. There is in genius a touch of strangeness, both sublime and disconcerting; and the admiration it arouses is always tinged with awe. It is hard to do full justice to the perspicuous and sane, like Molière, Voltaire, Gibbon: they have their immediate reward. Genius is the title granted in compensation to those who aspired beyond human power. Washington, in his perfect measure, appeals to us far less than Napoleon the visionary and gambler. Genius is not perfection in achievement, but a groping for something which as yet has no name. The striving for that Something is the first step in revealing and defining it. The "inspiration" theory gives a positive but mythical explanation of that feeling; the "insanity" theory recognizes it negatively. He who does, however supremely, that which has been done before, is not a genius. He who comes with a new gift, were he travel-stained, halting, tongue-tied, has a right to that great name.

A new gift! Is there anything new under the sun? Modern science says yes, in defiance of the old-bachelor philosophy of the Preacher. Not only does everything evolve in nature: but evolution, at times, takes unexpected leaps. The thing of yesterday is not the same as the thing of to-day. It is not even *imperceptibly* different: it may be a radical departure. As H. G. Wells has it, the steamboat did not evolve out of the sailing vessel by a gradual transformation of the galley stove into a boiler. In natural history, there are (or there may be) *mutations* in the sense that De Vries attached to the word. In the history of the human mind, genius is a significant mutation.

At first sight, this does not conflict with the theory that genius is recognized eminence. We have only to reword it: Genius is *recognized innovation*. On second thought, a contradiction appears: the world "recognizes" only that with which it is familiar, and crowns only the paradox which has already become a commonplace. No better example could be found than Jean-Jacques Rousseau. Rousseauism was manifestly floating in the public mind, a doctrine in quest of a Messiah. Jean-Jacques only served as a nucleus of crystallization. The apparent genius worshipped in history is not the true originator: he is the symbol of a thought which, after an obscure struggle, has at last reached public consciousness.

Genius as a creative mutation we do not deny. But the only true geniuses then are the unknown geniuses. Ages before any great revolution in thought, the decisive word was spoken: perhaps half-consciously, perhaps half-jestingly; and that word found no audible echo. It may have been said, apparently in vain, hundreds of times, before the obscure beginnings of growth. The thought now appears as vague misgiving, as idle rebellion, as unnameable aspiration. Thus it spreads until it reaches definite consciousness in some individuals. These individuals may be suppressed or derided; they may be recognized later as true *forerunners*. Finally comes the miracle of luck: the man who speaks the decisive word into ready ears, however few. Then we have messiahs, prophets, poets, inventors, *geniuses*,—the long, anonymous gestation unrecorded and forgotten. The Greeks had an altar to the Unknown God, and every nation has a shrine to the Unknown Soldier. Our Halls of Fame should reserve their finest monuments for the Unknown Geniuses; they are far more vital than those upon whom falls the full light of history.

There is nothing so academic, in popular estimation, as the discussion of a word. What care we for a definition? What we want is the substance. But words are potent. The heap of loose thought covered by the term genius may block the way to useful action. On the whole, we feel that the word genius is useless and dangerous. For one thing, it has a demoralizing effect: genius, because it is beyond convention, is free from any law. The painter in *The Moon and Sixpence* may seduce his benefactor's wife and abandon her: he is a genius, and skill with the brush (*if ultimately recognized by the dealers*) justifies the infliction of torture and death. A Montparnasse lad may drink himself into an insane asylum, and offer chance splashes of paint as a finished picture: in his own eyes, he is a genius, and there may be a few friends for whom the sacred word will be sufficient to silence all criticism.

215

In history, genius has repeatedly served as an excuse from common sense and decency. It was eminently right that hundreds of thousands should perish in the snows of Russia: Napoleon woefully mismanaged that senseless campaign—but was he not a *genius*? "Do not touch the Concordat!" said J. C. Bodley to his French friends. "Who are you that you should meddle with the work of Genius?" And how would a petty mediocrity in Italy to-day dare to pit himself against the manifest genius of Mussolini? Imagine how much more intelligent the great Russian experiment might be, if the Bolshevists did not have such blind faith in the "genius" of Karl Marx; how much more religious the world would be, were it not for its excessive and oppressive trust in the "genius" of Saint Paul or Mohammed. The idea of genius fosters insane pride in a few chosen souls, servility among the many.

Anything that paralyzes thought is harmful, and such is the effect of that ill-defined term. *Superiority,* in terms of social service, we are ready to accept and reward. Genius as mutation, original, creative, we want to recognize and honor. But every one of us is a potential mutation, a new experiment in the world; this aggregate of atoms which I call myself has never existed before, can not exist elsewhere under exactly the same circumstances of space and time. In so far as he is unique every individual brings a new revelation, has a spark of genius. If only he dared; if only his fellow men were more receptive, less blinded by the worship of past geniuses.

We are not upholding, as in pseudo-democratic doctrine, the commonness of the common man as against the aristocratic gifts of the few: we are pleading for what is uncommon, nay unique, in every common man. Do not bow with superstitious reverence before a few individual geniuses: be ready to recognize *genius* in them, in yourself, in all men. Release the infinitesimal particles of genius in every one of us: heaped up together, they will rise to heights beyond our dreams. Equality is an empty word, and leveling down is a stultifying policy. But no scale of superiority devised so far has any general and final value; a hard-and-fast division between "geniuses" and "non-geniuses" is unscientific as well as deadening. Keep every path open. "Incommensurability" may be an ugly word: but it is a sane doctrine.

Part III

The Public

Chapter 15

THE TACIT INTERLOCUTOR

I

AN author speaks the language, wears the costume, follows the customs of a particular civilization: in Taine's terms, he belongs to his "race, environment and time." So does every one of his compatriots and contemporaries. *As an author,* he possesses certain general characteristics which may be said to constitute his vocation; he conforms more or less closely, more or less consciously, to an established professional type; he occupies in that capacity a recognized position in society—recognized even when it is ill defined.

This recognition implies that there is some connection between the author and society as a whole. In so far as the poet is absolutely individual, independent, unique, isolated, he has no standing at all. Society, in its contact with the author, constitutes his *public.*

Our working hypothesis, in this book, is that literature is the joint production of author and public. Writer and reader do not merely belong to the same large cultural group, national or supernational: they collaborate in a very definite manner.

This thesis offers itself under two aspects. The first is what we called, in our introductory chapter, the *pragmatic approach:* literature does not exist *for us* until it has been recognized as such. In the eyes of Apollo, the unknown poet may be the greatest; among mortals, "he whose songs are unread never wrote at all." The specifications for an author are: a soul, an instrument, a public. The third is no less essential than the other two.

This *pragmatic approach* is brutally factual and grossly general; but, on its own field, it can hardly be challenged. The second aspect of the thesis is more controvertible: *the author always writes for a public.* A book is a conversation, urbane or angry, with an unseen but ever-present interlocutor. It is a discussion, a plea, a declaration of love, of hatred, of contempt: never a scroll of undecipherable hieroglyphics tossed indifferently into the void. The author uses the words of his people and of his time; he accepts or combats their prejudices; the public is the mold in which his private thoughts must inevitably be cast.

Now this will very properly be challenged. "The public be damned!" was the motto of poets such as Horace and Ronsard, long before it was adopted by a now vanishing brood of capitalists. (Note that for the capitalist, at any rate, the public he damned so light-heartedly was none the less indispensable.) The true artist, it will be asserted, works for himself alone. We firmly believe this haughty claim to be in a large measure justified. We hope to discuss the point at length in *Art for Art's Sake.* The very essence of art may consist in its absolute independence. At present, we are not concerned with the essence, but with practical facts: the body of works that we actually read, enjoy, criticize. On this purely pragmatic ground, we shall be satisfied with the assertion that the *bulk* of literature is written for a public.

We need not dwell on the enormous amount of writing done confessedly for *profit*—money, social prestige or fame. The thirst for immortality, *Exegi monumentum, Non omnis moriar* . . . , is a desire not merely for a public, but for a perennially renewed public. To write for a public does not imply that you are seeking to please that public: you may elect to tease, to browbeat, to insult your readers. Only you are conscious of their existence and you attempt to secure their attention. In not a few cases, rough methods bring popularity. Aristide Bruant in his famous Cabaret, Miss Texas Guinan in her noted nightclub, G. B. Shaw in his Prefaces, Mr. H. L. Mencken in his *American Mercury,* welcomed their audience with a volley of epithets: *"Bourgeois!*—Sucker!—Pharisee!—Boob!"* This seems to establish a delightful footing of intimacy and mutual confidence: "Now that we have been properly introduced, let's have a good time together."

A public, of course, does not mean "the general", notoriously untrained to the subtleties of caviar. It means an audience, if possible an audience of friends, a jury of your peers, as few as you please, sifted by the most rigorous shibboleth you can devise. Even the poems of Emily Dickinson were communicated to a small number of chosen souls. Every piece of writing that is *published,* were it in the most esoteric of "little" reviews, is seeking a public.

It may be a public of one: the one whom we are most eager to impress. We are willing to concede that certain famous love poems were originally indited without any thought of their appearing in print. It may be a public so small and so scattered that it has not yet achieved consciousness. It may be a public still unborn and perhaps never to be born: the pathetic "appeal to posterity", a supreme act of faith or a supreme gamble. Thus, in Vigny's poem, the dying navigators entrust their last message to a frail bottle. Such "bottles in the sea" are many posthumous Journals, that of Vigny himself, Amiel's, and, in parts at least, *The Education of Henry Adams*.

Finally, even the works which are written most strictly for one's self alone are written *as if* for a public: else they would hardly be written at all. Suppose a poetical mood comes upon us. What shall we do? There are three possible lines of action, or perhaps three stages. In the first case, we silently enjoy the unformulated ecstasy; no less silently, it disappears; from the literary point of view, it simply does not exist.

Or—second hypothesis—we are tempted to note it down, but we still desire to preserve our secret. Our notation, meant for no other human eyes, would remain a sealed letter to any stranger. So far as the world is concerned, it might as well never have been written: that which remains inviolate in the inner shrine is not "literature."

There are works that hover on the threshold: some incoherent and sublime pages of Pascal, for instance. They reach us because, elliptic, scornful of syntax and logic, they are none the less written almost as if they were meant for a public. They presuppose a common experience, they make use of the accepted signs. Pepys's Diary, obscure in a purely material way, entered literature only because it could be deciphered. It was jotted down in lucid English: the mode of transcription alone was a puzzle. Swift's *Journal to Stella* is literature in so far as its "little language" is a language at all, a code of communication. Its oddities can be mastered, so that the original public of one has been multiplied many thousandfold. The stream of consciousness or interior monologue, a most promising field for revolutionary experiments, offers a variant of the same problem. It attempts to catch thought before it has been fully organized into formal language: but it can not be accepted as literature unless it has some degree of intelligibility.

The cryptic notation, therefore, is merely an intermediate phase which can be resolved into either of the two extremes. If it does keep its secret, it does not count for us. If it can be deciphered, its unconventional form adds to our difficulty, but ultimately it is put into a tongue "understood of the people"—at least of a few people.

In the majority of cases, a third hypothesis prevails. People who write "for themselves alone" (*you,* reader, I could swear; and myself as well) are using the standard medium; oftentimes, they use it with scrupulous care; and not seldom, they even affect elaborate forms. Why should men adopt an intricate technique, without the remotest hope of being read?

First of all, through the force of imitation and habit. An English engineer, the only white man in a tropical construction camp, will, we are told, don his dress suit for dinner. (For all I know, this English engineer may be a myth: but a myth of such long standing becomes respectable. Anyway, I am using him as an illustration, not as an argument.) He is manifestly a social product; he dresses as though he were bidden to a Duke's, because London, ten thousand miles away, is still his inexorable master. Similar is the case of the man who indites a sonnet and never shows it to a soul. The fact that the engineer is isolated in the jungle, the fact that the sonneteer is not seeking publication, are alike irrelevant. The former does belong to Society, whose remote control he obeys as if by instinct; the latter does belong to the literary world, and follows the canons of that world, which will never know his name.

Why do we put on the formal dress of a conventional poem, or even the semi-formal of correct prose, when we expect no company? Possibly to keep in training against the day when we may get into society. Perhaps because the only way of clearing up our own thoughts is to express them to ourselves as though we were strangers. Perhaps because the future Self for whose benefit we desire to preserve the memory of a golden moment is, we surmise, likely to be more than half a stranger. Chiefly in order to reassure ourselves that we are not dumb, like the beasts in the fields, even though our voice should never be heard. "I, too, am a poet!" we exclaim. We are, in our own eyes, a sovereign *incognito*. When literature is discussed before us, we hug our secret, with an inward smile: "If they only knew!" Too proud to fight—too diffident, too sensitive to face a real public, we revel in the approval of an imaginary one. But the make-believe public for whose praise we are striving has the same effect upon us as an actual public would have.*

II

This part of our book will be mainly devoted to the effect of a special public upon the writer. We shall at present content ourselves with a sketch of the more general influences. It is a delusion to believe that a great man—poet or warrior—would have been great at any time and under any circumstances. Would Napoleon have been the same Napoleon, if he had been a second lieutenant under Louis XVIII? It is hardly less unreasonable to imagine that Shakespeare would have been Shakespeare under Queen Anne or Queen Victoria. Adaptability is not a necessary attribute of genius. On the contrary, we consider the time-server, the opportunist, as more likely to be a clever mediocrity. Scribe, Sardou, Pinero, Benavente, would have been successful, within their limits, in any period and under any régime.

When the man's inner tendencies coincide with those of the times, when author and public are in substantial agreement, the writer is carried by the stream with surprising ease. There were powers in Pope and Johnson that would have manifested themselves even in a Romantic age: but it is more than likely that the full development of their talent and of their fame needed the favor-

---

* Baudelaire has put the matter with his usual savage misanthropy: "I write," he said, "to prove to myself that I am not inferior to those I despise."

227

able climate in which they lived. This harmony explains the great vogue of men now forgotten, and even the enduring fame of others not intrinsically great. Malherbe was a surly pedant; there were dozens of poets at his time more gifted than he. But literary France, like political France, was craving for discipline, and hailed as a Master this hard-boiled martinet of Parnassus. In like fashion, Calvin Coolidge will remain in history as one of the most successful of our Presidents, because his negative virtues exactly fitted the needs of the hour. Or so we thought.

More profitable is the consideration of times out of joint, of irreconcilable conflict between the author and his public. The most radical effect is to crush the dissenter altogether. From the pragmatic point of view, which must be ours, we are able to consider only those works which have come to light and survived; from the ideal point of view, success is no sure criterion of excellence. In damning the losers in that literary struggle for life, we are adding insult to injury, which is the acme of callous vulgarity. Under given circumstances, a truly great man may be discouraged from even attempting to write. Our familiar "mute inglorious Milton" has no standing in history: yet, have we any right to deny that the germ of genius was in him? How many genuine freethinkers were there in the Middle Ages? How many potential dramatists in eighteenth and nineteenth century England? We shall never know. It is cheap optimism to assert that energy will conquer all obstacles. Disraeli was jeered at when he first addressed the House. He swore: "You shall hear me yet," and he was heard. But his disabilities were superficial in their obviousness; his talent was eminently adaptable. He deliberately sought to win his public, and succeeded. A more genuine soul, a more uncompromising character than Dizzy might have lost the fight—might indeed think that Dizzy's victory was but a capitulation in dazzling disguise.

For it is possible for men to win apparent success, and fail to express their best selves. Their public will not permit it: they are the prisoners of a fame they half despise. If we agreed with Van Wyck Brooks, such would be the ordeal and the tragedy of Mark Twain. Alexander Dumas wanted to be a dramatic poet, and almost succeeded: but he was forced into the position of a romance-manufacturer. I have preserved a queer feeling of sympathy—which, no doubt, would have been extremely unwelcome—for Miss Marie Corelli. Some thirty years ago, she was enormously successful with the sentimental shopgirl we all conceal in our hearts; but, even at the height of their triumph, her lucubrations were held up as the perfect models of the cheap and the tawdry. With this severe judgment I am compelled to concur. Yet I wonder whether the quality of her imagination would not have made her notable at a certain moment of Romanticism. *The Sorrows of Satan* is not a weirder book than *Frankenstein;* and it holds together better than most of the Gothic novels which are now seriously studied by scholars. She came nearly a century too late. If the educated public had not turned down her work in derision, if she could have hoped to please critical judges, she might have been more severe with herself. She wrote at a time when most respectable fiction was realistic or psychological; she was almost compelled not to be respectable—from the artistic point of view.

We have noted so far cases in which this disharmony between author and public had only negative effects: silence, a warped activity, success that does not heal a secret bitterness. It may also lead to the direct expression of melancholy, rebellion, despair. The gentler souls sigh almost inaudibly: Senancour in *Obermann;* Frédéric Amiel in that enormous *Journal* which tells in so many thousand pages why he could not write; *The Education of Henry Adams,* a testament, an indictment, an alibi. There is much of this element in Matthew Arnold's elegiac poetry. With no lack of sympathy for these sensitive writers, we can not but resent the feebly egotistical touch in their lyric frustration; at times, their delicate moaning is hard to distinguish from a whine. Far better is the resolute stoicism of Alfred de Vigny: a hostile world, even when it crushes us, shall not be permitted to gloat over our defeat.

Disharmony may also seek the veil of paradox, cynicism, futility. This is often the key to the Art for Art's Sake attitude, to Gautier's defiant Preface to *Mademoiselle de Maupin,* to much of the career of Oscar Wilde, to Cabell's graceful, all too conscious trifling, a scherzo through which an obstinate lamento is heard. It explains in part certain aspects of post-war literature, the effect of brutal, rasping discords on the too finely strung organism of Aldous Huxley.

Finally, we have open rebellion, the rather histrionic defiance of the Storm and Stress period, revived with even greater dramatic effect by Lord Byron. From Schiller to

Victor Hugo and even Balzac, the outlaw—Karl Moor, Hernani, Vautrin—became the pampered darling of Romantic literature. It would only be fair to discriminate between the purely destructive anarchism of the orthodox Byronians, and the prophetic, the Promethean tinge in Shelley. For Shelley, revolt is not an end in itself, not a cherished pose, but an inevitable phase swiftly to be left behind, the stormy passage to an ideal of serene beauty.

In all these cases, the attitude of the poet is governed by that of the public. Byron might have been a rebel even in a Paradise created according to his own specifications: but it is hard to dispute that Schiller and Goethe were at heart *classicists,* aspiring to a world of order; less obviously, for the curve of his evolution was cut short, this is also true of Shelley. In a Shelleyan universe, much of the Shelley we know would never have been manifested at all: neither his revolts nor his yearnings. He would have had to find other means of self-expression; or, in a paradoxical but inevitable phrase, other modes of *self-unfulfillment.* There is no fulfillment this side the grave.

The luckiest author is the one who comes just at the turn of the tide. The old synthesis is still enthroned, but men are increasingly weary of its lifeless rule. The first who speaks words of release and of promise is hailed as a deliverer. He has at the same time the benefit of the rebellious attitude, which seems heroic; and the benefit of harmony with vast numbers, which brings safety, recognition, power. A few years before, he would have been a sacrificed forerunner; a few years later, a dealer in platitudes. Such was, again, Rousseau's miraculous chance. The "return to Nature" was well under way: it became fully conscious through him. We are appalled at the discrepancy between his sudden rise to fame, his enormous influence (an incubus which tormented Irving Babbitt), and, on the other hand, the rudimentary quality of his thought, the obviousness of his art. It was the public that evolved Rousseauism: Jean-Jacques was only its living symbol.

On a smaller scale, the fate of Rostand is parallel with that of Rousseau. Decadence, esoteric symbolism, naturalistic filth, obscurity and pessimism of all kinds, had palled on the French public. *Cyrano,* gay, brilliantly witty, wonderfully clever in technique, unblushingly sentimental and melodramatic, full of grandiloquent braggadocio, was the perfect antidote both to Mallarmé and to Zola. Readers of to-day can hardly realize what a stir it created in literary Paris: Faguet wept tears of joy, and sang *Nunc dimittis.* The play survives on its own merits, which are great. But it owed its first impetus, the legendary prestige with which it is still surrounded, to the fact that it registered a veering in public opinion. Epoch-making masterpieces are epoch-made. The *Cyrano* we admire is in part a tradition, greater than the mere words of Rostand, greater than Rostand himself. In *L'Aiglon,* the poet, the dramatist, the subject, were all deeper than in *Cyrano:* but the unique chance was gone. Maurice Rostand considers his father's glory as the "crystal tomb" in which the son is imprisoned. But Edmond Rostand himself was such a captive: he could never escape from his own *Cyrano.*

The incentive to create, the author's mood—hopeful, resigned or defiant—, the reception of the work, its later growth, its relapse into oblivion, are all products of the Public: the writer is but a medium.

III. "THE PHANTOM PUBLIC"

We gladly borrow Walter Lippman's phrase. The public is a Phantom which stands constantly at the writer's elbow, dictates to him, stops his pen, even when he is not conscious of its presence. But it is a *Phantom:* it has no shape, no features, no consistency. Clutch it, and your fingers will meet in the void. We speak, at times with superb assurance, of the Public Mind, the People's Voice, which is an echo of God's own. We build political and literary theories on that conception: and lo! it is a phantom.

A phantom, or if you prefer an idea: and how many hard facts have shattered themselves against the un-movable reality of a myth! The public mind exists, since we believe in it; and human intercourse would be im-possible without such a belief. But what are the solid elements in it that can actually be caught in the net of our analysis? Our task is not to deny, not to explain away, but to understand.

Here three hypotheses offer themselves to us. The first is Orthodox Democracy. Every one of us has his opinion, which arises spontaneously in him. In the open forum of public life, these individual opinions are con-fronted; the elements that are purely odd or selfish fail to aggregate, cancel each other, disappear in the mass. The common denominator is automatically arrived at. Groups or men are selected, almost at random, to represent this common factor: in purest democracy, they might be chosen by lot. They have no superiority over the mass, except perhaps the gift of guessing what the public wants. A statesman is one who keeps his ear on the ground *and hears*. The hero is the average man on a gigantic scale: Emerson's conception of Napoleon. The writer of genius is the one who voices the platitude that was on the tip of everybody's tongue: this is a familiar interpretation of Jean-Jacques Rousseau.

The second hypothesis is the Messianic or Prophetic. The mass is inert; there is no spontaneous public opinion. Individuals arise who venture and create: the herd follows. The Tables of the Law were not the fruit of a constitutional Convention: they were brought down from on high.

The third hypothesis we shall call the Aristocratic; or, in order to create that irritation which is sometimes stimulating, the Bolshevistic. It starts neither with the whole mass, nor with the single gifted individual. The unit of action is the small, determined group, the *conscious and organized minority*. The binding force of such a group may be an institution, a class, a clan, a faith; it may even at first be the personality of one man; but that man would be powerless to reach the mass if he were isolated. In all cases, the group is greater than any one of its members. Robespierre, Lenin, Mussolini, exist only through Jacobinism, Bolshevism, Fascism. The 18th Brumaire brought to power a team of "strong, silent men" who, under the chairmanship of Bonaparte, governed France triumphantly for a decade. When Napoleon, drunk with conceit, annihilated their influence, relied solely on his genius, on his prestige, on the devotion of the masses, he destroyed his own Empire. Autocracies and democracies are both delusions.

What is "the American Public Mind", which, according to newspaper reports, is so "grimly determined"? The Government? Congress? famous editors? notabilities with or without definite positions? No: it is mostly innumerable lobbies, idealistic or selfish, including the Churches, Labor, and the American Legion: in short, any organization run by a few able men for a definite purpose. In those groups which know what they want lies the substance of power. The historical parties wait meekly to have their minds made up by others; the official "leaders" are indicators, not forces. Are these lobbies the natural emanations of the General Public? Are they the followers of inspired prophets? Neither: they are *conscious and organized minorities,* swaying the mass, devouring the individual.

One strikingly clear example: in 1870, "France" felt herself insulted, and declared war on Prussia. The Emperor wanted peace; but his fiber was weakened by suffering, and he yielded, his eyes tragically open to the inevitable catastrophe. The Empress wanted war: but she had no decisive voice in a constitutional government. It was therefore "France", and not the sovereigns, that made up "her" mind and carried out "her" will. What was "France"? Thirty-six millions of French peasants, workmen, *bourgeois?* Not at all: France was the Cabinet, Parliament, the Paris Press, the Paris mob: the few thousands who had constantly spoken in the name of "France" and who believed that they were "France"; minorities which were conscious and vocal, because of their official position, or simply because of close physical proximity. *They* spoke, or rather they shrieked; they were heard. The thirty-six millions protested in private and silenced their own misgivings: who were they that they should oppose the will of France? The majority can only rally to one of the conscious minorities; and, in 1870, the conscious minorities—Thiers alone dissenting—went mad. The majority, in 1815, wanted neither the Bourbons nor Napoleon, neither reaction, nor military despotism; they allowed the Bourbons to flee, amid jeers, and Napoleon to return, amid the plaudits of a few; passively, sullenly, because they were not steered into a more acceptable alternative.

This theory of the *conscious, organized minority* is not new. It lies back of the good old *conspiracy* of our forefathers. It may be carried to an absurdity. Balzac, in particular, was extraordinarily fond of esoteric history. Beneath the trumpery of high-sounding principles, vast popular movements, resplendent official personages, he wanted to discover the secret deals of the "strong silent men." Hence his admiration for Fouché, who held in his hands the threads of the Empire, so completely that Napoleon, knowing himself betrayed, did not dare to unmask the traitor.

This view, familiar to every reader of the American press, is not seldom called "realistic", with a great affectation of superior wisdom: it is just as likely to be, as with Balzac, a Romantic and melodramatic delusion—pursuing in dark vaults at midnight a mystery that is not there. The fallacy is the assumption that only ruthless men, working in secret for selfish ends, can form a *conscious*

236

*organized minority.** An open conspiracy in the name of an idea may be fully as effective. At the time of the Dreyfus Case, the defenders of the victim were decidedly a small group of energetic men: but they were not, as their adversaries charged, an occult "Syndicate" subsidized by unnameable powers. The Jesuits, the Free Masons, the Jews, the Communists, International Finance, have at various times and in many different countries, not excluding our own, been turned into horrific bogeys. Naïve as this may sound, a certain degree of sincere idealism is essential to prolonged success. A mere gang is soon exposed, or splits into rival gangs. Napoleon III and his followers were not simply a band of greedy ruffians, as Kinglake and Victor Hugo would have us believe. In this negative way, democracy reasserts itself: you can't fool all the people all the time. At least not with the same thing.

In many shapes, ranging from high philosophy to cheap melodrama, the notion of the conscious, organized minorities has become a commonplace of political thought. We do not yet apply it so freely to literary problems. Yet the laws of the formation of public opinion are not radically different in different fields. Neither in literature nor in politics is there an unmistakable, spontaneous *Vox Populi.* No work is ever tossed by an isolated man to the vast, unorganized crowd, and, without preparation, without guidance, eagerly grasped by all and acclaimed as a masterpiece. There must be a nominating committee to anticipate, and to engineer, popular response.

* This fallacy, we must confess, has the support of the best dictionaries. *Conspiracy:* a secret combination of men for an evil purpose. Why necessarily evil?

237

As a matter of fact, the theory of the conscious organized minorities is much more applicable to literature than to politics. In politics, the ultimate authority of the mass is officially acknowledged. If Demos is not the master, he is at least the arbiter between his rival masters. In literature, there is no universal suffrage. Even in our days of generous mass education, the most popular works appeal only to a small minority. The potential reading public, among 125,000,000 Americans, would be over 60,000,000. A book is sensationally successful when it reaches half a million readers. Outside of the fiction field and of the semi-scientific, a *public* is counted, at best, in tens of thousands. Even for fairly obvious literature, the *public* is barely one in a hundred of the population; for any literature with any taint of subtlety, it is more likely to be one in a thousand.

Now this scattered, amorphous constituency can not be reached directly by an individual. Its needs have to be supplied from a few centers, and through definite agencies. I may be craving for exactly the kind of verse that a man ten miles away is writing now: but, in all likelihood, I shall never hear of him except through New York.

The *public* therefore is not identical with the *nation*. But even that smaller community within the community is not one. The days of "one faith, one law, one king" are passed, and Pluralism reigns supreme. Not only is there a pyramid of publics, immense on the Dickens level, smaller for Robert Browning, until we reach the apex where James Joyce alone fully understands his *Work in Progress;* but there are interpenetrating publics, con-

238

tiguous publics, totally isolated publics. The famous "General" is a myth. If you look up at any time a list of best-sellers, it will give you no intelligible picture of the American mind. Here is one which I noted down a few years ago: it could no doubt be matched to-day. Leaders: Chic Sale, *The Specialist;* Culbertson, *Auction Bridge;* Ernest Dimnet: *The Art of Thinking;* James Branch Cabell. *The Way of Ecben* (this last did not remain long in that proud company). Draw your inferences if you dare.

Is the literary world a chaos then? It certainly is: Mr. Cheney, in his *Survey of the Book Industry,* from the business standpoint, arrived at exactly the same conclusions as the Neo-Humanists. There was some semblance of order in "the old days",—an order which we overemphasize in retrospect—because the leading minorities were indeed conscious and organized: their organization was one with that of society itself. Literature is a gamble now, because we are conducting it on the democratic (or better pluto-democratic) principle, without even the rudimentary consciousness, the rough-and-ready organization, of political democracy.

The way of salvation is not through a return to the ancient cultural hierarchy and its shibboleths which masquerade as standards. The old culture was bound up with a social world which now lies in the dust. Any proposal to organize *literature* (as distinct from the book mart) on the same principles as our economic and political world would probably arouse amused scepticism. For both society and literature, the way out is forward.

239

Chapter 16

Yesterday: UNIVERSITIES AND ACADEMIES

I

REPEATEDLY in history, minorities had to seize power, to maintain themselves against all comers, and to force recognition. But their ideal is to leave their revolutionary origins behind. Napoleon was not satisfied until he had covered himself with a triple armor of "legitimacy": a democratic investiture, through a series of mock plebiscites; a religious investiture, through the Pope's presence at his coronation; a dynastic investiture, through his marriage with a Habsburg Archduchess. Material authority is precarious; it must receive the consecration of the spirit.

So the tendency of every leading group is to entrench itself in an official position, and seek recognition *de jure* as well *de facto*. Thus social differences become hardened into classes, which would fain turn themselves into castes. Thus a free religious movement becomes a church, with an established clergy. In the literary domain, there is the same tendency to consolidate a situation, to protect vested interests. A literary Church is formed; it has a canon of Holy Scriptures, a formal creed, without which there is no salvation. It has its clergy, with a novitiate and an ordination, with powers to bind and to loosen. That literary clergy is composed of the Professors: a definite example of a small, conscious, organized minority assuming the right to instruct the masses.

The kinship between the Church and the University is not fortuitous. Both had the same origin: the medieval clergy had a monopoly of learning, and theology was the supreme end of their studies. It is with the greatest reluctance that the Churches have given up their paramount influence over education; and they obstinately defend their last crumbling ramparts. Napoleon fashioned his Imperial University after the pattern of a religious order: the staff, although laymen, were to be subjected to quasi-monastic discipline. Oxford and Cambridge were long semi-ecclesiastical in character. Our American Universities show even now unmistakable traces of their churchly origin. Cloisters are still in fashion; Romanesque and Gothic in great favor; the academic gown is a priestly garment. In some of these Abbeys of Learning, the vows of chastity, obedience and poverty are still in honor.

All this may seem, if not fanciful, at any rate irrelevant: harmless survivals or innocent make-believe. But something far more vital endures: the notion of a literary orthodoxy entrusted to the keeping of the literary clergy. There are books that one *must* have read; there are books that one *must* admire. The people come to the Doctors for Doctrine; and they go away much disappointed if the Doctors have no doctrine to offer. At present, dogmatism is still fostered in the grades and in the high schools; and the Universities are compelled to teach and to maintain an orthodoxy in which they no longer believe. A situation not unlike that of the Church at the time of the Renaissance, when Cardinals and Bishops, won over to Pagan art and Pagan learning, were far freer of thought than their flock.

The scholastic attitude, which is that of the Neo-Humanists, is the negation of democracy in literary taste. *Your* opinion is not "as good as any other man's and probably a darn sight better." The few who are trained in the Law have the right to approve and to reject. They substitute their expert judgment for that of the uncultured masses. They prescribe the way in which a young *élite* may become their associates and successors. They preserve the Apostolic Succession from the days of Aristotle; they are in possession of the sacred tradition and its hallowed standards.

Put in these ecclesiastical terms, the doctrine is likely to cause resentment or amusement rather than awestruck obedience. Yet its influence is almost ineradicable. The teaching of literature is still to an appalling extent the enforcement of conformity. The man who does not know or does not properly admire the *right* thing is ill-educated: either an ignoramus or a heretic.

The direct influence of the Academic Church in contemporary literature is, at first sight, imperceptible. The indirect influence is very real. In preserving the spirit of Tradition, the Pontiffs of Yesterday warp our thought far more than we are aware. Then, although they contribute little to creative literature, they, as a class, are great producers of imitative work, not seldom of high excellence. They write sound and urbane criticism, correct poetry, even cultured fiction. Especially, they compose all the innumerable textbooks of literary history; they control that market at both ends, production and consumption. *Writing* history, if it be done consistently enough, is almost equivalent to *making* history. It takes a great wrench in our minds to realize that possibly *literature* is not identical with what the Professors have been handing down from generation to generation.

There is at least an enormous lag between official teaching and the trend of independent thought. When I was a schoolboy, in the early nineties, I still believed in the unquestionable superiority of the French Classicists, as a body, over Victor Hugo and his barbaric hordes. When I first applied, in a public library, for a volume of Hugo's dramas, I blushed and stammered as though I had been asking for the Marquis de Sade. It took the Scholastic Sacred College half a century to realize that Victor de Laprade, one of themselves, was a nonentity compared with Charles Baudelaire. And, although I am sworn to fearless speaking, I shrink from mentioning American equivalents for that obvious French case. Let the reader be bolder—if he has no academic standing to lose.

The Literary Church, although it deems itself sovereign in its own domain, is, like some of the religious Churches, very much in the hands of the temporal power. This is not mere self-seeking. The Professors are in natural harmony with the conservative class, because it represents, like themselves, authority and tradition. Decorum, good taste, good style, are the qualities which are emphasized in humane letters as well as in polite society. To be thoroughly versed in classical allusions, to know the table of precedence of all literary worthies, are things no less important to the scholar than the mastery of genealogy is to the courtier. The niceties of grammar, the punctilio of diction, correspond to the fine points of etiquette. Not to split an infinitive has exactly the same significance as addressing the second daughter of an Earl in the right form. The University man is part of the conservative scheme: but rather as a dignified retainer, like the Chaplain, than as one of the masters. The professed reverence with which both are surrounded is a courteous fiction: if they cease to "know their place", they lose their standing. They can teach only *ex cathedra,* in which case no one minds what they say.

If a scholar is out of sympathy with the society he should adorn, and expresses his heretical views, he is guilty of a breach of taste, and very properly snubbed or expelled. But even the scholar who, without attacking the existing order, ignores it, refuses to serve it, is first of all and uncompromisingly a scholar, stands condemned. He is the unsocial, boorish *Pedant,* a stock character in comedy from classical times to our own. The perfect scholar is the one who is also a gentleman. The Jesuit Colleges were first of all schools of good manners. Until the war, Oxford and Cambridge were emphatically the seminaries of the aristocracy and gentry. During the same period, American youth sought certain colleges for their social prestige rather than for pure learning. Even at present, "cultural" courses are frequently taken for the *finish* they are supposed to impart. They train you for admission into that desirable and supercilious circle, so well described by Aldous Huxley, in which the "good things" of "Uncle Virgil" are treasured.

It is no pun, but sober etymology, to say that there is *class* in the *classics*. To know the *right* thing admits you among the *right* people. I do not mean for a moment that the classics are wrong, and that the people who enjoy them are wrong. I only mean that the conception of their rightness is apt to be social rather than intrinsic. The man who seeks titled company solely because of its titles proves himself to be no aristocrat but a toady. The one who professes classical orthodoxy because it is "the thing" shows himself impervious to the spirit of the classics.

The social factor has thus been prominent in that culture of which the Professors are the official guardians. I wish Thorstein Veblen had given us a *Literary Theory of the Leisure Class*. His essential notion of *conspicuous waste* would apply admirably to much of our classical education. It is *disinterested:* a splendid claim. But the gentleman alone can afford to be disinterested, because he has no livelihood to earn. Traditional Culture subordinates the paltry questions of the moment, and deals with those problems which are eternal. This also sounds very lofty: but it means a refusal to meet the challenge of the times. To the plain question which rises in every young mind: "Why is there so much injustice in this world?", the answer is offered: "My dear fellow! How dreadfully vulgar! Let us show the fruits of a liberal education, and talk about Petrarch!"

In speaking of "the Professors", we are guilty of an injustice to the present generation. The American Professor of Literature to-day is not a serious danger; first of all because he is not a power, and also because his mind is, in many cases, far more open than New York journalists affect to believe. The Professor, we repeat, is himself a victim of the Professorial tradition. Individually, he frequently seeks to escape; as a member of a group, he is compelled to conform.

Here we have, therefore, the first of our "conscious, organized minorities." In theory, its claims to authority are based upon expert knowledge; in fact, upon the genteel tradition and an alliance with the ruling class. When that alliance is broken, the Professorial Doctrine is rejected as sheer pedantry. When the ruling class abandons the genteel tradition, or loses its own power, the professors' influence sickens and dies.

This influence affects living authors in two ways. Directly, it fosters a scholarly style, and emphasis on correctness, elegance, wealth of allusions. In this form, it was very great during the Classical Age; it has left traces throughout the nineteenth century; it is still felt in England, in Continental Europe, even in America. Much of the charm of Anatole France and Cabell has no other foundation. We taste it and relish it in Huxley, Maurois, Thornton Wilder, Christopher Morley, Willa Cather, not to mention the critics and essayists, and a few smart New Yorkers who might consider it an insult. Oddly enough, it is present in our appreciation of James Joyce: there is in the author of *Ulysses* a Professor, whose recondite allusiveness is enjoyed with conscious pride by all meritorious pupils.

Indirectly, it has fostered, in America particularly, a

deplorable anti-cultural bias: the dread of highbrow stuff, the exaltation of the crude. Because of the scholar's superciliousness, illiteracy has become a virtue, or at least a successful literary trick. Among the innumerable readers of our most popular fiction, a goodly proportion would be perfectly capable of enjoying higher things. But there is on every side—authors, publishers, public—a nervous dread of the professorial taint. This "conscious minority" has become so self-conscious that it is fated to remain an isolated, a hopeless minority. And so it shall remain, until the teaching of literature throws off its traditional shackles.

II

The Professors used to claim authority in the name of a doctrine. This, with the breaking down of the classical synthesis, became more and more of a pretense. The true source of their power, such as it may have been, was their harmony with the tastes of the ruling class. This frankly pragmatic and social ideal is even better represented by the Academies, and particularly by the *Académie Française*.

This illustrious institution is the clearest example of a small group possessing official prestige and influence in the realm of literature. The interest that it presents is therefore not local, anecdotic, antiquarian: the Academy stands for a principle. Whoever is yearning for "order", for definite standards, for a proper hierarchy of values, for an established guardian of sound tradition, for a Supreme Court of correct usage and elegant taste, must consider the French Academy as his Utopia. Matthew

Arnold sighed audibly for such an authority; Professor Irving Babbitt sighed in the secret of his heart. The Academy has been in existence for three hundred years: what has it done for literature?

Its creation is part of the great restoration of order that marked the seventeenth century, and culminated with the maturity of Louis XIV. It is coeval with Descartes's *Discourse on Method:* also a determined effort toward intelligent discipline. It is significant that its founder should have been Richelieu, whose hands of priestly steel wrested France from chaos.

A number of gentlemen were in the habit of meeting informally to discuss questions of literature. Richelieu heard of this little group. He was suspicious of even the most innocent gatherings not under his immediate supervision; he was genuinely interested in letters; so he requested this small knot of friends to form themselves into an official body, under his high protection. They were flattered rather than delighted: but the wishes of His Eminence were law. So the Academy—modestly and sanely called "the French Academy", without any of the extravagant titles then current in Italy—came into being in the folds of the Red Robe. Until the end of the Ancient Régime, it was part of its ritual that on the admission of every new member, some reference should be made to the formidable Founder.

This Academy was, in its prenatal days, a *Club of Gentlemen:* and a club of gentlemen it has remained. Of gentlemen: not of ladies. Madame de Sévigné, Madame de Lafayette, Madame de Staël, George Sand, could never have been admitted. Even in our own days, the

French Academy objected to the election of Madame Curie to the Academy of Sciences, for fear her admission might be used as a precedent. No sound reason has ever been offered for this ungallant ostracism. Women were at that time, through the *Salons,* most influential in polite literature. They have never seriously protested against their exclusion: they are satisfied not to be members of the Academy, if only they can make academicians.

Of *gentlemen,* once more: a man who has forfeited the name is debarred from this most exclusive of clubs. Molière was a "mountebank", appearing on the stage in broad farcical rôles: in his lifetime, he could not be thought of as a candidate. After his death, he was admitted in effigy, and his bust bears the handsome apology: "Nothing was lacking to his glory: *he* was lacking to ours." Diderot, the hackwriter and Bohemian, Rousseau the vagabond, in spite of their immense prestige, were not eligible. Neither was Balzac, ever in fear of the sheriff; nor Alexandre Dumas, whose life was a Christmas Pantomime, all glittering tinsel and paste. Zola knocked most insistently at the inexorable door: it became a perennial jest of literary Paris. No jest to him: as the head of the Naturalistic School, he felt it his duty to secure official recognition. He was invariably, almost unanimously, blackballed. His private life was above reproach, and the verbal filth in his works might have been overlooked. But he was accused, not quite fairly, of seeking notoriety and enormous sales through unsavory scandal; and this conduct unbecoming an Academician and a gentleman disqualified him for ever. Jean Richepin, who had posed truculently as a tramp and a rebel, had to repent, recant, atone, in sackcloth and ashes, before his youthful sins were forgiven and his gentlemanly status restored.

So an election to the French Academy is not inevitably the reward of literary excellence. In every generation, there is at least one of the best authors who is pointedly left out, and is said to occupy the forty-first armchair—the number of the immortals being limited to forty. Foreign readers would undoubtedly nominate for that distinction Romain Rolland, one of the first citizens in the coming United States of Europe. But the Academy has not yet forgiven him for standing "above the strife." The argument that his style is "soggy" is not quite ingenuous. Romain Rolland is not great as a word artist. But he writes fully as well as the average run of the Forty; indeed far better than most of them.

While great writers are not seldom left in outer darkness, others are admitted whose literary production is of the slimmest. The first Secretary of the Academy, Conrart, is perhaps the only man who left his name on the honor roll of literature for never writing at all. "Imitate Conrart's prudent silence," was the wise counsel of Boileau. Rostand, in the first act of *Cyrano de Bergerac,* has a *bourgeois* tell his son: "I see many a member . . .; here are Boudu, Boissat, and Cureau de la Chambre, Porchères, Colomby, Bourzeys, Bourdon, Arbaud. . . . All those names, not one of which will die: how beautiful!"—and not even scholars remember a single one of them.

The Academy is an epitome of good French society. It admits writers in so far as they are also gentlemen;

prelates, aristocrats, great lawyers, conservative statesmen, notabilities in every field, provided they are using good French, and have shown some interests in the purity of the language; at times, it elects illustrious Frenchmen, even without such a proviso. It happened that Marshal Foch, as a writer, was well up to the academic average, and Marshal Lyautey distinctly above it; but the one great service of Marshal Joffre to the Republic of Letters was that, as long as he lived, he refrained from publishing his Memoirs.

The French Academy is not therefore a body of technicians. It is not dominated by creative artists: we shall see later how radically different is the private Goncourt Academy. Grammarians, critics, professors and historians of literature are abundantly but not overwhelmingly represented: no pedantry attaches to that august body.

This is not quite in accord with Richelieu's ideal. He meant his Academy to have definite jurisdiction over literary activities. It was at the same time to write the law, and to apply the law. As the collective undying successor of Aristotle, it was to keep the *Rhetoric* and the *Poetics* up to date, by issuing formal treatises on these subjects. And it was to pass judgment on the productions of the day.

In its dogmatic capacity, the Academy has very wisely gone to sleep. The public would be mildly amused if the Forty should ever bring out a Neo-Aristotelian code. Absolutism in literature is dead, although absolutists are very much alive. The publications of the Academy are not commandments, but the register of good usage in vocabulary and grammar. The *Grammar* came out for the first time when the venerable Institution was nearing the close of its third century. This incredibly protracted travail was assisted at the end by Abel Hermant, a licentious and flippant writer who reserves all his purism for matters of diction. The result inevitably evoked Horace's *ridiculus mus:* there is hardly a teacher of Junior French in this country who, single-handed, could not have done better.

The *Dictionary* has at any rate the benefit of a continuous tradition. Every generation or so, a new edition appears. Only those words which are current in polite society are included. Archaisms are dropped out, not without regret; neologisms are admitted, with cautious reluctance. Even slang forces its way into the select company, after a quarantine of a hundred years. *Epatant* has thus acquired citizenship, while the door was firmly closed on the upturned nose of the Midinette. The Academy recognizes only the vocabulary of general conversation: local and technical terms have no standing. This is wisdom, for, in spite of the presence of an occasional scientist, this Club of Elderly Gentlemen is hardly prepared to deal authoritatively with unfamiliar words. France, who loves to tease her Academy with fond familiarity, has not forgotten the definition of a crayfish: "a little red fish that walks backwards."

The Academy, in this respect, is a far better mirror of classical France than the law-giving, law-enforcing body dreamed of by Richelieu. For French classicism was never based solely on abstract logic: it was tradition interpreted by common sense, reasonableness rather than pure reason. The Academy was somewhat similar in character to the old Parliament of Paris, which never had the initiative of laws, but which harmonized the customs and preserved the traditions of legal France, even against the caprices of royal power.

But the Parliament was a court of justice: the Academy attempted to judge—once, and once only. Richelieu referred to his new creation the case of Corneille's *Cid,* which was stirring an unprecedented hubbub in literary Paris. In doing so, the Cardinal showed remarkable moderation. The play was an exaltation of dueling, which he had declared a capital offense; and of Spain, then at war with France. Had Corneille written under Napoleon, Clemenceau or Mr. Mitchell Palmer, he might not have been treated with such ecclesiastical mansuetude.

The problem was the central one of all literary criticism: can we judge according to formal rules, or is pleasure our only law? France had fallen in love with Rodrigue and his Chimène; but the play was "faulty" according to the pseudo-Aristotelian rule of the three unities.

Corneille defended himself with the cunning of a Norman lawyer. The *unity of place* is respected, he claimed, so long as the action remains within the limits of the same city. The *unity of time* allows, not three hours, but a whole day; and *one* day means anything short of *two* days. And he proceeds to show, with his watch in his hand: that two young people could become engaged, their fathers quarrel, the youth kill his prospective father-in-law in a duel, a suit be brought against him in the King's Court, a Moorish invasion be repelled, the victory be reported in full, a second duel fought, and the hero and heroine reconciled, all within thirty-four or thirty-six hours. This, to say the least, strains credibility: yet the law is not formally broken. It shows what can be done with what Irving Babbitt called "an armour of elastic steel."

The judges were torn between their genuine admiration for Corneille and their classical scruples, reinforced by Richelieu's well-known bias. So they returned a halting, non-committal verdict, which pleased neither party, and least of all themselves. This experience discouraged the Academy from ever again acting in a judicial capacity.

But this one equivocal sentence, coupled with Corneille's pettifogging subtlety, burdened France for two hundred years with the rigid formality of the famous "rules." The French public was not clamoring for them: they were imposed from above, by the pedants, the legalists, the Academicians. Had Corneille defied the shades of Aristotle, had the Academy dared to support him in his resistance, much unnecessary stiffness and artificiality could have been spared. But then Corneille would not have been the Corneille we know: the poet of the reasoning disciplined Will; and the Academy would not have been the Academy: the guardian of decency and order on Parnassus.

The French Academy has therefore not done the things it was appointed to do. It has done a few other things, some of them rather unexpected, with respectable but indifferent success. The prizes it awards do not attract much attention: at least not the prizes for literature, for the Academy is also empowered to reward "virtue" (Prix Montyon). It has become the trustee for several fine collections, including the matchless treasures of Chantilly:

a living museum, it might in time become the corporate curator of all antiquarian museums.

Its influence on French literature has been surprisingly small. No great writer has suffered seriously, in fame or profit, from not being an Academician; no academic nonentity has been forced, by virtue of his official immortality, upon a sceptical and unresponsive public. The books which men have refrained from writing for fear of endangering their chances of election were, in all likelihood, better left unwritten. The books composed for the sole purpose of establishing an academic claim could very well have been spared.*

The authority of the French Academy is thus hard to define. But it exists. The Immortals have been the butt of unending pleasantries ever since the days of Richelieu: but in France, ridicule does not kill—it preserves. These very jests are a tribute: no one ever dreams of poking fun at the British or the American Academies. Any Frenchman interested in letters could name offhand half a dozen Academicians: I have met a number of American professors who did not even know we had an Academy.

The first reason for this persistent favor is that the Academy, alone among lay institutions, is connected with the past by a practically unbroken tradition. The French Revolution changed its name for a few years, but could not kill its spirit. France is an intensely conservative country that went through one tremendous up-

---

* General Max Weygand, for instance, wrote a *Turenne* which made him eligible—a *masterpiece* in the sense that the old Guilds gave to the term. This serious, dignified piece of work added nothing to the General's reputation or to the treasures of French Literature.

heaval: the few things that remained unshaken became all the more precious. England has her King, her Lords, her Yeomen of the Guard, her two ancient Universities: France has no such survivals except the Academy.

The Academy is unique in another respect. At all times, it was the meeting point of every form of superiority: birth, station, talent (beauty alone being left out of consideration). The ruling classes in their various degrees find in that literary institution their perfect symbol. Especially at present, when *bourgeois* culture is entrenching itself in France against the onslaught of Russo-American machine-worship, the Academy becomes a new Verdun. In the livid light under the dingy dome, one circular glance will embrace, among the members and in the audience, the leaders of a solid, obstinate, shrewd, hard-working world.* It is not "France" any more than the King was "France": probably less. But it has called itself France for so long, that it never questions its exclusive title to the name.

The power of the Academy is therefore not technical, not artistic, but social. The Academy is not a workshop: it is a Salon, and the emanation of the Salons. Its elections are prepared in the drawing-rooms. Society flocks to its open meetings: a first night at the Opera, a famous race at Longchamp or Chantilly, are plebeian compared with the best academic events. Academicians are great lions. One of them answered congratulations in these candid terms: "Yes, it is a fine position. The uniform is

---

* It was said: "The center of gravity of the Academy is Raymond Poincaré, the center of levity Maurice Donnay." We fully agree with the first part of this epigram.

very becoming. *And one is well fed."* Prominent host-
esses have their personal academician as the chief ornament of their gatherings. Anatole France, the most conspicuous example in recent times, thus belonged to the
household of Madame Arman de Caillavet: an association singularly profitable from the worldly point of view,
but which grew heavily irksome with the years. France
would have preferred obscurity and indolence to his
success in a society which had lost all its glamor in his
eyes.

To sum up: the Professorial Church and the Academy
are two "conscious, organized minorities" which claim
authority in literature. That authority has never been
absolute; it is increasingly ignored, especially in America.
But once it was great, and even now it must be taken
into account. The study of their influence reveals that
literature never is a fully independent realm: it is part
of a larger whole, which we call society or civilization.
The ideals and the methods of these two Institutions are
the same as those of the ruling class—an aristocracy of
wealth and intelligence. If the Professors and the Academicians cease to be in harmony with that class, their
position becomes unsubstantial, almost shadowy. This
has come to pass in our country, where *culture* in the
conventional sense is neither frankly democratic nor
openly plutocratic. If the ruling class—be it Plutus or
Demos—fails to integrate the old culture into its system,
and fails likewise to evolve a culture of its own, if superiorities of every kind do not meet and work in harmony,
the immediate result is bewilderment, and the next decadence.

Chapter 17

Yesterday: COURTS AND SALONS

IT is an ancient custom to name literary or artistic periods after the ruler of the state. The most widely known example is probably the Augustan Age; the Periclean, the Elizabethan, the Victorian, immediately come to our minds. The Italian Renaissance is often referred to as the era of the Medici; the serene sunlit heights of French Classicism are known as "the century of Louis XIV."

These time-honored appellations are of very unequal value. England had an Augustan Age without an Augustus. We speak of Georgian architecture, although the House of Hanover had little to do with it; in literature, the best that could be said of the Georges is that they were not unworthy of such official poets as Colley Cibber, Whitehead, Warton and Pye. Except perhaps in a few poems of Tennyson, it can hardly be said that the personality of Queen Victoria impressed itself upon Victorian literature. A perfect harmony, through three long generations, grew between her and the dominant class: the Victorian era is one of the most definite in history. But that harmony excluded art, as a discordant note: it

is chiefly in a chronological sense that Walter Pater,
Algernon Charles Swinburne, Thomas Hardy, can be described as Victorians. Some of these royal names are
sheer flattery, others were adopted for the sake of symmetry and convenience. But, under favorable circumstances, which have occurred repeatedly in history, the
Sovereigns, through their courts, have wielded a notable
influence in the domain of letters.

This is as it should be. Ideally, the Court is, much more
than the Academy, the common ground of all superiorities. Historical names, great servants of the state, men of
genius in every line: all those who rise, whatever may be
their point of departure, must meet near the single summit. When the dynasty is truly the national center, such
an ideal is at least partly fulfilled.

Less worthy motives may contribute to the same result. Under the Ancient Régime, authors would gravi-
tate toward the Court for the same reason which induces
their successors to seek popularity: the approval of the
élite was then the unmistakable sign of success. And the
Kings encouraged artists and poets for the same purpose
which causes dramatic stars to be nice to journalists. The
chief concern of kings is glory: an inglorious king is no
king at all. And the trumpets of fame are in the hands
of the poets: art is the supreme advertising agent. Imagine the difference if Napoleon III had been wise enough
to enlist Victor Hugo as his Vergil; or if Vergil had
written the *Chastisements* of Augustus instead of the
Æneid.

This is true only of the genuine monarchical state,
harmoniously hierarchized from the sovereign at the

apex to the masses of the people below. Then the Court
is a unique strategic point: conquer the Court, and the
world is yours. There is no clearer case of a "conscious,
organized minority" acting with the tacit approval of the
passive majority. When that grand national symmetry
is destroyed, the influence of the Court is impaired, and
may vanish altogether. In a tyranny, there is no real
court, only a band of sycophants and executioners. There
is but one thing that it can impose, and that is silence.
Ivan the Terrible could not be the center of a national
culture. Even Napoleon, although he was by no means
an Oriental despot, was too much of an autocrat for the
growth of a literary Court. The élite never fully rallied
to him; between the people and himself, his heterogeneous aristocracy was a screen rather than a link.

When a single element assumes exclusive predominance, whether it be the aristocratic, the military or the
ecclesiastical, the representative character of the Court is
lost, and with it the possibility of wide influence. The
Golden Century of Spanish Literature owes little to the
morose, monastic, bureaucratic inner circle under Philip
II. The moments of full harmony between people, court
and king are rare and fleeting. The first decade of rule
of Francis I offered that character, the best years of Queen
Elizabeth, the young maturity of Louis XIV: hardly
any other in modern history. Frederick II was a man of
letters, and gathered round him wits, philosophers, poets:
but it was a cosmopolitan, French-speaking crowd, alien
to the Germany which was rising in those days. The
King's personal prestige influenced German culture in a
way diametrically opposed to his own Gallicized taste.

Maximilian II in Bavaria, Louis-Philippe in France, Prince Albert in England, Don Pedro II in Brazil, were pathetically worthy men who tried, according to their lights, to play the Augustan rôle; Maximilian of Mexico would have sought a place among them, if his reign had not been so tragic and so brief. They met with indifferent success; indeed, they were frequently called arch-Philistines for their trouble. The Romantic rule of Louis II in Bavaria ended in disaster. The incursions of William II into the domain of culture only roused exasperated irony. One princely Maecenas alone achieved his end: the Grand Duke of Weimar attracted the protaganists of the German spirit to his duodecimo capital, and thus inscribed his name by the side of theirs in the annals of the Fatherland. Here the usual process was reversed: it was not a Court fostering literature, but literature immortalizing a court.

The influence of Elizabeth and that of Louis XIV are subjects so vast, and so generally known, that a mere allusion must suffice. That influence was very real: history, literary no less than political, would be very different without these two proudly conscious figureheads. But it belongs to the past: it would be a miracle if the world were to see again a Gloriana or a Grand Monarch. Even in the countries which have most carefully preserved the trappings of monarchy, its spirit is gone. As Theodore Roosevelt bluntly put it, kingship is equivalent to a lifelong Vice-Presidency. As for our republican courts, their action on literature is microscopic. No less than four Presidents of France were members of the Academy, and not a few of ours had books to their credit. Yet the Elysée and the White House are even farther from the centers of national culture than Buckingham Palace.

But the Court survives at any rate as a shadow: it is to the Court that we owe courtliness and courtesy. And it survives also in solid, ubiquitous, minute fragments: the Salons. With its formal dress and its etiquette, every Salon is a miniature Court, just as every court worthy of the name was a magnified Salon. The quality that made Louis XIV truly regal was not his pride, but his exquisite politeness. He was the perfect host: he enjoyed life, and wanted his friends to enjoy life with him. He was as respectful of their titles and privileges as he expected them to be respectful of his prerogatives. It is not sufficient for a King to be the first gentleman in Europe —witness George IV and Edward VII: but a gentleman he must be, or his court will remain an oppressively tedious show. Napoleon was no gentleman, but a blend of the martinet and the parvenu: hence the failure of the new Augustus to inaugurate a new Augustan Age.

It is a commonplace that literature is the mirror of society; but, until recent times, it was far more accurate to say: "Literature is the mirror of 'Society.'" Pericles was not a stern dictator, but a smiling friend. The atmosphere of Plato's dialogues, particularly the *Symposium,* is that of good company enjoying good talk over good wine. The men who have best rendered the spirit of a perfect week-end party, W. H. Mallock, Aldous Huxley, are the distant but conscious heirs of Plato. Horace, Ovid, Petronius, were "Society" writers in the most sophisticated sense of the term.

The Barbaric invasions meant darkness and silence for several hundred years. It was in Southern France and Italy that the "social" ideal revived. In the North, the aristocracy lived isolated in their craggy castles, keeping culture away from their moats and portcullis. The urbane tradition had never completely disappeared in the Mediterranean world. Nobles, merchants, poets, could meet on pleasant terms. Among the Troubadours, many were of noble lineage.

Hard work and violent sports are the privileges of men: "Society" is woman's domain. The courtly literature of the South was dominated by the cult of the Lady. The notion that reverence for women is of Northern origin is hardly corroborated either by history or by literature. No one could occupy a more honored position than the Roman matron; and woman, in the early medieval epic, still imbued with the Northern spirit, plays a very subordinate part. In the *Roland,* fair Aude appears but to die: it is a man's world, and roughhewn. In the little courts of Languedoc and Italy, softer influences were at work. Etymologically *chivalry* implies fighting on horseback: the knight is a mere cuirassier. But chivalry came to mean exalted courtesy: uncouth strength bows before gentle grace. *Gallant,* in English, is *valiant; galant,* in French, is *polite,* with a touch of sentimentality.

Southern Princesses carried this new conception to the Northern courts, England, France, Champagne. Chrétien de Troyes transformed the mystic and passionate motives of Celtic legend into codes of *savoir-vivre,* i.e. *savoir-aimer*. In our days, he would conduct a syndicated column of advice to the lovelorn on points of etiquette and sentiment. And his work was followed by the enormous flood of romances which, three centuries later, addled the brains of a worthy country gentleman, Don Quijote by name: Dulcinea was a more indispensable appurtenance of his knightly calling than even Rocinante.

Nothing is more misleading than to dub "Middle Ages" the whole thousand years between the fall of Rome and the Renaissance. We should at least distinguish between the Dark Ages, the Age of Faith, and the Age of Make-Believe, which was that of chivalrous fiction. Joinville, the very human companion of the last Crusader, St. Louis, finds pleasure in the thought that he will retail his prowess in the ladies' drawing rooms. Aucassin prefers to Heaven, the abode of sniveling monks, the other place where he is bound to meet noble knights and fair ladies. Ovid's *Art of Love* was the favorite classic in that age which we call "stern" and "naïve." Boccaccio, whose *Decameron* has a houseparty for its framework, and every kind of love for its theme, started a tradition which, through Chaucer and La Fontaine, has descended to James Branch Cabell and Michael Arlen. The *Romance of the Rose,* in its inception, was an allegory of delicate lovemaking.

Not that "Society" entirely dominated literature: there were poets of the cloister, and poets of the marketplace also. And there were rebellions, coarse but not unwholesome, against the subtleties of aristocratic courtship. Like every over-elaborate ritual, the Society Code engendered formalism, hypocrisy, and ultimately disbelief. The later

Middle Ages were not lacking in works which, like *The Cream of the Jest,* turn abruptly from highflown romance to realism and satire. The most international classic of the period, the *Romance of the Rose,* is Janus-like: William of Lorris all dainty conceits, John of Meung a solid, earthly, freethinking *bourgeois,* who will brook no nonsense.

It was Italy again that served as an inspiration for the greater Renaissance of the sixteenth century. What amazed the Northern men-at-arms, when they swooped upon the land of endless delight, was not the scholarship of a few Byzantine refugees, not even the crumbling remains of Roman grandeur, but the exquisite luxury of social life. The Renaissance influence on thought, style, manners, domestic architecture, is far more Italianate than Greco-Roman. It was Italy that gave the model and formulated the code of courtly behavior. Francis I strove to live up to Italian standards, in surroundings of Italian luxury. Just as Italian gardens spread into Northern climes, every Northern literature in turn had its Italian *Arcadias,* and the love conventions of the sonneteers. We might blot out the *direct* influence of antiquity, and still understand the Elizabethan age; take away the Italian factor, and the whole period is blurred.*

It was again from Italy that France derived the inspiration for her most famous literary salon, the ideal of its kind, the Hôtel de Rambouillet. Henry IV was affable, shrewd, witty in a soldierly way: but years of camp

---

* The Elizabethans themselves would demur: they took pride in following the Ancients, not the Italians, whom they did not respect. Yet their very knowledge of the classics was derived from Italy; and their taste for Latin and Greek was an Italian fashion.

life, at the head of an army which at times was hardly more than a ragged marauding band, had disqualified him for social leadership. And his devouring amorousness was very different from the punctilious deference exacted by the old knightly code. France, after half a century of turmoil, was sighing for order in the state and decorum in society. So young Catherine de Vivonne, Marquise de Rambouillet, familiar with the amenities of Italian life, withdrew as completely as she could from Henry's foul-mouthed and promiscuous circle, and started a little court of her own. Her success was immediate, brilliant and prolonged. Her "Blue Room" became the focus of refined society and polite literature. Even Corneille, who was by no means at his best in a drawing room, appeared at Madame de Rambouillet's; and Bossuet, then a mere boy, gave that aristocratic assembly a foretaste of his sonorous eloquence. We shall see later what excesses of sentimental, psychological and verbal subtlety were encouraged by the Hôtel, and above all by its numberless imitations. *"Précieuses"*, preciosity, became terms of reproach. But we must not forget that the great Salon was at the very heart of dignified literature, and that such admirable women as Madame de Sévigné and Madame de Lafayette were proud to belong to the *Précieux* circle.

With the accession of Louis XIV to personal rule, the literary salon lost its predominant prestige. Louis wanted no prime minister and would tolerate no social rival. No Salon, not even the splendid company of the Great Condé at Chantilly, was allowed to eclipse the Tuileries or Versailles. The highest in the land had but one desire:

to remain at Court, and edge their way to the immediate vicinity of the Presence.

It was this Court, emulated throughout Europe, that gave its tone to so much of European literature. The aristocracy believed that they had to applaud stiff pseudo-classical tragedies for the same reason that the first King of Prussia felt obliged to keep a Royal Mistress: not out of any spontaneous desire, but because Louis XIV had set the example.

With the decline and death of the Grand Monarch, social leadership once more deserted the court and fell into private hands. Louis XV was an absentee king, who watched with imperturbable gravity and a secret chuckle the dissolution of his monarchy: under him, primacy shifted back from Versailles to Paris. The eighteenth century was par excellence the era of Salons. Paris gave the tone, and Europe followed with eagerness. The most unmistakable products of the Salon spirit in English literature are Lord Chesterfield and Horace Walpole. But they were only extreme instances, almost caricatures: a generation later, the Society ideal can be traced, delicate yet definite, in the genteel background of Jane Austen.

Rousseau led the rebellion of the individual against artificial Society: but it must be remembered that his success had its first roots in the very society which he denounced. If he had not been a member of the literary clan in Paris, the frequent guest of financiers and the protégé of aristocrats, his primitivist paradoxes might never have found an audience. It was Society that started the back-to-nature craze: fine ladies, at the Opera, nursed their infants in public; and Marie-Antoinette played the milkmaid in the comic-opera hamlet of Trianon.

The French Revolution and the Empire ruined the influence of the Salon. Madame de Staël, brought up, just before the catastrophe, in the delightful atmosphere of Parisian society, strove heroically for her defeated ideal. Just as she was dreaming that Directoire France might be led back into the vanished Paradise, Bonaparte seized hold of the government. She hoped against hope that he would share his Republican throne with her: all material activities to be his, hers the leadership of public opinion through the social élite. But Bonaparte wanted no public opinion: his own sufficed. So he kept Madame de Staël at arm's length, and his arm was long. Social life was hushed: the police had ears everywhere.

This breaking down of the social ideal is responsible for a sentiment which began with Rousseau and assumed the proportions of a disease: the oppressive feeling of solitude. Man was liberated from the shackles of conventional society, and found himself aching for the familiar chains; individualism brought with it melancholy and despair.

The Salon survived in England and revived in France: but its glory had departed. In France, it suffered particularly from the divorce between the old aristocracy and the modern spirit. From 1830, the fall of the last Bourbon, to the eve of the Great War, the Faubourg Saint-Germain had been sulking. The result was that the highest circles were devitalized—sulking is an uncreative mood—, while Society as a whole was decapitated. In this generation, the attitude of the great noble families is not so hostile: but their half-hearted reconciliation with their own country is the fruit of resignation, not of renewed hope.

Efforts were made throughout the century to stave off this decadence. The Duke of Orleans, eldest son of Louis-Philippe, and his artistic, ambitious German Duchess, attempted to create for themselves an intellectual circle, of which Victor Hugo was the main ornament. The youngest son of the *bourgeois* King, the Duc d'Aumale, sought to revive the alliance between art, literature and Society. He became a member of the French Academy and was universally respected: but the sympathy he inspired was mingled with curiosity, as before the last representative of a fossil race. The cousins of Napoleon III, Prince Napoleon and Princess Mathilde, had personal friends among the best writers of their time, like Sainte-Beuve, Renan·and Taine; and even among those who were not supporters of the Imperial régime. Prince Napoleon, a Cæsar estranged from his own class, was hardly the man to set a fashion. As a matter of fact, we think of him rather as a minor member of Sainte-Beuve's group than as a princely patron.

The literary Salon still exists. In a recent study, Madame de Caillavet's was called "the last of the Salons." Who knows? Institutions enjoy at times an interminable evening twilight. There are still barons in France, although their baronies have become impalpable. Marcel Proust's tortuous chronicle of Society in the last fifty years is a record of accelerating decadence. The Academy does not feel complete without a Duke or so: but neither the Faubourg Saint-Germain nor the Faubourg Saint-

Honoré can make or unmake even a third-rate reputation.

In England, the social-literary tradition is not wholly lost. The two historical Universities, as we have seen, were until the war the symbols and the instruments of that alliance. Some aristocrats still deem it an elegance to have a book to their credit. Lord Rosebery's excellent *Napoleon* was a feather in his Scottish cap—but far less brilliant than his winning the Derby. And it is still the right thing for intelligent Society to entertain writers. There is nothing that comes so close to the old ideal as a week-end party in a great country house. There we find, or at least we expect, the blend of superiorities from widely different fields; a blend which must be daring, if it is to have the proper tang, and yet not haphazard, or it will cease to be smooth and palatable.*

The literary chronicle in the best British journals has frequently the tone of a Society column. Just as we want to know the latest fashion in clothes and the latest rumors about engagements, estrangements and flirtations, we like to be informed, a little ahead of our neighbors, that Mayfair is dropping Evelyn Waugh or rediscovering John Galsworthy. Mr. Hugh Walpole, himself a notable product of the social-literary alliance, gives that gossipy flavor to his enjoyable monthly letters. He manages to convey the impression that you are "in the know" without retailing any actual scandal. Others do not show the same restraint. The British aristocracy, we are told, are

---

* A writer of very humble origin and very unconventional manners like D. H. Lawrence found himself quite naturally hobnobbing and corresponding in familiar terms with titled ladies.

eking out a scanty living by exposing to view each other's washing.

English society is a fact, solid, patent, undeniable: American society baffles, not description merely, but imagination. Its elements are, like our sea power, second to none. But they are not integrated. As we have seen, a reception day at the French Academy reveals a many-sided but closely knit world; and, in spite of gate-crashers, so does a formal affair in London. There are functions in New York where the aristocracies of wealth, wit, beauty, power, may seem to mingle for a moment. But they will soon be dissociated again: they do not belong together. In a very elusive sense, "Society" still controls literature: it is smart to read certain books, to wear certain clothes, to be seen in certain places. But that smartness has no actual, definite center. It is a myth, out of which fabulous sums of very real gold have been coined. So long as wealth, journalistic brilliancy and the book trade have their chief abode in New York, the scholarly and Puritan tradition in New England, the romance of bygone days in Virginia and Louisiana, religion in the Middle West, beauty in Hollywood, and political power in Washington, we can not expect an all-inclusive, and at the same time homogeneous American "Society."

So the very term has become something of a joke: only minds that are primitive are hankering for that un-American ideal. Yet Society in the organic sense, the fusion of all the élites, did exist in Boston, in the almost mythical New York that Mrs. Edith Wharton is attempting to revive for us, in the world of Owen Wister, James Branch

Cabell, Ellen Glasgow. I have seen charming traces of it in a thriving seaport of Texas. The same ideal prevails, we are told, in the Bohemian Club of San Francisco. But not one of these centers ever was national in character; most of them are memories; some may be mere legends.

Whether we like it or not, we Americans must be resigned to democracy. The élites on this side are incommensurable. No common standard of the past will be acceptable to them all—least of all money. And we have almost ceased to pray for a new common standard. Pluralism is here. It does not make for a symmetrical world, like that of Louis XIV. It does not even make for a richly varied one: at first we see nothing but monotonous confusion. We may yet be able to organize, freely, our private universe. But the ideal of *one* great national literature, backed by all the forces of *one* recognized national élite, is evaporating like the ideal of *one* national Church. And hard as England and France may resist, they are bound to follow our course. Society's influence on literature is a thing of the past, because Society itself has dissolved.

We watch its dissolution with mixed feelings. It had many things to its credit that we are reluctant to lose. It had invariably made for elegance of expression without pedantry. To expound vital problems without boring charming ladies requires a difficult technique. Through that exacting school, French has acquired a matchless clarity, which is not inherent in the language itself. Even Descartes the professional scientist, even Pascal the mystic, addressed themselves to the well-bred rather than to the technicians. Fontenelle was a philosopher for drawing rooms; Montesquieu, a learned magistrate, sprinkled his mighty *Spirit of Laws* with neat epigrams; Voltaire created the "New History" in order to convince Madame du Châtelet that the study of the past need not be musty. The tradition is unbroken down to Renan, Taine, Bergson, Bremond, and the latest doctor's thesis.

No doubt this lucidity may be obtained at the expense of profundity. Madame de Staël, the very incarnation of "Society" in literature, appalled sundry German philosophers by requesting "the gist" of their systems in less than ten minutes. Ten minutes to make clear that which it had taken them ten years to make obscure! And Madame de Staël became the laughingstock of the erudite. Yet we wonder whether, of all those dizzy fabrics of thought, much more is actually remembered than what Voltaire could have expressed in a few pithy paragraphs. It is all too easy to mistake the turbid for the profound, and limpidity for shallowness. Certain translucid passages of Renan have the rich and strange beauty of submarine gardens. There is a clearness that adds to the quality of thought, as well as a clearness that detracts from it. Both are, superficially, forms of politeness: the author tries to spare his public unnecessary pains. But the second is tinged with secret contempt: "This is all you would understand, anyway." The former is inspired by genuine courtesy: it is rude to offer the reader an unfinished product.

Such clearness is not an inborn, individual quality: it is part of the social order. The author is conscious of a public which knows the best and is entitled to the best. Such a public wants clearness from a Renan, a Henri Poincaré, a Bergson, not from Walt Mason the Rhyming Optimist or Bruce Barton the Supersalesman of Heaven. England and America desire the same thing, but do not know what to ask for; they were delighted when the French technique was deliberately adopted by Lytton Strachey. It came with the freshness of a discovery: yet Strachey considered himself as a disciple of Fontenelle and Voltaire; and, for nearly half a century, the long series of *French Men of Letters* had been offering, in dainty little volumes, an admirable and truly Stracheyan blend of scholarship and subdued irony.

We are using French literature as an example: we are well aware that France has no monopoly of clear thought and elegant expression. "Whatever is not clear is not French," deserves a place among popular fallacies; the man who coined that phrase had certainly not read Stéphane Mallarmé and Paul Claudel. French "Society" is no more infallible than French dressmakers or French cooks. There are dowds and *gargottes* in Paris; Victor Cousin and Caro were once mistaken for philosophers; and Henry Bordeaux is a member of the French Academy. On the other hand, we have come across no book about France more cogent in thought, more elegantly spare in expression than that of the *German* Ernst Curtius; and none lighter in touch, wittier, more whimsical and yet more searching, than that of the *German*

Sieburg. The best example of Voltairian irony that we know was uttered by the dour old Scot Carlyle;* and we could name half a dozen Londoners now living who beat the Parisians at their own game.

We have praised, unblushingly, the influence of "Society" upon literature. Now for the inexorable law of compensation. The penalty for urbanity is not always shallowness, as Pascal and La Rochefoucauld will testify: but a certain degree of formality. If they do not destroy personality, good manners succeed in veiling it; and conformity in externals obviously leads to sameness or monotony. Professor Babbitt's insistence on standards must bring forth standardized products.

In many fields, the loss is small: only eccentricity is sacrificed. It is disastrous in the lyric. For a "sociable" literature, the Ego is hateful; and lyricism is the exaltation of the Ego. Romanticism, which restored the possibility of lyric poetry, was a revolt against Society. Because France was so eminently sociable, Romanticism in France was only a magnificent accident. Retrospectively, we imagine that Lamartine, Hugo, Vigny, Musset, were the dominant powers during the two great Romantic decades: their classical contemporaries have vanished from sight altogether. But those "dim ultimate Classicists", now so deeply forgotten, were then in almost absolute control of the Academy and of all official positions. The Romanticists were held to be only a noisy band of talented, ill-bred youngsters, who presently would calm down. All later poets in whom the lyric note was unmistakable—Baudelaire, Verlaine, Rim-

* Margaret Fuller: "I accept the Universe."—Carlyle: "Gad! she'd better!"

baud, Mallarmé—had little to do with recognized "Society." High-grade French literature often has the faultless elegance and the banal distinction of Beaux-Arts architecture.

"Society" is conscious at times of its own commonplaceness, and seeks to escape from it through excessive refinement. The fear of triteness drives it into Preciosity. The disease goes by many names—Marinism and Concettism in Italy, Gongorism and Cultism in Spain, Euphuism in England. These words denote rare and virulent attacks: but the danger is permanent. The American form of Euphuism is smart wisecracking: some articles in undiluted New-Yorkese are as far-fetched in their allusiveness as the very worst pages that the early seventeenth century had to offer; and they will prove as puzzling to posterity, unless posterity be wise enough to leave them alone.

A "sociable" literature is dominated by woman; and the chief interest of a "society" woman relieved from household duties and family cares, before the days of sports and politics, was Sentiment. Not passion: passion is brutally unsocial; but the pretty game of minute analysis, spending hours before a psychological mirror, splitting hairs into four and then into four again, weighing bubbles in balances of gossamer. Provençal society started the fashions of the Courts of Love, which debated and adjudged fine points of sentimental casuistry, with no less subtlety than the Schoolmen displayed in their theological puzzles. Chrétien de Troyes was a deft dissector. Centuries later (but the line had never been broken), Madeleine de Scudéry mapped in detail "The Land of

Tenderness." The strategy of courtship was as elaborate and slow as that of a Montecuccoli.

The tradition survives: French Academicians are still able to write three hundred pages on the momentous problem: "Will *A* commit adultery with *B* or with *C?*" To the uninitiated, it makes remarkably little difference. America has her Paul Bourget in Mrs. Edith Wharton, and the same kind of appeal, which can not be described as *sexy,* is found in *The Edwardians.*

Society's worst crime is to have fostered cheap society literature, by and for those who have never been there. Such an accusation was leveled against Balzac himself. He was more familiar with business, Bohemia and the underworld than with the noble Faubourg. Still, in his defense be it said, the great realist was conscientious enough to carry on flirtations with a couple of authentic Duchesses, and to marry a Countess. Few of his critics can boast of such a record.

Let us allow the pendulum to swing for the last time. If French Society had not been so familiar with the intricacies of sentimental psychology, would Racine's analysis have been conceivable at all—that probing of the heart as tragically profound as anything in Shakespeare? * Could we have had such a study as *Manon Lescaut,* so level, so gray in coloring, so unerringly human? Or lighter and delightful things, like the comedies of Marivaux and the proverbs of Musset? Or the pitiless autovivisection of Benjamin Constant in *Adolphe?* The crude

---

* The training begins early. To my knowledge, thirteen-year-old children were assigned this subject: "Analyze the elements of coquetry in Racine's *Andromache.*"

hypotheses, the pseudo-scientific methods, the weird terminology of many psychological sects are poor substi-
tutes for that power of disenchanted, dispassionate observation.

Yet the fact must be faced: "Society" is doomed; and
with it a long established standard of literature. We have
merely indulged in a few moments of meditation before a tomb. Let others repine: our quest is not ended.

Chapter 18

Yesterday: SCHOOLS, GROUPS AND CLIQUES

"SOCIETY", directly through the Court and Salons, indirectly through the Universities and the Academies, has to a large extent controlled literature. But the writers have also formed autonomous groups of their own. There again, we have "conscious, organized minorities" which determine the action of their members, and assume the leadership of public opinion. An author does not think or feel quite in the same way, nor does he wield the same kind of power when he is isolated as when he is a member of a team.

These groups may affect many forms, from a convivial gathering of friends to a regular Trade Union affiliated with the Federation of Labor. The latter is not in sight: it is well known that writers are not easily amenable to formal discipline. It would be interesting to have H. G. Wells censored for exceeding the Union output, or Bernard Shaw suspended for accepting less than Union wages. But the Union's chief weapon, the strike, would not be effective in literary hands. If professional writers were to strike, the publishers' offices would be besieged with blacklegs; if methods of terrorism kept these away, it would only give the classics a chance; if the classics were destroyed, the readers would simply enjoy a holiday.

Although the literary craft is not capable of rigid organization, and although it is notoriously torn by violent jealousies, there is a point upon which it acts with a single soul: and that is in magnifying the importance of literature. Only once in several generations do we find a traitor to his class like old Malherbe, who averred that "a good poet was of no more value to the state than a good nine-pin player"; but, in his arrogant verses, Malherbe contradicted this cynical sally. The greatest triumph of the advertising industry is to have "sold" the advertising idea to a gullible American public. We spend ten times too much on advertising, but dare not cut out a single cent, any more than we dare cut out competitive armaments. No campaign against advertising would be successful except through advertising methods; and the man who could conduct such a campaign would prefer not to kill the goose which lays the golden eggs. Similarly, we could not call the authors' collective bluff except through a successful book, which would confirm the power of literature. We suspect that the poet's influence often resembles that of Chanticleer, whose song causes the sun to rise—provided it be sung just before dawn.

"Society" with a literary tinge and literary society proper merge by imperceptible degrees. The personnel of two gatherings may be practically the same: in both cases a blend of professional writers and men of the world. The difference would depend upon the geographical location—Chelsea or Mayfair—and upon the quality of the host. But what if the host himself be at the same time an author and a man of affluence? Thus Helvetius and d'Holbach generously entertained the Encyclopedic coterie, and contributed books which would have done credit to starvelings. Thus Samuel Rogers was a poet as well as a banker. We come then to the fine point of distinction: "Which are more memorable, the writings of the host, or his dinners?"

In most cases, however, the difference between the two worlds is definite enough; and, although there is no lack of friendly visiting back and forth, few men are equally at ease in both. As professional authorship is seldom accompanied by great wealth and a smoothly running household, the natural place for writers to gather is the Tavern. So it has been from time immemorial, and we all remember the bouts at the *Mermaid's* or Dr. Johnson's fine eulogy of the *Cheshire Cheese.* A matchless quartet of Classicists, Molière, Racine, La Fontaine, Boileau, used to meet at the *Fir Cone,* or sometimes at Boileau's suburban cottage at Auteuil. Once they went so deep into their potations that they reached the point of absolute pessimism. Only Boileau's unconquerable common sense, still groping and staggering through the fumes, prevented four of France's greatest from jumping into the Seine. Such memories create a bond. It was not purely on theoretical grounds that Boileau defended Racine against discouragement, and told Louis XIV that Molière was the first writer of the age. For every literary group is, and should be, a Mutual Aid Society.

In the eighteenth century, the tavern found a more refined rival in the coffee-house, the Salon and Academy of the true Bohemian. Although the Encyclopedists had friends in many drawing rooms, and could call that of Mademoiselle de Lespinasse their very own, it was in the Cafés that their leader Diderot was seen at his best. In an ultra-conservative country like France, the Café has remained an institution, although hardly a power. It offers a rallying point without infringing on the writer's cherished freedom; and it allows the semi-Bohemian to catch a glimpse of the literary world without any fear of losing caste.

This curiosity, of course, creates a danger. A Café can not be kept a secret. It soon becomes a show place, and visitors from Bucyrus, Bucharest and Buenos Aires flock to see the Lions sip their absinthe. The Lions enjoy their popularity, superficially, and for a very brief time; then despise themselves for it, and move to some unpolluted Helicon, some undesecrated Hippocrene. Chasing the ever shifting center of literature through the cafés, wine-shops, taverns and cabarets of Paris is as exciting as hunting big game in the jungle. Rodolphe Salis made a fortune by frankly commercializing his Montmartre cabaret, the *Black Cat;* and some of the *Black Cat* poets, taught by so able a master, achieved success in solid *bourgeois* terms: Maurice Boukay-Couyba became a Senator and Cabinet Minister; Maurice Donnay a member of the French Academy. Now that jazz bands have displaced poets as Montmartre's chief attraction, a chapter in literary history is closed.

To drink with a man in a public place does not com-

mit you in any way; to eat with him creates a closer relationship. All churches and all trades have had their
agapes; indeed, it was seriously prophesied that the new
and sorely needed American religion was slowly emerg-
ing out of the Rotary Luncheons. The Literary Dinner is a very fine thing, so long at it does not turn into
a banquet—a promiscuous gathering where one listens,
in weary silence, to a few star performers, wearier than
the rest. If the membership is small and stable, and if
it implies genuine personal intimacy, the Dinner is a
power as well as a delight. It was such a Dinner, at the
Magny Restaurant, that knit together the best Parisian
minds under the Second Empire: Sainte-Beuve, Renan,
Taine, About. Flaubert and George Sand, who had
elected to bury themselves in their provinces, attended
whenever they happened to be in Paris. Prince Napoleon
established a rather precarious contact between that liberal group and the political world. It was the same company, with Sainte-Beuve acting as host, that created an
uproar among the Conservatives by eating meat on Good
Friday. For the Magny habitués were freethinkers almost to a man, and their scientific Positivism was more
threatening for orthodoxy than anti-clericalism of the
common kind.

There again we see the tendency of a social gathering among literary men to turn into a school. Boileau
and his friends did not meet primarily because they were
Classicists: they took their classicism for granted. But
they were congenial as boon companions partly because
they shared the same views on literature; and their close
association brought those views into sharper focus. The

Magny diners were not sworn in advance to support scientific freethought. George Sand, for instance, was a survivor of Romantic Humanitarianism, and she was liked and admired by all of them. But if the group did not rally to a formal doctrine, it created an atmosphere; and an atmosphere was exactly what the doctrine needed for healthy growth.

To pass from the social literary group to the School, one definite element is required: a leader. This quality of leadership is, of course, not literary in itself: it is the same which makes for prominence in business or politics. It is not creative genius, although it is not incompatible with it. Among the poets of the French Pleiad, Joachim du Bellay was at least as gifted as Ronsard, and wrote the able manifesto of the movement: but Ronsard assumed command. Lamartine had won fame when Victor Hugo was still a schoolboy: but Victor Hugo quietly seized the helm. The Goncourts had been *Naturalists* before Zola had reached artistic adolescence: but— much to their chagrin—, they were swept aside.

Leadership is not solely based on self-confidence. There are writers who possess magnificent conceit, yet remain isolated. Rousseau started a revolution, but did not create a school. Chateaubriand was revered as the first writer of his day, yet the actual chief was that young upstart Hugo, who had scribbled on his school books: "I want to be Chateaubriand or nothing." Chateaubriand had to be satisfied with incense: Victor Hugo was followed.

Leadership requires talent, self-confidence, hard work, and above all *a desire for coöperation*. You can not lead a team unless you want a team: a Rousseau, a Chateaubriand, wish to stand alone. Even in death: Chateaubriand is buried on a rock beaten by the waves, and Victor Hugo's bier was followed to the Pantheon by half a million men, *quorum pars parva fui*. Among great writers, some are supreme soloists, some are born conductors.

Both types may be the center of a group. But the admirers of the soloist have no creative element in common; they are not an orchestra, they do not form a school. There is no clearer instance of a *group* than that which gathered round Dr. Johnson. It had congeniality, fixity, loyalty: but it was merely a group. It had very little influence upon literature; and, paradoxical as it may sound, Johnson had very little influence upon his group. They liked him, they admired him, they did not preach his gospel. (But did he have a gospel? His idea of conversation was not to carry conviction, but to unhorse an opponent.) The Doctor's massive strength did not appreciably retard the downfall of classicism. He denounced, shrewdly as well as vehemently, the hoax perpetrated by Macpherson: but "Ossian's" prestige for another thirty years, was immensely greater throughout Europe than Johnson's. Johnson was the triumphant defender of lost causes: an autocrat, not a dictator.

The personal group, worshipping, and not seldom exploiting, a Master, is therefore far less important in literature than the School. It may indeed prevent the formation of a school: the inner circle closes jealously round the god, and wishes to keep exclusive possession of him. Anatole France after 1910 (I dare not mention living

English and American writers) had thus become an idol for the masses, and the prisoner of a self-appointed clergy. He tried to break through that inexorable ring: but the task was beyond an old man's strength, and he had to resign himself to the company of his friends.

The three stages are sometimes found in the career of a single author. First, the voluntary coming together of like-minded men: thus the young French Romanticists met in the drawing rooms of Charles Nodier, at the Arsenal Library; Victor Hugo was a member of that *Cénacle,* as it was called, and barely "first among peers." Then Victor Hugo, with his undoubted genius, his monumental self-confidence, his Napoleonic talent for organization and advertising, forges ahead, issues manifestoes, musters troops, prepares the first night of *Hernani* like the storming of a fortress. The *Cénacle* now meets at his home, and has become the Romantic School. Finally, Victor Hugo, world-famous, surviving his literary epoch by a third of a century, is surrounded by henchmen, the best of whom, Auguste Vacquerie, Paul Meurice, can *pastiche* his more obvious tricks so as to defy detection. It has been wisely said: "To the founder of a school, everything may be forgiven, *except his school.*" Here the term *school* is too flattering: the right word is *tail*.

The lassoing of Naturalism by Zola, the locking-up of Symbolism in the dark hermetic cabinet of Mallarmé, the confusion between the Æsthetic Movement and the personal antics of Oscar Wilde, are other examples of the same process. A vague desire leads to a loose association; an inner group turns the association into a machine;

the machine is no sooner perfected than power is cut off; it runs on momentum for a decade or a century, as Pseudo-this or Post-that; until it is properly added to the scrap heap of literary history.

The process is not always complete; there were many abortive schools which remained mere tendencies. These are sometimes vaguely described as "generations." *Art for Art's Sake,* for instance, represents a moment, a mood, a doctrine, not a school. Nothing is more baffling than these creatures of the mist: on that account, historians, retrospectively, and critics, prospectively, are always clamoring for schools, inventing them when they are not forthcoming. With a school, you stand on firm ground.

The founding of a school is of course very flattering to the vanity of the charter members. That is why schools grow with tropical profusion, but not always with tropical exuberance of life. *Classicism* and *Romanticism* on the one hand, *Realism* and *Symbolism* on the other, are four fundamental attitudes, and it was right that they should be organized into schools, in order to reach definite consciousness. But the creation of *Naturalism* was wholly unnecessary: Naturalism is merely the exaggeration of certain aspects in Realism. The name was found, and the man, and the theory: so a new *ism* enriched or cluttered the literary Pantheon. The game is going on as merrily as ever. Jules Romains, when he is not mystifying his fellow doctors with his theories on *extra-retinian vision,* is attempting to start a *Unanimist* school: as if the rudimentary feelings and impulses of masses had not been depicted by Hugo and Zola, among others; as if Stephen Crane had needed Unanimism to render the soul, not of one man, but of a whole regiment in battle. André Thérive—with commendable moderation, it must be said—is pleading for a *Populism* which is at least a hundred years old. We had *Spasmodics,* and *Imagists,* and *Vorticists, Impressionists* and *Expressionists, Pre-*everything, *Post-*everything, *Neo-*everything. The only school that fully appealed to us was *Dada,* a desperate attempt to reach the absolute zero of nonsense. This at least would have given us "the school to end all schools."

The effect of spontaneous groups is stimulating; the effect of schools is deadening. For one thing, schools cause writers to waste in proclamations and controversies much time that might have been devoted to creative art. Then schools compel a consistency which is the negation of life. The loss would be small if only second-raters used the official school stencil: but even great writers, as soon as they are committed to a formula, become, in the name of their principles, slavish imitators of themselves. The very greatest alone escape that paralyzing influence. Homer never knew he was "classical", and that blissful ignorance has made him the classic eternal. Dante thought of himself as a classicist, but fortunately he was mistaken. Shakespeare would have been puzzled by our term Romanticist; Molière was "classical" in *The Misanthropist,* "romantic" in *Don Juan,* "realistic" and even "naturalistic" in *Georges Dandin.* Goethe went through all schools and transcended them all. Balzac died before Realism was named.

The School enforces artificial conformity on men of radically different temperaments; it paralyzes those who

can not whole-heartedly enlist under its banner. It has
all the faults of sect and party, and it seems almost as inescapable. Like all orthodoxies, it creates an elaborate
set of false values. The school of yesterday, the rival
school of to-day, are swept aside with deadly cocksureness. The school Credo is the letter that killeth.

And by school, sect, party, we mean here the standard,
reputable, fully established organization. It is too easy
to deride the infinitesimal group of youngsters who fire
a few crackers as earnestly as though they were storming
the Bastille. They know in the secret of their hearts that
it is only boyish play, although they might choose to die
rather than confess it aloud. It is the school of the middle
aged that counts, and that hurts.

A fully equipped school requires: (a) a tendency;
(b) a personnel; (c) a name, even though it be meaningless like Romanticism, question-begging like Classicism,
insulting like Decadence; (d) a leader, with staff complete; (e) a doctrine, expressed in critical manifestoes;
and (f), certainly not least, a periodical. When two or
three young men are gathered together in the name of
literature, their first desire is to found a review. The Review is the embodiment of the team spirit. It is an excellent medium for consolidated advertising. The literary
field is strewn with those dead leaves, but also enriched.
Absurd they may seem to sober eyes; but we believe, and
shall later attempt to establish, that the insurgent literary magazine is almost indispensable as a pathfinder.

The reader will immediately think of our *Little Review,* whose story Margaret Anderson has told with such
feminine vivacity in *My Thirty Years' War;* of *Transi-*

tion, which, it was suggested, would have been an apter name if spelled backward; in ages already remote, of the *Yellow Book,* with Aubrey Beardsley and Oscar Wilde —a little paper abused and derided in its day, and which has now given its name to a decade. The most complete example is offered by the *Mercure de France* in its earlier period. Under the editorship of Rémi de Gourmont, in the nineties, the *Mercure* was decidedly the organ of the Symbolists and Decadents. It praised them, expounded them, published their work, both in the magazine and in book form. The group was too generously open to be termed a clique: but it formed a team. Those weird unworldly poets worked for their ideals with a persistency, a sense of strategy and discipline, which are lacking in many a plain business man. The group did not exist merely on paper: the writers met in the flesh, in the old-world headquarters of the review, rue de Condé. The editor's receptions gave definite body to a loose mass of protest and yearning. The *Mercure* has become a well-established, and, we hope, a profitable business. But the idealism of its early years has not completely faded away. Perhaps only for auld lang syne, we can not think of the *Mercure* as a mere commercial enterprise.

What is the influence of the schools upon literature? On the authors themselves, we have expressed our opinion that it was wholly bad. On the public at large, the solid mass of readers, it is imperceptible. When hundreds of thousands chose to buy Blasco Ibáñez's *Four Horsemen of the Apocalypse,* or Dreiser's *An American Tragedy,* they could not be deterred by the thought that Naturalism had been dead and buried these many long years—

jam foetet. But, for the steady, enlightened, literary public—perhaps a hundred thousand in each of the leading
countries—the Schools still possess some significance.

This, we believe, is a survival of the days when Society
felt compelled to take interest in literature; when authors
were either members of Society, or had a society of their
own. These conditions are passing away: people who
never meet can not divide on shibboleths. But they are
still casting their shadow behind.

"Schools" start doctrinal controversies: it is their sole
raison d'être. From the point of view of creative literature, this is sheer waste: controversies are not art, any
more than, in the theological field, they are religion.
But the debate provides good exercise for thought. The
names, the formulae, the organizations, force themselves
upon the reader's attention. America would never have
listened to the muffled echo of very ancient discussions,
if these had not been offered as "the New Humanism",
with a first-class staff, resounding manifestoes, symposia
for and against. And we must surmise that it is better
for a few thousand Americans to talk about Humanism
than about the antics of some picturesque Mayor, Gov-
ernor or Evangelist. It is probably as difficult to bring
out a literary idea without a "School" tag, as it would
be to market any product without a trade name. Our
prophecy is that the "Schools", if they survive at all, will
turn more and more into merchandising devices. A
shrewd publisher will some day launch *Neo-Post-Vorti-
cism,* with the motto "Floating Power", or "Not a Yawn
in a thousand pages!" But this takes us away from Literature as an autonomous realm into our next field of exploration: Literature as Business.

Chapter 19

To-day: LITERATURE AS BUSINESS

So long as "Society" was unshaken, the publishers
played a very subordinate part in literature. Few writers
relied on book sales for a living. If they had no independent means, they hoped for a sinecure or a pension.
Reputations were made *before* works went into print.
Publication was the corollary of success, not its prime condition. To work for the booksellers was to avow oneself
a hack, and lose caste. Gentlemen merely consented to
have a book brought out at the request of their friends.

These conditions, so alien to our methods, have not
entirely disappeared. Speeches, sermons, letters, travel
notes, occasional verses, a skit for private performance,
appear from time to time with the mention that the
writer has yielded to the importunities of a too indulgent
audience. This blushing reluctance to be dragged on
the public stage is not invariably ingenuous: the merest
polite hint will serve as an urgent request. But it is more
trustworthy in the case of books for private circulation
only: Henry Adams's *Mont-Saint Michel and Chartres*
was known among a chosen few, before it became a successful business venture.

This uncommercial tradition has remained stronger (willy-nilly) in poetry than in other branches of literature. In all languages, many books of verse are printed at the author's expense, and chiefly for distribution among his immediate acquaintances. The word *publisher,* in this connection, would be a misnomer, with a touch of cruel irony.

One of the last prominent cases in which fame was achieved before publicity was that of José-Maria de Heredia. His hard, luminous and flawless sonnets, which provide such a favorite exercise for American translators, were known in literary circles through private readings, manuscript copies, and a few samples in the non-commercial reviews. Heredia was already designated for the Academy before the *Trophies* were actually put on sale. Paul Valéry's reputation was for many years purely esoteric. When the general public finally heard his name and was curious to read his books, it was found that a Valéry could not be bought in the open market. It was necessary to use all the "pull" at your command before one of the slim and cryptic volumes could be added to your treasures. This artificial rarefaction, by the way, has turned into an excellent business scheme. As his fame increased, Valéry received more and more for giving less and less. For a few years, he was the author who made most money by refusing to sell. As an Irish critic would put it: "If he had refrained from writing altogether he would be a millionaire."

Another case in which the usual commercial methods do not fully apply is that of the Subscription Book. This is an extension of the "Society" idea. Presumably the author is well known, and samples of his work have been circulated among his friends. It is right that they should manifest their desire by affixing their names to a subscription list. Through this safe and dignified system, which presupposes an organized aristocracy of culture, Pope made himself independent of individual patronage, and likewise of popular favor. Samuel Johnson also used it; but, great as was his integrity, his indolence was at times greater still, and he pocketed advanced subscriptions to books that he forgot to write. The subscription method marked the transition between the gentlemanly era and the commercial. It is still used in special cases, such as expensive scientific works, and handsome limited editions. It strongly appealed to D. H. Lawrence. We shall see that, in a modified form, it might serve again as a transition, this time from the mercantile to the . . . human, for lack of a more definite term.

In all the above cases, the publisher is, like the printer, merely the author's agent. He is supposed to have no initiative and no responsibility. But, with the crumbling down of "Society", all existing criteria lose their validity. There is no orthodoxy that any University or Academy can enforce, no aristocratic group whose word is law, and the authority of the literary cliques does not reach beyond a very narrow circle. We know for certain that the actual reading public is by no means coextensive with the enormous body of potential readers: but we do not know the boundaries of that public, its ramifications, its principles, its tastes. We can only guess and gamble; and the people who are doing the guessing and the gambling for us are the publishers.

And, as they do so, it is they, no longer the professors, Society or the cliques, who are roughly determining what path literature shall take. They are the ineluctable guardians of the gate. In antiquity, even in the Classical Age, an author could read his manuscript to a few friends, and win recognition: in our enormous, multifarious, chaotic world, the individual author is lost. Even if he could afford to have the book printed at his own expense—there are a few reputable firms in that branch of the trade—his chances of success would be slim. The *author's book* starts with a stigma, and is marked out for defeat. Marcel Proust had an enviable reputation in the best Parisian circles, and he was wealthy: yet he knew he would have no chance of attracting attention if he paid out of his own pocket for bringing out his work. No new Walter Scott, no second Dickens could arise unless a publisher gave him leave to try his luck. If you win the publishers to your side, nothing is gained; but, if you fail to win them, everything is lost.

The publishers are therefore the latest and clearest examples of our "conscious, organized minorities." Like the politicians, they claim to represent the public, to give them only what they want. But this is not true even of politicians, who frequently offer us only a choice between two things we equally dislike; and it is less true of the publishers, since there is nothing like organized plebiscites in literature. The desires of the public are known only through the publishers' guesses. Had the publishers in their wisdom decided that the public did not want *All Quiet on the Western Front,* because they were surfeited with war stories, or *The Bridge of San Luis Rey,* because it was too remote, sophisticated and highbrow, there would have been no way of quashing their verdict. There never is any appeal from the publishers to some other authority: the only appeal is from one publisher to another publisher, whose guiding principles are on the whole very much the same. American literature does not reflect the American public mind: it reflects the publishers' opinion of the American mind: and the publishers seem to take a pessimistic view of human nature. Are they right, or do we deserve better? We shall never know to what extent they are misrepresentative men.

We have no intention of presenting publishers as powers of darkness. Young idealists are apt to make that intolerant mistake. Publishers are business men; Art claims (it is one of its minor hypocrisies) to be absolutely disinterested; therefore publishers are the natural enemies of Art. A neatly contrasted Manichean scheme: the authors on the side of the angels, the publishers reducing Beauty and Truth to a question of dollars and cents. Reality is not quite so simple. Even in the theological domain, we are beginning to suspect that the Devil has been maligned, and should be given his due.

An author whose fancy lightly turns to thoughts of pelf is no rarity in the literary world. If it be sordid to be paid for one's efforts, not a few writers are guilty of that crime. The publishers are in business: but, as in the case of many other business men, their trade also happens to be their hobby. They deal in books because they like them, and not exclusively because they think books a more profitable "line" than paint or glue. They too are *bookmen:* the literary atmosphere is congenial to them; their minds like to dwell on literary themes. For over a century, the heads of the great firms in Europe and in America have been men of liberal culture. Up to the present at any rate, the publisher, cynically indifferent to the quality of his wares, provided they bring quick returns, the dealer in scandal and filth, the expert in ballyhoo, the practitioner of cut-rate and cut-throat methods, has never stayed in the business long enough to affect literature.* On the contrary, there are innumerable examples of publishers bringing out the work of an unknown author, not even as a gamble, but as a service; or, if the word sounds too sanctimonious, as a satisfaction to their personal pride. Serious books that can at best break even over a period of years are brought out for the honor of the firm. Not to mention Anglo-Saxon examples, Victor Bérard's thought-provoking and erudite studies on the *Odyssey* were a family sacrifice of the Armand Colin house on the altar of humane letters. Honesty is the best policy in the long run. Many of us do not run quite long enough to discover it: but publishing concerns are among the very oldest in the business world, and a decent regard for the opinion of mankind is one of their assets.

Even the man new to the trade prefers good books to poor ones: not entirely as a matter of good taste and individual prestige, but as a plain business proposition. A steady good-seller (this, as we suggested, might be ac-

---

* Questionable methods, unfortunately, are not always spurned by publishers who ought to know better. The scandal caused by Paul Margueritte's *La Garçonne*—a mistaken book, but an honest one—was due to the fact that the publishers had called attention to the most *risqué* passages. The advertisements of Aldous Huxley's *Brave New World* overemphasized the spiciest episode. Both authors belonged to literature, and should have been treated with greater respect.

cepted as a pragmatic definition of a *classic,* but it applies also to a standard cook book) is obviously safer than a meteoric best-seller. Any publisher would prefer to build up the honest, solid reputation of a Galsworthy rather than stun the public with *The Cradle of the Deep.*

In all countries, but particularly in England and in France, good publishers have become social centers. The head of the firm has a Salon as well as an office. Successes are celebrated like family affairs. Many books have been written bearing on the influence of publishers as the nucleus of a literary group. These, and the correspondence of noted writers, give an impression of mutual trust and cordiality. The unworldly genius chained to a rock and fighting off the vultures is sheer nightmare. It is true that many publishers are decently well off, and that not a few geniuses go hungry. Yet it may be said that publishers have suffered more from the unreliability of geniuses than geniuses from the greed of publishers.

We are frankly giving an idealized picture, knowing full well that there are bad publishers as there are bad ministers, bad grocers and worse authors. We should like to believe that this ideal will remain permanently with us; but we are afraid that it belongs to a period that is disappearing. In the hierarchized society of the ancient régime, which lingered through the nineteenth century, there were dynasties, not only on the throne, but in the professions, in the trades, in the crafts. They had solid family traditions and a sense of *Noblesse Oblige.* One was destined from the cradle to be a judge, a carpenter, a bookseller. Making money was not the uppermost preoccupation: it was not negligible by any means, but, with decent care and industry, an adequate return could be taken for granted. Making a name for one's self was almost plebeian: the name was made, and had only to be maintained. This quasi-feudal conception is waning: the miracle is that it should not have disappeared altogether. Increasingly, business will be strictly business. We felt, poignantly, the difference when a friendly London publisher of the old school sold out, at eighty, to a large and aggressive firm. Shall we see again the days when a publisher's office was in verity his den, lined with favorite old books, family portraits, and mementoes of famous associates? When his private apartments were actually over the shop, and were pervaded with the same atmosphere?

It would be hard for the book industry, in a capitalistic civilization, not to become frankly capitalistic. We may expect to see it dominated by huge impersonal concerns which, instead of keeping in their files chatty letters from their author-friends, will think in scientific graphs, and feel not at all. Into this world of soulless giants, personality will break forth once in a while, in the form of a young Napoleon of trade, ruthless, efficient, self-centered. Increasingly, "mere" literature will be looked upon with an indulgent smile.

Good or bad, the publishers control literature as they never have before. What are they going to do with it? We have no experience whatever of the book trade, and prudence compels us to let the publishers speak for themselves. We have picked out two works bearing directly on the subject, because they are as sharply contrasted as possible. They present the opposition of two spirits, two methods, perhaps two civilizations and two ages.

Bernard Grasset * is already a publisher of mature experience, although still a youngish man. He selected publishing as a profession because of his sincere love for letters. He placed at the service of his enthusiasm certain aggressive qualities which would have made him a success in any country and in any trade. He was not merely a competent merchant—the dreary *Homo Economicus* buying in the cheapest market, selling in the dearest: he was able to realize that conditions were changing, and to take advantage of the change. Convinced that the modern publisher does represent the "conscious minority" occupying a strategic position, he believes that the publisher should frankly assume leadership.

We have seen that in the old days, social values created literary values. The discovery of a new talent came from the self-styled élite: the publisher merely registered their selection. Now, in a society in turmoil, no one is able to take the initiative, *unless it be the publisher himself.* It is his part to pick out a likely winner in the literary race, to groom him and train him, and give him a start. Just to print a book, place it for sale, send a hundred copies to reviewers, insert paid advertisements in the proper magazines, is mere routine work: it requires no imagination, no mental energy. A book cast into the literary sea in that mechanical manner will sink like lead, and no praise from the experts will make it float. The great business of the publisher is not so much to choose a book as to *launch* it.

* Bernard Grasset: *La Chose Littéraire,* Paris, Gallimard, 1929.

To-day: LITERATURE AS BUSINESS

In Paris, Bernard Grasset is working in a transitional world, where social and literary elements are still interwoven. The disintegrating aristocracy of birth and intellect cling to the belief that they are dictating literary taste; the parvenu aristocracy of wealth, the Post-War *Nouveaux Riches,* would like to share that privilege; but, old or new, rich or poor, they are in no condition to formulate that taste for themselves. They are arbiters who need expert prompting. In steps our publisher: through social contacts and press influences, he "makes up the mind" of the would-be dictators. When he has induced one small group to "discover" his author, he uses that group to win the larger circle of those who want to be "in the know." It is not a campaign of crude ballyhoo, but one of whispered suggestions. Then the pump is properly primed: we are ready for the general public. And, as often as not, the general public remains placidly indifferent.*

In other words, the publisher attempts to do in a few weeks what Madame Arman de Caillavet did for Anatole France in fifteen years. Naturally, Time fails to respect that which is done without his collaboration. But who cares for Time nowadays? It may be the next fallacy to be exploded by the mathematical hyperphysicists. The method, therefore, is not new: it is the good old "puffing" (shall we say "puffing and blowing"?) of our ancestors. What is new is its commercial application by efficiency experts.

* Frank Swinnerton agrees with Grasset: advertising and favorable reviews don't sell books. What sells books is *talk*—among the right people. Swinnerton's *Authors and the Book Trade* (A. Knopf, 1932) is a very pleasing, easy and adequate survey of the problem.

This subtle game, in which genuine art, snobbishness and business sense are so cunningly blended, is exactly similar to that of the great dressmakers. In the old days again, the initiative of fashion actually belonged to the society ladies themselves. They chose their styles, with the assistance of their *couturières,* who were not yet *couturiers.* Their success was a personal one: a dazzling young Countess was herself the artist and the work of art, and not a mere titled *mannequin.* Then, in the very measure in which the prestige of old Society was waning, the collaboration of the *couturiers* became more exacting. Under the Second Empire, the old aristocracy kept away from the Court, and there were adventurers and parvenus among the personal friends of Their Majesties. Paris no longer admired Madame Untel, but Worth's creation for Madame Untel. The initiative had passed to the *couturier:* but he still had to work through high society. At present, the models are created rue de la Paix, and are displayed by the *mannequins* in the salons of the firm, or at the races: Society takes notice and follows. Success still depends on Society's approval, but the styles no longer originate with Society. Bernard Grasset and his rivals are the Worths, the Paquins, the Patous of literature. If they decide that novels shall be worn shorter this season, that Lesbianism or the interior monologue are *passés,* that a touch of Communistic Red or Royalist White is all the rage, then we shall repeat, with imperturbable assurance: "Oh! no one reads a full-size novel any more!—Proust? The passing of the Marcel wave!—Moscow is the new Athens."

Bernard Grasset is not fooling his public: he is trying

to secure recognition for the things he genuinely likes. But he is not such a humbug as to claim that he is giving the Public what they want. The public do not know what they want, and probably should not have it if they knew. He tells the public what they ought to want, which is exactly the service expected of a conscious, organized minority.

Only his system is based on the insecure survival of the Society ideal. When that is gone, other means will have to be devised. But we need not be concerned about such a contingency. Barring a Bolshevist revolution, the twilight of *bourgeois* society in France may be interminably prolonged. At least, it is likely to outlive M. Bernard Grasset.

La Chose Littéraire is hardly more than a pamphlet: only thick paper, large type and generous margins give it the bulk and dignity of a standard French yellowback. Its method of treatment is, like its physical presentation, very elegant and very slight. When we pass from this brief and pleasant causerie to Mr. Cheney's formidable volume,* we realize that there is an ocean between Paris and New York. Mr. O. H. Cheney does not deal with such a frivolous thing as "literature", but with the solid reality of the Book Industry; and in order to give the Association for which the Survey was made a full dollar-for-dollar value, he embodies in his text pages of tabulated or graphic statistics. We have had no glimpse of either man's inner sanctum; we imagine M. Grasset in a study with touches of the Bohemian studio; and Mr. Cheney

---

* O. H. Cheney: *Economic Survey of the Book Industry*, 1930–31. National Association of Book Publishers.

in the impressive office of the competent executive. Yet there is more epigrammatic wit in the American product than in the French; and also a franker confession of bewilderment. M. Grasset still believes that publishers can lead; Mr. Cheney does not know whither publishers are driven—a piece of wisdom which must be accounted a bargain at ten dollars net.

Why are books selected for publication? Why do they sell? Why do they cease to sell? A triple mystery. The one thing that Mr. Cheney's statistics clearly bring out is the haphazard conditions of the industry. It caters to no definite public, and it does not market an indispensable commodity. As it is without guide, the trade seems bent on imitating the magnificent wastefulness of Nature. Infant mortality among books is appalling. And there is another aspect of the question which is not within the scope of Mr. Cheney's survey. From the business point of view, a perfect score for a firm would be an uninterrupted series of large sales. From the artistic point of view, the enormous success of certain books is even more to be deplored than the undeserved neglect of others.

A firm which has some notable triumphs to its credit, some of them not of an obvious kind, had the splendid idea of asking the public pointblank why they bought and read certain books, and what they were interested in. This document, which must have reached nearly every American home, is well worth reproducing:

> Dear Reader: To aid in an important survey, please check in the squares below the reasons prompting the purchase of (fill in title of book in which you find this card):

Review in	Appearance of Book ....
Advertisement in	Listed as best-seller ....
Recommended by	Widespread Discussion ....
Circular or Catalogue from......	Bookstore display ....
Suggested by bookstore	Published by So-and-So ....
Author's previous book.........	Attractiveness of title ....
Author's reputation	Interest in subject ....
Gift	Other Reasons ....

I am interested in (here follow 21 kinds, from Religion to Cross-Word puzzles.)

Certain items in this questionnaire ought to be of much practical value to Messrs. So and So. It is well to know whether the good word of such or such a critic actually carries weight; and whether *The Consolidated Western Clay Products Journal* is a proper advertising medium for treatises on Auction Bridge. But even if such a tabulation gave us a clearer view of what has happened, it could hardly provide a rule for the future. I am willing to check on Messrs. So and So's list that I am interested in Detective Fiction: *with the proviso that it be good,* and Messrs. So and So have no way of knowing what *I* mean by good. I am not sure that I know myself. I have never been addicted to Westerns so far, but I am ready to be converted by a masterpiece. A success in one subject may favor a new success of the same kind, or it may hinder it: Wells's *History* seems to have helped Van Loon's: it might just as well have killed it. If everybody is reading debunking biographies, or works about Russia, or flamboyant praises of Mexico, we may be on the point of declaring ourselves utterly weary of the stuff, and the next book, which may be the best of all, will be voted commonplace and tedious. This is also true of a man's reputation. Too sensational a vogue is rather a danger than a promise. We are apt to deal harshly with our fads of yesteryear. We visit upon them our own sins of gullibility and gregariousness. We want to assure the world and ourselves that we were not actually taken in by Monsieur Coué.

Perversely enough, the economic trend of book producing is uneconomic. From a business point of view, the ideal would be steady sales steadily expanding. Instead of that even flow, the trade tends to develop seasonal floods. The Christmas rush, which should be checked, is encouraged. It is quite true that a book is always a fairly safe gift. It is flattering for the recipient to be credited with literary taste; and a well-selected volume does not look so futile or so stingy as the average two- or three-dollar knickknack. Still, there are quite a few Americans who buy books for themselves and read all the year round. And every new morn is somebody's birthday.

More dangerous than the seasonal peak is the brevity of success, followed by total neglect. Books hailed as "epics", "devastating", "epoch-making" (the blurb writers are overworking a few words which need eternal repose) will be dimly remembered in a few months; another little flare of semi-popularity with the cheap reprint, and they are gone for ever. If we resign ourselves to this jerky tempo, the quiet, unobtrusive book will have absolutely no chance. Stendhal prophesied in the eighteen thirties: "I shall be understood about 1880." And it came to pass, because French literature at that time offered the possibility of slow, barely perceptible growth. If a new Stendhal failed to catch within three months, his career would be at an end.

This American craving for the very latest model, this

necessity for sudden success, favor waves, crazes, sensationalism. Worst of all perhaps, they almost compel the good writer to overdo. The public, having no corporate existence, has no memory; it is more and more difficult for fame to acquire momentum. So a self-respecting author, if he does not want to be forgotten, is forced to bring out his works in quick succession; or, if he allows too long an interval to elapse, he has to stake his reputation again on each new battle. After a few years of silence, he must "stage a comeback", a notoriously difficult thing to do.

The other uneconomic tendency in the trade is its gambling character. Too many books are published, with a wild alternation of a few "best-sellers" and a majority of "flops." Obviously it would be better if we had fewer books, none of them sensationally successful, all selling decently well. That could be the case, if it were possible to anticipate the desires and measure the appetite of the indefinite monster whom we are all trying to serve. Catching the public's fancy is frankly a matter of luck: so it becomes good business to have as many tickets as possible in the lottery, and hope for the one big prize that will recoup many losses. It is not wisdom, but a counsel of despair. But again, if the publishers keep their eyes fixed on the 100,000 mark within six months, the fine, quiet, exceptional book will gradually be ruled out.

The leaders of the industry themselves deplore these conditions. In other respects, however, the book trade conforms more closely to sound economic principles, but with results that are scarcely less disastrous for literature. If the gambling element could be eliminated—the unpredictable windfall, the wastefulness of innumerable failures—the industry would strive for orderly, standardized mass production, which is the key to efficiency. This point has already been reached by the great popular magazines. These wonders of the Western World are quite frankly a branch of the advertising trade, with art and literature offered only as a bait. They need enormous sales to make their advertising space valuable; so they can not afford to employ writers who are not themselves nationally advertised products. They know, and most of their readers know, that the work of their most highly paid contributors is, to put it courteously, not strikingly good. But you can trust the label: from coast to coast, you know what you are buying, which is true neither of the pulp magazines nor of the highbrow reviews. And the few big packers of serial fiction overshadow the book market as well. In a capitalistic Utopia, literary production could be consolidated into four or five Syndicates, which would provide at the same time the efficiency of concentration and the blessings of competition.

This danger would be enormously increased, if the movement for cheaper books were to succeed. A shrewd citizenry, in which the Scottish strain has remained potent, loves a bargain, as a compensation and an excuse for its intermittent recklessness. Not seldom it loves a bargain *dearly*. When the corner drug store offers you a neatly bound volume, with a flamboyant jacket, an alluring title, a well-known author's name, the whole for 99 cents, with a tube of dental paste thrown in, you would feel yourself a simpleton if you walked away to the book shop, and bought exactly the same kind of work for $2.50. But cheap editions can be justified only by enormous sales; and the cult of sudden, massive success is a threat to all the more delicate values.*

Book production, if these tendencies were unchecked, would soon find itself in the same plight as its great rival, the talking pictures. There also, the experimental, the subtle, the rare, that secret power which reveals itself by slow degrees, are accounted damning sin. It would not do for a picture to be understood "about 1980": it is a big investment, it must take at once, or be a dead loss. The vast American public must be pleased; and, as that public is very dimly known, only the most approved gags and tricks can be used. When a film is declared "daring", it is because it exaggerates, not because it explores. Unless foreign countries follow the lead of Germany in repelling the American invasion, Hollywood will be the unquestioned world capital, and will spread a dead level of vulgarity for the greatest happiness of the greatest number.

This is gloomy prophesying: but we are nearer of kin to Mark Tapley than to Dean Inge or Mr. Joseph Wood Krutch. Let the worst come to the worst! We shall later attempt to sketch a literary Utopia: let us now conjure up a literary nightmare. Five or six publishers only, each with a staff of a dozen authors, are publishing a limited number of titles which sell by the million. The industry is consolidated, organized, made efficient, beyond

* This objection applies only to new books. The cheap *reprint*, on the contrary, has many admirable points. In my youth, I read some of the finest English books in sixpenny editions, which sold then for 4d½ (9¢). France has series of excellent modern fiction, with wood cuts, for 15¢; and certain American *Libraries* are a boon and a blessing.

the rosiest dreams of Mr. O. H. Cheney. In such an atmosphere, would literature perish?

Who knows? We might have an age after the heart of the Neo-Humanists—if Neo-Humanists have anything so romantic as a heart. It would be a world of standards, with very definite rules. The few masters of the craft would reach an extraordinary degree of technical skill, or, if you prefer, of efficiency. And, as in such an age, politics, religion, art, would all be integrated under the general formula of BUSINESS, it would bring our present chaos to an end, it would be a discipline of life, a new classicism.

Such an ideal would not only satisfy Irving Babbitt (who, if he had survived into that millennium, might have been the Will Hayes of Humane Letters), but it would also rejoice the soul of Tolstoy. For it would be a thoroughly democratic art, purged from all sophistications and morbidities, intelligible at once to every man. To the supercilious, it might seem primitive and crude. But this is merely a matter of comparison. The *common* level need not be low; and nothing prevents it from rising steadily. The cheapest cars to-day are marvels of refinement compared with the luxury cars of twenty-five years ago.

Under this Dictatorship of the Intellectual Proletariat, it is not inevitable that all the élites should be guillotined, or reduced to sullen silence. But the élites would have to dissolve as distinct bodies; and, if they wanted to be heard, they would be compelled to use a tongue understood of the people. An artist to-day is tempted to address exclusively his peers, and to use their cryptic jargon. When all literature has become one gigantic *Saturday Evening*

Post, he will have no choice but to place his power at the service of popular art. The patriotic tragedy of Æschylus, the thumping melodrama of Shakespeare, the edifying, sentimental, detective romance in *Les Misérables,* show that it is not impossible to live in close touch with the masses, yet soar to the heights.

You will say that the very essence of the poet is to be *different.* Granted: but great art could be different *within* the common medium, not *aside* from it. Even to-day, a page may be of the rarest quality, without such artificial 'signs of distinction as Mallarmé's syntax or Joyce's vocabulary. The poet will write for the masses, and also for himself. A few notes may be lost by his enormous public without spoiling their enjoyment of the whole. And, through these few notes, he has saved his soul.

Nor will those few notes die unheard. They will reach, within the vast throng, the few who are no longer allowed to isolate themselves. They will create a mysterious communion rarer in quality than the fussy little circles of Greenwich Village. To be aggressively, boastfully esoteric is a childish prank. To conceal, with apparent artlessness, the Secret within the Obvious, is a searching delight. Even to-day, a book which will be read by a few thousands is perhaps meant for less than a score. Pascal, in his Vision, exacted from Christ the assurance: "I have shed such and such a drop of blood *for thee.*" *I,* the isolated reader, feel that my own poets have written such or such a word for me, for me alone, and for none besides.

Big Business,—or its extreme limit, the Biggest Business of all, Bolshevism,—can kill only external differences. The hierarchy of literature would reappear within the ap-

parently homogeneous mass. All men would read the
same words: there would be as many different resonances
as there are individual souls.

Mr. Cheney, who is a very stimulating writer, has thus
enticed us into the land of his dreams, a thoroughly
organized and efficient book industry; and we have found
that his Utopia might be habitable after all. Somehow,
all ideals converge. It is a pity that their meeting point
should be just beyond Nowhere.

For there is little hope or danger of our ever reaching
such a degree of organization. People can standardize
their plain, basic necessaries, and even their material
luxuries: not their æsthetic satisfactions. Our needs might
very well be served by a single railroad system; one big
firm could supply bread, or even automobiles, for us all;
but no syndicate could long preserve a monopoly of
literature. There are two tendencies at work in the
world: opposite, not antagonistic. The one is toward
more unity on the material plane (standardization); the
other toward more diversity on the spiritual plane
(pluralism).

All that we need retain of Mr. Cheney's survey is a
confession of despair: the industry is in a state of chaos,
and no simple measures could create order.

Why balk at chaos? Liberty means chaos, compared
with the orderliness of death. But our chaos is excessive.
This, in our opinion, is due to the faint-heartedness of
the publishers, who dare to gamble, but not to lead. If
they refuse to be our "conscious organized minority", to
whom shall we turn?

312

Chapter 20

To-day: GROUPING TOWARD A RATIONAL ORGANIZATION

I

WE have seen that the publishers were "leaders" blindly guessing whither the flock wanted to be led. Neither they, nor the public, and the authors least of all, are satisfied with the situation. The thought that religion, politics and business are all in the same plight brings rather wan comfort. "Confusionism", as Irving Babbitt named the spirit of our age, is the most cheerless of religions.

Is there any way out of this morass? Must we wait until our civilization be "integrated" again? But, if every branch of human activity were to wait for every other, movement of any kind would become unthinkable. *Planning* is a fine, energetic motto; but planning means the coördination of efforts, and first must come the effort.

We have attempted to show that the old literary order depended upon a social structure which is now a memory. Pure commercialism has evolved no new order of its own: in theory and in practice, commercialism is anarchy. We shall now examine a few efforts toward a more rational organization of literature. We have no faith in any one panacea. What is of interest in any proposed reform is the recognition of an evil, the affirmation of a spirit, and a call to renewed activity. And this is the sign and promise of returning grace.

The times, being hard, are not unfavorable. Grievous as the sins of Capitalism may be, self-complacency is no longer one of them. Our world is in a penitent mood: world war, political futility, economic chaos, have shaken its confidence. This is all to the good. We have more faith in chastened Capitalism than in arrogant Communism. The Arch-Tempter's name is cocksureness.

If commercialism be the enemy of literature, the most obvious solution would be to take business out of publishing. Books should be published because they are good, and not exclusively because they bring money. There is nothing revolutionary about such an attitude. The most orthodox capitalist admits that business should not be the rule in matters of the spirit. We resent the intrusion of commercialism into science or religion. We do not—confessedly—give positions of national trust to the highest bidder, although we sometimes seek our representatives in the cheapest market. Books are not purely a "commodity": they fulfill at present many of the functions which, in the Middle Ages, were reserved to the Church and the Universities. It would not be absurd if literature also were excepted from the field of competitive economics.

Several agencies could take the place of the commercial publishers. The first is the State. In addition to official documents (which, in war times particularly, often rise to the dignity of fiction), it may bring out, as in Russia and Mexico, cheap editions of the classics and of popular textbooks. Vasconcelos believed that the Enneads of Plotinus were indispensable to the regeneration of the Indian *peon*. Washington, less idealistic, distributes tons of informative "literature", not all of which is wasted.

The second is the University Press. It usually limits itself to scientific and scholarly books. When it ventures, in a half-hearted way, to bid for the favor of the general public, it is not strikingly successful. It might be desirable if the Universities were to assume full control of learned editions, research publications, highly technical treatises. Books of reference, dictionaries and Encyclopædiæ should come under some *Inter-University Bureau of Intellectual Standards*. When the venerable *Britannica* or a prominent seat of higher learning adopt methods of high-pressure salesmanship, we have in both cases the same sense of incongruity. The Professor in print should be as dignified as the Professor in the lecture room. And yet . . . is *salesmanship* so radically different from *education?* The same definition: "Inducing a man to get what he does not want", might frequently apply to both.*

The third is the privately endowed Press. The institution I dream of would have to be wealthy enough to make some impression on the gigantic American market. It would restrict its activity exclusively to literature as an art, leaving to the trade practical works and books for mere entertainment, to the Universities all scientific publications. It would never seek popular success; but it is

---

* The religious Presses, circulating books at cost or giving them away, are even better examples of non-commercial publishing. A 500-page volume of Swedenborg may be had for a nickel.

not inconceivable, if the Press acquired any kind of prestige, that substantial success would follow. It would pay each accepted manuscript a minimum representing the time spent upon it under decent conditions of comfort; if the sales justified additional compensation, it would give the author royalties on the usual basis. Manuscripts would be submitted anonymously. A veteran of literature would have no better chance than the sophomore who deftly imitates his style; less of a chance than the freshman who, for a wonder, should bring something actually *fresh*. If the established author wants to capitalize on his past successes, let him make his terms with the commercial publishers. The Press would have two autonomous departments, called respectively *Tradition* and *Experiment*.

Our millionaires are a breed of men of whom we are justly proud. But they are far too imitative, that is to say oddly self-diffident. Their benefactions follow a few well-worn grooves. As a result, we have an actual plethora of Universities, and certain Peace Societies spend much of their income on activities rather remotely connected with peace. A *Memorial Press for Fine Literature*, on a sufficiently large scale, has not yet been tried, and should prove tempting. The suggestion is freely offered to any millionaire friendly to the Muses. If I were a millionaire myself, there are seven or eight better uses I could think of for my orphaned pelf.

These solutions are attractive. But they repose on the assumption that a non-commercial body would know how to pick the *good* books. On what authority? In virtue of what principles? One thing is certain: we do not want to entrust the fate of literature to the State, if the

State is to be represented either by the politicians or by the bureaucrats. Shall we be guided by the professors of literature and the academicians in the name of tradition? Or by "Society" in the name of "good taste"? But, if we still believed in these conservative authorities, our difficulty would not exist.

We might have the editorial board elected by the writing profession. The constituency might be hard to define: yet it would not be so vague as either "Society" or the "general public." The board would acquire thereby no pontifical infallibility: but a fair degree of competence might thus be secured. Creative artists are not necessarily poor judges of their own craft; some of the shrewdest criticism has been written by the best poets. When our Foundation had been under way for a few years, the electoral college might be limited to the authors whose work it had accepted.

Commercial or philanthropic, official or private, any publishing concern can not be worth more than its body of advisers. In this respect, the best firms have maintained a highly creditable level. When books are passed upon—to mention a few names at random, by Anatole France, by George Meredith, Edward Garnett, E. V. Lucas, Frank Swinnerton, or, in this country, by W. C. Brownell or Willa Cather, there is little cause for complaint. Indeed, *business* is not seldom better equipped, at that crucial point, than the University presses.

Other things being equal, however, our Foundation would have a decided advantage over the commercial publishers. When a reader reports favorably upon a fine piece of work, he also has to answer the question: "Will it

317

sell?" And he may have, sorrowfully, to answer: "It will not." In the trade, this means, in the majority of cases: Thumbs down. The endowed Press would be serenely indifferent to probable sales.

Another way of escape from unmitigated commercialism is the *subscription series*. This method has long been a familiar one in music and the drama. The national repertory theatres of France have three sources of income: State subsidies, yearly subscriptions, and box office receipts. When a young gas fitter with a passion for the stage, Antoine, started his *Théâtre Libre,* he organized it on the advanced subscription principle. With a modest and fairly steady backing—never fully adequate, alas!— he was able to produce daring plays, experimental plays, translations from unfamiliar literatures. Many a battle was lost: but no disaster was irretrievable. For the *Théâtre Libre* had a certain momentum; and when finally it went down, it had renovated the French drama.

The same system can be applied to literature. Charles Péguy had a curious publication, called the *Notebooks of the Fortnight*. It was not a magazine: each number was an independent volume by a single author. The editor's own works appeared in that fashion; and, in addition, he revealed his personality in prefaces, postfaces and interfaces, through many a page of perversely repetitious and ponderously insistent prose, shot through with passages of strange poetical power. Péguy's circulation, we believe, was about three thousand: modest enough, yet far greater than might have been hoped for by some of his collaborators, had they used the ordinary channels. The Péguy group was not rich, not powerful in political and academic circles, not drilled to repeat a shibboleth, but it had a common ideal of intellectual honesty, which had been its bond during the Dreyfus Affair. That small but solid group counted among the shock troops of the literary world. Romain Rolland's interminable *Jean-Christophe* first appeared in the form of *Notebooks*. It is doubtful whether this mighty work would have been accepted by any commercial publisher. A trade-wise business man would have guessed that in France, a country notoriously indifferent to music, and worse than indifferent to Germany, no public could be found for the slow biography of a child musician in a small Rhenish court. The Péguy phalanx broke the ring of prejudice. *Jean-Christophe* was reprinted in a trade edition, and won world-wide acclaim.*

Between the subscription series and the Review of the usual type, there is only a technical difference in the distribution of the installments. The *uncommercial literary magazine* is one of our strongest hopes of salvation. By this means, poets can still hail each other, and play between the enormous iron feet of the Book Trade Robots. In so far as it embodies the prejudices and vanities of a clique, the "little" Review is futile and even dangerous. In so far as it represents the flame of youthful faith and indignation, the refusal to serve either Mammon or the Law of the Pharisees, it is holy even when it is ludicrous.

With a pitiful circulation, it is not negligible. Its contributors and readers (usually they are one and the same, a small devoted company) will not altogether forget its

---

* More recently, Louis Hémon's *Marie Chapdelaine* had been published twice (as a serial and in Canada) without attracting any attention. It was included in the *Green Notebooks*, a series inspired by Péguy's, and, through that select public, was revealed to the general reader. The trade edition went into the hundreds of thousands.

message, even when they sober down into right-thinking (*i.e.* unthinking) *bourgeois.* Between the experimental vanguard, which at times seems *perdu,* and the main body, there are *liaison* agents. Shrewd editors like to do literature a good turn, and at the same time give their magazine a name for moderate daring and safe liberalism. So an author not infrequently passes from the esoteric little Review to the periodicals run on a sound business basis.

This transfer from the uncommercial to the commercial, however, is not without peril. We are astonished and delighted at times to find the names of genuine artists on the announcements of frankly industrial publications. But in many cases, it is their name only, not their integrity, that they carry over into the mighty organs of Philistia. The million readers of these triumphant magazines want to be flattered by the thought that they too are patrons of "real art"; but they do not want to face the humiliating experience of not understanding a word. So a tactful compromise is reached, and we have stories signed—shall we call it, for the sake of safety, George Meredith?—which might have been concocted by—let us say Marie Corelli. The voice is Jacob's, but the hands are Esau's.

The uncommercial series or review is bound to be an ephemeral affair. It is identified with its editor, and uncommercial editors die young. They are killed in three ways: by the mere accident of disease, murder or war; by failure—here we have an illimitable field of little white crosses—; * and, no less inexorably, by success. An editor whose originality has become an asset is compelled to

---

* "The little magazines which die to make verse free." (Alice B. Toklas).

standardize that originality, that is to say to embalm it. Péguy had just reached that point when the war broke out. Had his *Notebooks* continued, they would no longer have been a living force, but a historical document. Henry Holt could not have kept the *Unpopular Review* alive, without achieving a measure of popularity. And it must have been galling for the most Swiftian of our critics to find himself with such a handsome following of "Yahoos" and "Boobs", to use his favorite terms. Naturally, the independent review must seek a public. But the test comes inevitably when the expansion of that public has to be purchased by a compromise. As soon as an editor asks himself: "This is fine stuff: but how will it affect my circulation?"—may his mess of pottage agree with him! He has bartered away his birthright.

All this does not mean that we consider the "little" review futile, or the successful review stupid. Both fulfill their function. But the review of insurgency can not lead for long, and the review of conformity can not lead at all. It is vain to hope for an institution that will combine steady moderation and daring originality. Just as Protestantism has long ceased to protest (except against religious free thought), so the various *Mercuries* have become as respectable as the *Atlantic Monthly* and the *Revue des Deux Mondes*.

But, on the whole, the periodicals hold out a much fairer promise to literature than the book trade. This for two reasons: they permit of freer experiments, and they have a fairly consistent public. No firm can expect one of its books to be bought simply because it bears the firm's imprint. But a magazine has a subscription list, and a large or small following of regular purchasers. A magazine is actually an organized unit of the reading public, a diffused Salon, the best substitute we have for defunct "Society." It is a pluralistic organization: there are innumerable periodicals, and every intelligent reader is supposed to glance at quite a few. But it is not pure chaos, like the book mart. Mourn who will for departed unity: we must find our bearings in a complex of interpenetrating universes.*

II

We have so far considered *organization* from the point of view of the producer—publisher or editor. We have seen that the noncommercial leader must, like his commercial brother, soon abdicate leadership. When he has defined and won his public, he becomes that public's prisoner. Wriggle as we may, we can not elude the fact that literature is brought out *for the sake of the consumer*. If not, why produce or publish at all? Sing to yourself and for yourself, and be satisfied. In the words of popular wisdom: "He who pays the pipers calls the tune." In the modern vernacular: "The customer is boss." So literary organization might come in the form of a Consumers' League.

One such League is almost ready to our hands: some kind of an *entente* among the Public Libraries. The Libraries are strategic points: but the Librarians are a

* We firmly believe that the periodical should be the main channel of publication, the book the exception. It were better if innumerable works of an ephemeral nature, well worth reading, never came out in book form at all. And, by ephemeral, we do not mean simply light fiction, but many serious contributions to political or scientific controversies. Books are too lumbering to keep up with the development of modern physics, for instance; and the Soviets, we are told, are wisely introducing the magazine textbook.

"minority" that has not yet achieved "consciousness." They too are paralyzed by that false conception of democracy which would leave all initiative to the masses. The masses are incapable of initiative; their one desire is to be, if not driven by a Mussolinian whip, at any rate firmly and wisely guided.

The "public demand" which Librarians heed with the same subserviency as politicians, is not spontaneous and divine: it is engineered by some aggressive advertiser, or is the result of some unaccountable craze. Public servants are supposed to serve the interests, not the whims, of the public. It seems a criminal waste of public monies for a City Library to purchase one hundred copies of some cheap thriller which no one will touch in less than a year. It is a capitulation to vulgarity, on the part of those who are paid to know better. It might be a safe rule for libraries not to buy any novel less than five years old. Current fiction could be made entirely self-supporting on a "cent-a-day" basis.

We are aware of two dangers. The first is excessive centralization. Just as the Napoleonic minister could pull out his watch and say: "At this moment, the same Latin text is dictated for translation in every school of the Empire," a Federal Director of Libraries could boast: "Ten thousand cities are receiving from our office their identical weekly pabulum. One hundred and twenty-five million minds with but a single thought! What a glorious achievement!" But, with the present resources of America, a standardized list would not necessarily involve standardized thought. It would be impossible to draw up a list of two or three hundred self-respecting books without having to include works of many kinds, and on opposite sides.

The second objection is that the body of Librarians is not prepared to assume such a responsibility. The days when a person of a literary turn of mind drifted naturally into a librarianship have been ended by our cult of material efficiency. Trained librarians are administrators, accountants, office workers, but not critics. After all, a great library is a complex machine, not a field wherein to roam and browse at will. We still believe that every library should provide a living and friendly guide for its readers; it might be well, in many cases, if the teachers of literature were also part-time librarians. This genuine influence can be felt in small places where personal contact is maintained; and the modest lot of such a librarian ought to be an enviable one. But that ideal is not unthinkable even in the largest cities. In mammoth department stores, the salesman is supposed to inform, suggest, advise: our libraries are too often conducted on the cheaper and quicker "Help yourself" or "Grocerteria" system.

But we have to note as a fact that the Librarians, at present, refuse to lead: false democracy, soulless efficiency, wise agnosticism, we know not. Perhaps they are justified in their self-effacement. Certain it is that with a bolder library system, no promising manuscript need be rejected for lack of a sufficient public: the library market alone would justify the printing of a small edition. The Directors of Art Museums are not so modest. They do not wait for a clear command from the crowd. They buy what they think is best, and then open their gates wide.

Another Purchasers' Organization is the Book Club. It is radically different from the old circulating library, which occasionally used the name, but exercised no control on your choice. It rather resembles the subscription series or the periodical: you commit your literary welfare, for a year, into the hands of an editorial board. Péguy was really the dictator of a book club which chose for you one volume every fortnight. Whether the Editor selects the works in manuscript, or already printed; whether he brings them out each under separate covers, or all jumbled in twelve monthly installments: these are details of organization, which do not affect the principle.

An excellent bookseller and super-*bouquiniste*, M. Edouard Champion,* the Paris agent for many scholars throughout the world, offered his foreign customers to pick out for them the best French books of the month. In this special case, the Book Club is particularly justified. Even a professional student finds it difficult, across the Atlantic, to follow the whirligigs of Parisian taste. Without believing in M. Champion's infallibility, one could trust him to know what books literary Paris was talking about. It is an extension of the "Society" idea.

The problem is not quite so simple when the Book Clubs operate in our own country. Then the two usual objections are raised: the fear of standardization, the surreptitious reintroduction of the business spirit. The first objection, as in the case of the Libraries, does not seriously frighten us. No single book club is within astronomic distance of securing a strangle hold of the

---

* His father was, in the book business, the successor of Anatole France's father.

market; not all the rival Book Clubs combined could do it; no appeal to the Sherman Act is needed. And the material advantages of the Book Clubs are many. They bring literature to the doorsteps of people remote from any decent book shop. They create a habit. They make book buying easy: to sign a check once a year is simplicity itself. People eat more on the "American plan" than when they have to order every item of every meal *à la carte;* and they spend sums on their own cars that they would grudge in the form of taxi fares. The Book Clubs' selection has such an advertising value that it increases the sales through the regular trade channels. All this, however, merely affects the *volume* of business, in which we confess that we are but tepidly interested. What about the *quality?* The Book Clubs claim that they have repeatedly secured the rewards of a best seller for serious works which otherwise would never have reached that heaven of American literature. They represent definite, enlightened, responsible leadership. The members of the board are few, well known, and trusted.

All this is excellent: but the second objection is more formidable. The curse of big business swiftly overtakes every American success. Péguy organized a healthy little market among three thousand friends; so he could publish—not every fortnight by any means—works of *rare* value, which otherwise would have been totally ignored. A board with a hundred thousand customers to please will attempt to give you the best—provided the best be acceptable to the hundred thousand. If not, sorrowfully but firmly, like their colleagues in the regular trade, they must declare: "We can't touch it." Once in a while, the

Book Clubs have made an unpopular book popular; but, on rare occasions also, the commercial firms have the same feat to their credit. The Book Club is absolutely one with the Book Trade in pursuing the great modern fallacy, the bane of literature: *sudden and massive success.*

III

The valuable element in the Book Club, as we have seen, is responsible, enlightened leadership. The curse is compromise with the business spirit. Can not the two be divorced? They can be, and are, in the *Literary Prize.* When the decision of a Book Club committee helps the sales outside its membership, its effects are exactly those of a Prize.

The prize goes back to antiquity, and flourished in the Middle Ages: Victor Hugo, in his boyhood, received one in the *Floral Games* of Toulouse, instituted in the fourteenth century. The Newdigate, at Oxford, has a splendid roll of winners, with such names as Matthew Arnold and Julian Huxley. As a rule, however, the *prize competition,* in which the subject is set, remains formal and barren: imagine bursting into lyric flame about *Timbuctoo!* Edwin Markham, we believe, has won more such tournaments than any man in his generation: but it is not as a prize winner that he deserves to be remembered.

There is one exception, however: one which justifies, for once, the horrible epithet *tremendous.* It is to such a competition that we owe Jean-Jacques Rousseau. An obscure middle aged bohemian, part musician, part botanist, hopelessly mediocre in both capacities, he read the announcement of the Academy of Dijon, hesitated,

picked out the paradoxical side, and became famous overnight. He was pinned down to his paradox by his success:
happier he, and the rest of mankind, if the unconscious
revolutionists of placid Dijon had not stirred up his
easily addled brain!

The prize, in modern literature, has multiplied like a
weed. Every University, every Academy, every firm, every
periodical, must take its hand in the game. We are nearing the time when the law will have to intervene and protect us against prizes no less than against lotteries. Else
every American youth or maiden, every matron craving
for pin money, every professor and minister, every retired
business man, every unwilling inmate of a State or Federal
Institution, will be scribbling away on the elusive
chance.

We need not insist upon the American prizes: they are
familiar to every reader. The Harper Novel Prize has an
excellent record; an Atlantic Monthly competition discovered Mazo de la Roche, a creditable if not a sensational
service to American letters; the Dial award went to Van
Wyck Brooks, whose delicate work had been consistently
indifferent to the cheaper forms of success. The Pulitzer
Prize is well worth having, although Sinclair Lewis found
it profitable to spurn it. We do not sympathize with
Sinclair Lewis's haughty refusal: but it is indicative of
current opinion in American literary circles. There is
no fault to find with our prizes: they simply fail to rouse
enthusiasm, or even interest.

France is prize-ridden even worse than we are; and
the prize steeple-chase is sometimes conducted with an
unscrupulous energy that would do credit to Wall Street

or Tammany Hall. But there is one prize which has attained unique prestige and power: the one awarded by the Goncourt Academy.

In opposition to Richelieu's forty Immortals, the ten Goncourt Academicians are all professional writers. At first, they were the personal friends of the founders, and represented the principles of Naturalism: but their interests are steadily widening. A self-recruiting body, they are all veterans with a firmly established reputation. But popular success counts for very little with them: Elémir Bourges, for instance, never reached the general public at all. Here we have a perfect example of the "conscious, organized minority": this small group, tightly knit, has acquired a prestige greater than that of its members taken separately; and its award confers fame. Literary France takes little interest in the elections to the Goncourt Academy, but waits with breathless suspense for the Goncourt Prize. Exactly the reverse is true of the Académie Française.

The one great service of the Goncourt Academy was to reveal Marcel Proust, who otherwise might have remained an illustrious unknown. There was courage also in endorsing Barbusse's *Under Fire,* when the war spirit was still raging. Some of the selections were indifferent, one at least, in our opinion, a glaring mistake.* Still, the Goncourt Prize holds its own, against innumerable imitative rivals. It does not truckle to business: it dictates to business. Its award almost automatically ensures sales that reach into the hundred thousands.

---

* *Batouala:* René Mayran, a very civilized colored Frenchman, has done far better work than this pseudo-primitive African tale.

In this case, the prestige of the Prize is due entirely to that of the jury. This is not so evidently true of the Nobel Foundation. The Swedish Committee fills no one with awe. It has performed its task honorably, not brilliantly. It has been slightly handicapped by the unfortunate word "idealistic" literature, attached to his bequest by the Dynamite King. This term introduces a non-artistic, possibly an anti-artistic element. The Committee has perhaps been guided by the desire of keeping a fairly even balance between the Latin and the Teutonic language groups; it certainly has failed to pick out the best representatives of Spain; it has been rather niggardly to us, and over-generous to the Scandinavian countries. But on the whole its decisions have been accepted with little grumbling. The prestige of the Nobel Prize is not due to the quality of the jury, but, on the one hand, to the munificence of the reward, on the other to its international character. Its standing with the best authors is shown by the fact that Shaw, who scoffs at all official honors, gladly accepted the Nobel palm without keeping the money; and that Sinclair Lewis, who scorned the Pulitzer, was proud of the Nobel. Its influence with the public can be measured in terms of increased sales. It had been difficult to interest a French publisher in *The Peasants,* by Ladislas Reymont: as soon as the Nobel award was known, the translation became marketable.

These two prizes illustrate very clearly the two different purposes of such institutions. The Goncourt Prize is a *discovery:* it reveals and imposes a struggling author; therefore it needs the backing of a jury with strong professional authority.* The Nobel Prize means the *confirmation* of established fame: therefore the prestige of the jury is of minor importance. The Committee merely registers a well-known fact; it is the prizeman who confers dignity upon the prize, not the reverse.

Strictly, the Confirmation Prize carries coal to Newcastle. It matters little, to the recipients or to the world at large, that Anatole France or G. B. Shaw should get additional honors or profits. They were tolerably conspicuous and comfortably well off without any further distinction. Within the limits of a national literature, therefore, the confirmation prize is useless, and its funds might be used to far better purpose. But the Nobel Prize is saved from futility by its international character. Mere *confirmation* in the author's own country, it is *discovery* for the rest of the world. *Babbitt,* for instance, was barely known in France before the Swedish spotlight fell on Sinclair Lewis.†

IV

Whichever road we take, there is a point where we encounter the same sign. The publishers—commercial, State, University, endowed—can help literature if they or their responsible assistants are good judges; a subscription series, a periodical, a book club, each is worth what its editorial board is worth; a prize counts or not, according

---

* It was questioned whether the Goncourt Prize could legitimately be given to Marcel Proust, who was middle-aged and wealthy, and had already published with some acceptance; it was wise, in our opinion, to rule that Proust was "young and struggling" within the meaning of the act.

† There is a third kind, which has its justification: the *consolation prize,* given to a man whose career has been long, distinguished, yet not dazzlingly successful. The French Academy awards not a few of those—naturally without confessing their true nature; and they are not absolutely unknown in America.

to the authority of the jury. Ultimately, we are always thrown back upon a small body of men, who are trusted to *know*. If knowledge and power are divorced, chaos must prevail, as confessedly, it does at present. The expert has, not the first word, but the last, in medicine, law, engineering: why not in literature? The man who knows, or claims to know, about literature is the critic. Give me a good critical police, and I shall give you a thriving literary state.

Proposed with such bluntness, the autocracy of the critic sounds preposterous. The familiar phrase arises invincibly again: "Not even a beautiful dream." For, in other domains, the charlatan can be told from the genuine expert by means of objective tests. "Laws" take their place in scientific thought only if they can be submitted to experimental verification. A bridge which stands a given load is an adequate bridge. But to what reagents, to what strain, can we submit a book? In what scales can it be weighed? Our sole objective criteria are crudely pragmatic: "the court of public opinion", "the test of time." Neither is applicable to the manuscript which comes to you fresh from the author's mind, with the secret of a new day between its leaves, if you had eyes to see.

We must renounce, and we gladly renounce, the idea of a definite, monopolistic body of critics, passing formal sentences. In the absence of critical law, we have to be satisfied with a vaguer entity, the *critical spirit*. All men have it, just as all men have the creative power; but some men have it in a higher degree. Only, while public opinion gladly recognizes creative superiority, it is far

332

more reluctant to admit critical superiority. Every man wants to judge for himself, to be his own critic. Ultimately and in theory, he is right: and he should be his own poet too. In practice, he judges only of the things which have been picked out for him by the publishers, the editors, the Book Clubs, the prize juries, *i.e. by critics*. Since the intervention of critics is indispensable, the public should strive to have the best, the most sensitive, the most highly trained, the most disinterested; and the only way of securing their services is to grant them proper recognition. Authors and public too often unite in deriding critics, all the while unconsciously guided by vague, anonymous, irresponsible criticism. This is a suicidal policy. The key to better literature is better criticism, and the key to better criticism is better critics: a platitude which involves a revolution.

This revolution is under way. Within the last twenty-five years, the change in American criticism has been startling. There had always been distinguished critics in America; but, for a long time, their tone had been decidedly academic, and they were devoid of any vital influence. To-day, pedantry and superciliousness are on the wane; "culture", by a natural reaction, has become almost a term of reproach. The critic walks cheerfully among men of the present. The progress in the number, quality and circulation of the critical reviews must needs carry with it an increase in power.

What would the critics do with that power? Reveal it by cutting down the profits of popular writers, as Thackeray, with his burlesques, killed the vogue of G. P. R. James, as Jules Lemaître extinguished poor Georges

Ohnet? It may have to be done at times: some reputations are a national blight. This would apply only to the
exposure of pseudo-artists: as a rule, the entertainers are
doing a good job in a non-literary field, and should be
left undisturbed. Will the critics on the contrary boost
the sales of deserving writers—a Midas-like gift credited
to Octave Mirbeau and to William Lyon Phelps? As an
incidental result, this is not to be despised. But why
think in terms of sales? Sales are indispensable to professionals: the fewer professional authors we have, the
better perhaps for literature. Genuine writers, as distinguished from educators, propagandists and entertainers,
would as a rule be all the greater if they limited themselves to one book every five or six years—half a dozen
works in a lifetime. In any decent civilization, this should
be easily achieved by any man who feels the urge within
him; and it would not interfere with a gainful occupation.

What can the critics do then? In a country of
125,000,000 people, all with some kind of an education, it
is a scandal that there should be no market for a book
which competent judges *know* to be worth while. The
first service of the critics, therefore, must be to organize
small, definite, enlightened *publics,* which will make the
circulation of the unusual work a practical possibility.
But the greatest service is not commercial. It is to provide a *critical* audience, one that knows the difference, one
that understands and appreciates the effort, even when it
can not fully accept the result. This mutual recognition
of a few congenial souls, without any official ties, without
any formal creed, is at the same time a stimulus and a
reward. Without it, official honors and wealth, to the

genuine artist, are a derision, and his conscience can never be at peace. It alone can relieve the gnawing self-doubt and the bitterness of the isolated worker. To turn the critics into a conscious and organized minority is the first requisite for a healthy literature.

Chapter 21

INFLUENCE OF LITERATURE UPON LIFE

I

THERE is no influence that is not reciprocal. This, a truism in physics, less obvious in sociology, may seem a paradox in literature. If the earth "attracts" the moon, so does the moon attract the earth. The jailer, on duty, is the prisoner of the convict; the victorious nation imposes upon itself a heavy tribute in order to protect the fruit of victory. An imitator of Ibsen does not react upon the man Ibsen, who is dead, but upon the fame of Ibsen, which is alive. He may enhance his master's glory, by swelling the train of worthy Ibsenians; he may detract from it, by making Ibsenism commonplace or ludicrous. If the forces of civilization have a definite action upon literature, we may be certain that literature is not without influence upon the course of civilization.

Some forms of this influence have already been indicated in the study of the *Literary Type*. A man's life is shaped by his conscious desires: if he wants to be an artist, he will be tempted to indulge in the temperamental oddities or excesses by which artists are supposed to be characterized. This, as we have seen, is particularly marked along the literary fringe, among "the coast dwell-

336

ers of Bohemia": but genuine artists are not free from this tendency. Literature may set the fashion of fatal pallor: and Lord Byron, first victim of Byronism, is compelled to drink vinegar. Goethe's *Werther* and Vigny's *Chatterton* were responsible for the suicide of several young poets. Musset and George Sand conscientiously assayed a grand passion which was not in their nature: but they were writers, and literature in their day was romantic: so romantic they had to be. Nero, at least in the picture drawn by Renan, is a striking example of the spurious artistic ideal carried into real life.

This *literaritis* (the hybrid name is hardly worse than the disease) spreads easily from writers and would-be writers to mere readers, and to whole circles in society. It is noted that children want to play-act the stories they hear. The *Golden Legend* inspired young Anatole France with the desire of becoming a "hermit and saint in the calendar." Little boys of a less holy disposition prefer to be pirates, explorers, soldiers, or even gangsters. Nor is this limited to childhood. Don Quijote is the perfect instance of a reader so enthusiastic, so convinced, that he must live the life of his book heroes. While Honoré d'Urfé's pastoral romance *L'Astrée* was an idealized picture of *Précieuse* society, it also served as a model. More than two centuries later, exactly the same phenomenon occurred with Balzac's *Human Comedy:* in both cases, groups of people adopted the names of their favorite characters, and patterned their speech and their actions upon theirs. André Maurois, in an episode of *Mape,* analyzes such an example of conscious Balzacianism. *Madame Bovary* shows the intrusion of literary romanticism into

337

a dull provincial life: poor Emma is the victim of her reading, almost as clearly as Don Quijote. *Hedda Gabler,* as interpreted by Jules Lemaître, is a satire on pseudo-Ibsenism by Ibsen himself. The heroine tries her best to live her life in beauty, and makes such a sorry mess of it that even death fails to achieve tragic dignity. Marie Bashkirtscheff was preparing herself to be a Hedda Gabler in real life. It is said that the braggadocio of *Cyrano de Bergerac,* the waving of the arrogant plume in the face of danger, led young French officers, in 1914, to useless and therefore criminal sacrifice. H. G. Wells has an amusing picture of the soldier who, chiefly through the use of gory expletives, consciously strives to be Kiplingesque. Examples are legion. Perhaps they are not quite fair to literature. For we note only the excess, the pose, the craze, the disease, and call them *literary:* it stands to reason that literature has an edifying influence also. But the word edifying is a stench in the nostrils of "pure" artists, and they hasten to disclaim any power for good.

In more diffused fashion, literature, as we have seen, tends to the fixation of the national type. *The* Frenchman, *the* German, are mostly book products. There probably are some French people who, like M. Lacarelle in Anatole France, feel it a duty to court every woman, in obedience to the Gallic tradition. *Noblesse oblige* and its obligations may be far from pleasant. By 1914, the Germans had forged for themselves a barbaric ideal, out of the *Nibelungen* and Nietzsche, which at times oddly superimposed a formidable frown upon rosy, chubby, bespectacled countenances. It was they who invented the

Hun myth—and waxed exceeding wroth when the rest of the world accepted it. Indeed we have already expressed our opinion that Nationalism was to a large extent a creation, and is to-day a survival, of the Romantic movement. The degree in which nations are swayed by literary and artistic ideals is seldom fully realized by historians. History is a pageant, a drama, and its æsthetic interpretation is more reliable than the economic. The economic is too sensible to be adequate.

We do not propose to discuss this idea at length in the present volume. Let a few familiar examples suffice, not as a demonstration, but as an indication. Among the direct causes of the French Revolution, the activities of the *Philosophes* are seldom omitted: "It is all Voltaire's fault, and Rousseau's," became the monotonous refrain of the conservatives; and those *Philosophes* were men whose prestige rested, first of all, on their literary fame. Beaumarchais's sparkling and daring comedy *Figaro's Wedding,* is cited among the signs of the impending catastrophe. The political and religious Restoration which prevailed in Europe after 1815 reflected the love of the Romanticists for historical pageantry: the coronation of King Charles X at Rheims was a triumph of the Walter Scott spirit. Sympathy with the cause of Greek independence was enhanced by the enormous fame of Lord Byron. The Napoleon of legend, far more vivid in our minds than the Napoleon of plain fact, was likewise a Romantic creation. It was literature that made the Second Empire possible, although Béranger, Victor Hugo and Thiers turned away in disgust from the work of their own hands.

339

Nor is this special to France. The Hohenzollern régime, from 1871 to 1918, represented neither the tradition of Frederick II, nor the aspirations of German democracy, and still less the necessities of a modern, scientific and industrial state: it was a scene from a second-rate pseudo-Wagnerian opera, a belated piece of literary Romanticism, introduced on the political stage by the supreme "realist" Bismarck.

This influence of literature may be focussed in the conception of *the Poet as Prophet:* were not the prophets of Israel great poets first of all? France is the least Biblical of modern nations: but in this respect, she is the true heir of ancient Judea. The power, greater than any king's, wielded by Voltaire and Rousseau, served as a precedent. Chateaubriand was persuaded that it was he who had restored in France Catholicism and the Bourbons; he constantly compared himself with Napoleon, and felt himself a national hero of the same magnitude. Lamartine, in the *bourgeois* Parliament of Louis-Philippe, represented "the constituency of the ideal"; and the Romantic revolution of 1848 chose him as its inevitable leader. Victor Hugo became the spiritual head of continental democracy and free thought, the irreconcilable enemy of Napoleon III, the ghostly father of the Third Republic. Zola, as the chief of the Naturalistic school, felt that he was *ex officio* the public defender of truth and justice. In Anatole France, the sense that the man of letters is called to leadership wrestled oddly, and at times victoriously, with his inborn indolence and his ingrained scepticism.

In Germany, the literary revival preceded and guided the political: Goethe was forced into the position of a national symbol, while his spirit remained cosmopolitan. The Young German movement was a blend of literature and politics. Wagner, Nietzsche, Treitschke, without holding political office, had their rôle in German history. In Italy, Dante was a national standard at a time when the country had become a mere geographical expression. Young Italy, like Young Germany, was first of all an open conspiracy of poets. Mazzini's eloquence was part of his power. Gabriele d'Annunzio was persuaded that artistic primacy even when it is tinged with decadence, is a call to action and a claim to command. The downfall of the Spanish throne was heralded by two authors as radically different as could be imagined, Blasco Ibáñez and Miguel de Unamuno; the new Spanish Republic was able to send as ambassadors great writers instead of mere grandees. After the aspirations of Ireland were shattered by the Parnell scandal and the fiasco of the Liberal Party, the national soul was placed in the keeping of the poets, and it was the literary Renaissance that prepared the political resurrection.

In England, Byron and especially Shelley had the souls of prophets. Carlyle formally draped himself in the prophet's mantle, blessing under his breath, cursing thunderingly, for fifty years. Ruskin was a gentler Carlyle; William Morris united in himself socialism, art and literature. Even Matthew Arnold condescended to point the way. Dickens made popular fiction a denunciation of abuses; Charles Reade also worked for reform through romances; an amiable minor novelist, Walter Besant, had his share in the People's Palace idea. Imperialism, whose father was a literary statesman, Disraeli, was sharply focussed by a poet, Kipling. It is worth noting that British Imperialism, a great force at the end of the nineteenth century, remained a sentiment which never found either its political or its economic expression. Among the elder writers of our own times, not a few have a robust faith in their right to guide, and, if need be, to drive: Shaw and Wells urging us forward, Chesterton and Belloc prodding us back.

America is the country where literary fame is most completely divorced from political authority. Emerson's following was large, but loose: it lost itself in the infinite shadowy pastures of Transcendantalism. *Uncle Tom's Cabin,* of course, was a portent; James Russell Lowell and not a few others placed their talent at the service of a great cause; Walt Whitman alone strove consciously to be our prophet: but he never attained the position of a Victor Hugo or even of a Carlyle. There is an ambiguous zone between literature and social action, where Winston Churchill meets William Allen White, where Frank Norris and Jack London are not very far from Upton Sinclair. Burghardt du Bois and Ludwig Lewisohn are prophets indeed, but for their own people only. Sinclair Lewis reminds us at times of H. G. Wells: but he is a reporter with a gift for caricature, rather than a constructive propagandist. Theodore Dreiser and Sherwood Anderson seem tempted by the rôle of an American Zola. And it can not be denied that H. L. Mencken has some kind of influence on American life. Indeed, he has many kinds of influence: but, after canceling their contradictions, it is not easy to measure the net result. To the average American, the idea of the poet as guide is grotesque beyond words. The poet, as we are taught in the kindergarten, is a demented person who goes flaunting the strange device *Excelsior!* and gets very properly killed for refusing to heed the practical man.

II

We have no mystic faith in the vision of rhymester or fictionist. A man is not necessarily God-inspired because he tells things that are not so. But the action of literature upon life may be justified without any appeal to supernatural powers. We all know the paradox propounded by Oscar Wilde and James Branch Cabell: *Nature imitates Art.* In less defiant terms, *literature is not mere experience, but experiment.** If this be so, literature occupies an essential place in the life of the community.

It was Zola, we believe, who first gave prominence to the term *experimental* in literary theory. By "the experimental novel", he meant something far deeper than the trying out of a new technique. His "Naturalism" was modeled and named after the natural sciences; his master was the physiologist Claude Bernard, whose *Introduction to Experimental Medicine* was one of the decisive books of the age. Zola's vast cycle *The Rougon-Macquart,* was "the natural and social history of a family under the Second Empire." And so, with a wealth of clinical documents, Zola proceeded to "demonstrate" and "prove" heredity. In this arrogant form, Zola's pretension is palpably absurd. A novel with heredity as its central

---

* The same idea was ably expressed by that stimulating teacher, Richard Moulton.

343

motive "proves" heredity exactly as a ghost story proves the existence of ghosts.

It is not within art's domain to prove anything. We translate the French expression *pièce à thèse* by *problem play*. But our phrase is a platitude: every play, even the broadest farce, is a problem. The French term is a fallacy: no play can establish a thesis. Art, to be valid as art, must be human, personal, individualized; and no single instance is an argument—it is at best an illustration. Victor Hugo wanted to show that the *Coup d'Etat* of Louis-Napoleon in December 1851 was a crime. He picked out one episode: a child had been killed by a stray bullet, and the corpse was brought to his grandmother, whose despair was heart-rending. The story is told with matchless restraint and power. It is great art; it would be highly effective with an emotional jury; but it *proves* nothing at all. The affair was an accident; the murderous bullet might just as well have come from a Republican rifle. In the Holy Revolutions of which Victor Hugo had made himself the high priest, innocent blood was also shed—far more than in the brief and vigorous police operation of December 1851. Similarly, *Madame Bovary* proves nothing against the reading of romantic fiction by provincial *bourgeoises*. Not all country doctors' wives were perverted by George Sand; and adultery probably existed before literature. But if art does not *prove*, with the rigor of science, it *explains*. Every poem, novel or drama is a working hypothesis. The subject itself provides the data: a character, a situation, a sequence of events. The writer's task is to present these data in such a fashion that they carry conviction. If the reader does not exclaim: "It must have been so!" then the author has failed. As Gertrude Stein put it with unwonted lucidity: "Composition is explanation." Explanation is not identical with formal logic or with the Q.E.D. of Euclid. The state that the author wants to explain may be one of confusion, of bewilderment, of mystery, of madness. *To explain* means: *to make convincing.*

Shakespeare, for instance, will take jealousy, Molière or Balzac avarice, Meredith egotism, and see how these forces work out under definite circumstances. Or we may start from a situation: social conflict in *Germinal* or *The Weavers,* miscegenation in *The Quaint Companions,* war in *Under Fire* or *All Quiet on the Western Front,* and draw out its consequences. Or again, we may be given the facts, authentic or fictitious: a scandal, a murder case, an estrangement, an idyl. Every event implies a mystery story: the problem is to provide the motives that will make the facts intelligible. It is not necessary that these motives be analyzed with the minuteness of a Henry James or a Marcel Proust. They may be implied, without comment, in the order of presentation: a method which the plainest art and the most subtle have in common: Harold Bell Wright meets Katherine Mansfield.

This applies not only to biography, not only to those novels and dramas which borrow their subjects directly from life, but also to the most fanciful, the most whimsical fiction. For a satire, a fairy tale, a hallucination always are the refraction or the transposition of some real experience, and have a logic of their own.

And this applies no less to the lyric. The lyric, intensely personal, immediate, spontaneous, spurns the very idea of "explanation", which seems to involve argument. "Why should I stoop to explain? Here is what I feel: take it or leave it." Yet every lyric is a fragment of an autobiographical narrative, and offers a problem. The lyric is a mood: I am glad or depressed. The poem itself is the hypothesis that accounts for the mood. I may choose to ascribe my elation to love, to the shy caresses of the spring, to the thought of God; if I am "perturbed unto death", I may blame disease, doubt, a faithless one, bad weather, democracy, the machine age, religion. Music alone conveys mood in absolute purity: literature must *explain*.

All this simply deepens the meaning of the word *convincing*. Convincingness is the one test of art. Whether it be a lyric cry, a realistic tale, a fantasy, it must be intelligible if it is to be human. And this inner necessity reduces almost to the vanishing point the share of absolute caprice. We fully agree with Lloyd Morris: "The responsibilities of a novelist towards his material are all but inexorable; the attempt to escape from them, all but disastrous." This is nothing but a re-phrasing of Horace's familiar warning against the *Deus ex machina*. If you juggle with your experiment, if you introduce, surreptitiously or brazenly, a new element out of keeping with the conditions defined by yourself, the result is inartistic. If you solve a psychological tangle by means of an automobile accident, or, as in *The Constant Nymph,* with an irrelevant disease, the reader feels cheated. Several of Molière's endings fall under that condemnation. They do not detract from the value of his plays solely because

346

they are so ingenuously artificial. The great artist tells us: "Here I rest my case: so far as I am concerned, the comedy is over." The actor-manager adds with good-humored contempt: "But as you would not know when to go home, I am going to give you the traditional last scene." It is a notice to put on your wraps and avoid the rush.

A work of fiction is not a proof as mathematicians understand proof, not a document that historians or sociologists can quote as an authority, not a piece of evidence in the eyes of the law: it has nothing to do with the facts that are accomplished, with *dead truth*. But it is an element in deciding upon a future course, *in creating living truth*. Inevitably, that which carries artistic conviction also carries moral conviction.

Fiction serves as experiment, *i.e.* as a substitute for actual experience, as directed experience within a definite field. If a novel presents, cogently, searchingly, the difficulties, the ultimate success or failure of some unequal mating—patrician and plebeian, white and black, Jew and Gentile, youth and eld—we can not help being biassed thereby. Subconsciously perhaps, we shall be urged one way or the other if ever we have to face the same problem in actual life. Every written romance breeds romance, every book filled with the fascination of war brings war a little nearer. I have been deterred from tormenting even the most repulsive animals by Victor Hugo's poem, *The Toad*. The supreme Master taught through parables.

Shall we be told that, in a scientific age, we should be guided, not by hypotheses, but by established facts?

Every decision is a choice between rival hypotheses: the future, hypothetical itself, can be dealt with in no other way. To build or not to build a bridge across the Golden Gate was a very practical problem. But, when we had amassed all available data, the two alternatives were still two pieces of Utopian fiction, two Wellsian *Anticipations,* the one optimistic, the other pessimistic. "Supposing the bridge is built: traffic will be immensely quickened, a splendid area will be opened to the city's overflow, a monument of startling majesty will be added to our treasures."—"Supposing the bridge is built: earthquakes will make it unsafe, ferries will remain cheaper and prevent adequate returns, an enemy could wreck the structure and bottle up our fleet, a unique marvel of nature will be marred for all time." Within the ascertained data, the hypothesis which is the more *convincing* deserves to win. Engineers and realtors have stolen the word *vision* from the poets, just as they have stolen the word *service* from the priests.

III

Fiction, if it moves us at all, is invariably an incentive or a deterrent. We are all Don Quijote and Emma Bovary. He was mad, and she was weak, because they had poor standards of art. They accepted as convincing works that should have been rejected. But even the flimsiest tale weaves itself into our lives.

This is why civilization—the consciousness of collective life—must take cognizance of literature. As a power, therefore as a danger. Censorship is as indispensable to the state as any other form of police; which does not mean that it should be entrusted to the usual police and exercised by the same methods.

When authors claim irresponsibility, and therefore complete freedom, they advance either of two pleas: the scientific or the imaginative. According to the first, their books offer nothing which does not exist in nature: they are not adding to the sum total of evil. The Praying Mantis devours her mate in the very act of union: to know this fact is no crime, not to know it is sheer ignorance.

But literature 'is not science: it does not present the dead facts, dispassionate, dehumanized: it arranges the facts into a living, convincing sequence. Any psychiatrist could tell us far worse facts than Baudelaire: but Baudelaire offers us the "flowers of evil", the fascination of sin, the apology of perversity.

The second plea is that art leaves actual truth behind, exists in a free world of its own, unhampered by contact with practical responsibility. Titania and Ariel laugh at statute books. This was Charles Lamb's apology for the licentiousness of Restoration comedy, and James Branch Cabell's defense *pro domo sua*. But if art does go beyond life, it opens the path for life to follow. The charming aërial puppets that mince and strut in Poictesme evoke in us definite attitudes of mind, which we carry back into the gross world of Lichfield. And Cabell himself tells us, with amusement that has long lost its edge, of all the fair readers who claim to follow the Cabellian gospel, and urge the author to do likewise.

I believe that literature does matter, and therefore I believe in censorship. I most heartily disbelieve in the present methods of censorship. It is entrusted to the wrong men: bureaucrats acting at the behest of bigots. It is chaotic, clumsy and therefore ineffective: its blunders and contradictions form an amusing tale. But for such ineffectiveness let us be duly thankful! A thorough inquisition backed by public opinion could stifle thought for centuries.

Censorship, as we have said, not seldom advertises that which it would suppress. We have seen that to the prosecution of *Jurgen* we owe Cabell as a national figure; and that our college students can not be bribed to read *Ulysses*—tougher than any assignment in the most dismal of sciences—now that it does not have to be bootlegged. It might be wise, sigh the ministers, to place the Old Testament on the *Index Expurgatorius*.

The maladministration of censorship is its only redeeming grace. The real danger is that censorship is invariably reactionary. It defends that morality which, left stranded by the stream of life, has ceased to be moral at all. Censorship is the bulwark of the past: vested interests, abuses, prejudices, superstitions. It was a board of censors that dealt with Socrates and Jesus. As long as censorship means *the right to suppress,* it must remain an incubus.

We need a far more active and potent censorship, an intellectual police with more accurate weapons. And its name is *competent criticism.* If you think a book is urging the wrong thing, do not suppress the book: it would circulate underground, or start a whole crop of books on the same subject. You can not cure a disease by concealing its symptoms. Instead of suppressing, *discuss.* If the book carries false conviction, which makes it spurious art as well as dangerous teaching, expose the fallacy. If you are disgusted with *What Is Wrong With Everything,* try to show *What Is Right With Everything.* If you are tired of everlasting sex books, laugh them off with *Is Sex Necessary?*

Literature is not independent: but it should be autonomous. Just as a scientific fact is amenable only to the laws of science, a literary danger should be met only by literary weapons. To bring Galileo, Darwin or Einstein before a Tennessee jury pushes back the limits of the absurd. To raid a bookstore and burn an edition, even by the authority of the law, is not a civilized method. It is stopping your opponent's mouth with your fist: the argument of the bully. Only a book can censor a book. Whatever is attacked by human thought, and can not be defended by human thought, deserves to fall.

Part IV

To-morrow

Chapter 22

GRAPHOPOLIS: A UTOPIA FOR LITERATURE

PLATO, greatest of poets, banished poets from his Republic. On the other hand, the knights-errant of the Ideal would scorn the ideal State, and the land of dreams is not fit for dreamers. Denounce the ugliness and vulgarity of our age as savagely as you please, and the poets are with you; but any definite scheme of reform will make the artistic temperament shudder. The **poetic** mind is invincibly attached to the picturesque past, and averse to the logical, purposive future. Victor Hugo abominated the metric system as much as Anatole France despised Esperanto; and Sir Hall Caine, worthily expressing the prejudices of his fellow-craftsmen, declared that "Shakespeare's spelling was good enough for him." In our own days, George Moore may be considered as the *beau ideal* of consistent art worshippers, and to his mind, social progress, including universal education, is "not even a beautiful dream." When genuine artists stoop to practical schemes of improvement, they immediately lose caste: Anatole France's *On the White Stone* is dis-

mally Philistine. Utopia is the paradise of the commonplace.*

This opposition between two kinds of prophets—poets
and reformers—is a paradox and a problem. The problem is not so fanciful for our own time and our own
country as it may appear at first. Are we Americans
losing poetic power because we are drawing dangerously
near the dismal coast of Utopia? For in comparison
with nineteenth-century Europe and its marvelous flowering of artistic genius, twentieth-century America is Utopia
indeed. Our cataclysmic industrial progress, our boundless democracy, our universities wide open to the masses,
have outstripped the imaginings of such prophets as
Saint-Simon and Cabet. Prosperity may be in eclipse for
a season as a result of excessive riches, but surely such an
absurd evil is not beyond cure. Rabelais's *Thélème* is
literally fulfilled in a great coeducational institution on
the Pacific Coast. I heard Pastor Russell tell us that the
millennium had begun in 1897; we had merely failed
to realize the fullness of our beatitude. We are already
treading the pavements of the New Jerusalem. It is
hard to conceive a material Utopia as far ahead of our
present civilization as we ourselves are ahead of "the
Man with the Hoe." We may travel much faster to-
morrow; we may add a telephote to our telephone, and
shake hands with distant friends through a teledactyl;
we may even skyrocket to Mars or Venus over the week-
end; in other words, we can make the world infinitely

* *Cf. also* Aldous Huxley: "The Boundaries of Utopia" (*Virginia Quar-
terly,* Jan. 1931; and "The Boundaries of the Promised Land" (*Fortnightly,*
Dec. 1930. J. W. Krutch: "Literature and Utopia" (in *Was Europe a
Success?*, 1934).

smaller and destroy the last vestiges of solitude and privacy. But the actual limits of a material Utopia are within the range of our conception, if not of our attainment. Just as victory over matter is almost within our grasp, we lose all conceit with it. The miracle of radio, as Aldous Huxley remarked, has chiefly served the broadcasting of twaddle. Interstellar communication might very well bring us no nearer spiritual perfection. The conditions vaunted as ideal by the Boosters' Clubs and other disciples of Macaulay seem to produce no Shakespeare; and there are many who wonder whether the same soil and the same climate can be equally favorable to poets and plumbers.

Mr. Stuart Chase has touched upon the problem in his suggestive book *Men and Machines*. But the difficulty does not lie chiefly with mechanical appliances: it lies rather with the mechanical spirit, the spirit of standardization; and that spirit seems inseparable from a normal, harmonious, classical, static, or Utopian world. We might smash all the machines, as they did in Erewhon, and spiritually find ourselves none the richer. Arcadian simplicity may be as tedious and stifling as the zippy atmosphere of Zenith; indeed, Sheila Kaye-Smith has found unplumbed stupidity in unplumbered villages. Here is our dilemma: we do not want brutal and wasteful anarchy, but perfect organization turns society into a soulless machine. Poetry is the eternal protest against the mechanizing trend towards Utopia.

In presence of such a problem three attitudes are possible. The first is, candidly and heartily, to damn art and literature. If they are in any way incompatible with sanity and sanitation, decency, comfort, orderliness, let them go!—a good riddance. Spiritual values which can not be translated into terms of good citizenship have no validity at all. But this opinion is seldom frankly voiced: the rankest utilitarian does lip-service to anti-utilitarian-ism. He has his pew in church, and allows his wife to lionize long-haired virtuosi. Unfortunately perhaps, the thorough-going Benthamite of to-day is dumb, in the original meaning of the term.

This leaves us with two solutions, in both of which the claims of art and those of the social order will be recognized. Strange yoke-fellows, which may shy at each other! We must on no account start with the heretical assumption that art may have a social message: let us be faithful (provisionally) to the sacred doctrine of art for art's sake. But no artist will object if we admit that art is worth while, and that conditions inimical to art are therefore undesirable. Let us, then, ask the artists themselves to write the specifications of their own Utopia. They like neither our present world, nor the world that reformers are attempting to create: what kind of a world do they want? In other terms, what civilization would be most favorable to the creation of art?

The last method of approach would be to admit the feasibility, nay the inevitability, of a materialistic and social Utopia of the standard type. But, instead of taking it for granted, as George Moore does, that all art will of necessity perish in such an atmosphere, we may attempt to forecast what forms of art could possibly survive, and even what new kinds might be evolved. Are we sure that art depends entirely upon ignorance, injustice and chaos? Are irregular verbs alone fit to be used in poetry and love? Let us assume the perfect state so dreaded by poets: could a niche be found for them?

The nearest approximation to an artistic Utopia remains William Morris's *News from Nowhere:* a paradise for house decorators and Roycrofters, a magnified Carmel-by-the-Sea before they put in the drains. The book is still a delight: but it is pretty thoroughly unconvincing. For it is ambiguous in its ideal and in its methods. Purely archaic in spirit, it brushes aside all the conquests of the machine age; yet it admits the services of a mysterious "Power" which is the ultimate triumph of science and industry. Then Morris was a professed Socialist as well as an artist: the pure note of the poet comes perilously near the propagandist's falsetto.

André Maurois offers a strictly literary Utopia in his fantastic trifle, *Voyage to the Island of the Articoles.* But the intention is too evidently satirical, not constructive. And the target of his satire is neither art nor society—only the well-known foibles of professional men of letters. For our purpose, this charming pamphlet is of no avail. A Utopia for Writers is by no means the same thing as a Utopia for Literature; just as a Utopia for Lawyers would not be a Utopia for Law; just as a clerical Utopia would be very different from a religious one. Utopia, for the special class, means privilege: a Utopia for singers is a state in which singers are rare, precious and treasured. Utopia for an ideal means on the contrary its universal diffusion.

All Utopias are retrospective as well as prospective;

their Golden Age is made up of elements borrowed from the past. We shall follow the same method in describing, without irony, the civilization of *our* Articoles. We shall take into account the lessons of history as well as the desires of men. We shall apply our familiar instrument, the theory of Taine: art is determined by race, environment and time. If this rule be true, it ought to be reversible: in order to secure the kind of art we want, what social conditions are necessary? This question resolves itself into the historical problem: under what conditions has the art we admire been produced in the past?

It is evident that in such a complex product, no single factor is absolutely indispensable. An unfavorable climate for instance, may be offset by an abundance of natural resources. It is evident also that, if our prescriptions were taken too literally, they would sound like a satire of Taine's ideas and of the whole sociological method in artistic criticism. With these words of warning, we may embark for Graphopolis, in the Land of the Articoles.

Graphopolis lies in the temperate zone. The tropics have failed so far to produce a literature that would rank supreme: yet they have natural wealth, beauty, a teeming population. The arctic regions can boast of Iceland, which, in proportion to its numbers, took a high place among centers of poetry; but we are safe in assuming that the mean temperature of Graphopolis is decidely higher than that of Rejkjavik. There are sharply contrasted seasons—an almost torrid summer, a mellow golden autumn, a glorious winter of hard frost and snow, followed by the yearly miracle of the spring: how much poorer would poetry be in a land without April! Scotland is not barred out as the possible seat of our Utopia: a surly clime drives you to the fireplace and books—or to the radiator and poker. Too ideal a climate might be a handicap: I would not endorse the claims of San Diego, where they play the organ outdoors every day in the year, or those of Yuma, Arizona, where they offer you a free lunch every day the sun does not shine.

The country round Graphopolis is a varied land of mountains and vales, with a rugged, deeply indented coast. Mountains alone will not necessarily evolve great art: watches, cheese and hotels, not the poems of Carl Spitteler, are the chief products of Switzerland. At sea level or below, the Dutch and the Venetians have created great schools of painting: they are less prominent as writers— perhaps for the lack of Parnassian heights to scale. Moderate cliffs and crags will do, as in England, Scotland or Attic Greece; even the molehills of Rome, Florence and Paris may suffice. But the devastating platitude of Russia and of our Middle West is an obstacle to be overcome: Russia had no great literature until the nineteenth century. We once tried to induce a millionaire to give Houston, Texas, an artificial hill, in the hope of making that friendly city the Athens of the southwest. Cathedral Heights and the Palisades will serve the purpose for New York, and Twin Peaks for San Francisco; but for Chicago there is little hope.

Graphopolis is watered by a noble river, which in olden times was worshipped as a god. Poets find inspiration in the thundering falls above the city; in the swift-

flowing stream, which they liken to human destiny, and
which grows sluggish before it merges with the measure-
less sea; in the somber fury of the turbid floods in early
winter or spring. It is also convenient for a watery grave:
romantic Paris needs the Morgue. The banks of the Chicago drainage canal rather discourage lyrical effusion.
The Los Angeles river, so far as we know, has not yet
become famous in song; yet it is not much worse than the
classic Ilissos. Although the land is well watered, it would
be advisable to have a small desert at hand: here Los Angeles scores a definite point. But Los Angeles, wasteful of
artistic possibilities, is reclaiming its desert—as short-
sighted as the fabled Auvergnats, who, blessed with the
possession of a volcano, carelessly allowed it to become
extinct.

Graphopolis is not a vast empire. A huge country is
slow-witted. Whether it lives under a tyranny, or enjoys
the alleged benefits of democracy, it is inclined to think
in masses, crudely. How much more favorable is the city-
state, Athens or Florence, or the tiny principality, like
Weimar! A ruler has a ruler's psychology, whether he
rule a thousand men or a hundred million; Dante was
as truly an ambassador as Paul Claudel; a court is a court,
even though it be that of the Hawaiian Islands or that
of Emperor Soulouque. And patriotism, in the city-state,
is concentrated, vivid, all-pervading, not a dull thing of
hearsay and statistics. Party politics assume the dramatic intensity of family feuds. The city wall is infinitely
more real than the arbitrary frontier. The artists in Montmartre once proclaimed the secession of the sacred mound
from the deplorably *bourgeois* French Republic; and

they were well advised. In Chesterton's fantasy, the Napoleon of Notting Hill reconstitutes a colorful world on a purely local basis. The original Napoleon owed his greatness to his Corsican cradle. Culturally, vast entities are barren. The formula of the future is communalism as in 1871—a world federation of independent cities.

What kind of community is Graphopolis—pastoral, agricultural, commercial, industrial? Pastoral life has given life to a huge body of literature. In so far as herding is a lazy life, it favors dreaming, the prerequisite of all artistic expression; but it favors even more the vague musing which is so characteristic of contented cows. Pastoral poetry is mostly the work of city dwellers, and remains exceedingly conventional: Theocritus and Vergil are not much more convincing than eighteenth-century shepherdesses. Pasture land, like the desert, should be kept as a minor background; as the very center of the literary scene, it would prove disappointing.

Agriculture is far less favorable to artistic expression than cattle or sheep ranching; it is too busy a life, a life of constant, absorbing, benumbing care. So, in our modern folklore, the cowboy is the hero, the hayseed the butt of ridicule. Yes, Burns did sing in his furrow, and cast a word of Franciscan sympathy to the "wee, sleekit, tim'rous, cowerin' beastie", whose housie he had laid in ruins. But how many Burnses are there on the roll of fame? France was long a land of peasants, but only the city birds were vocal. The fields are needed for material sustenance and spiritual refreshment, but the artistic power of Graphopolis, like the political, is concentrated in the city. "Urbanity", "civilization", imply the *urbs* and the *civitas*.

Graphopolis is therefore a mart and a workshop, a place wherein the wits of men are sharpened by constant fencing. But Graphopolis is no mere country town, the all-sufficient center of its own rural district. Such a condition would lead to parochialism and intellectural atrophy. Graphopolis is a commercial power, sending caravans and argosies to the farthest ends of the world. Preferably, it is a *thalassocracy,* like Athens, Venice, the Hanseatic League, Holland, Scandinavia, or Portugal at the time of her literary glory. Overseas trade is of commanding cultural importance, for it brings wealth, leisure and luxury, broadens the horizons, fosters the spirit of adventure. So to the wharves of Graphopolis cluster ships of all nations, spice-laden, freighted with dreams, even when they carry nitrates, hides or guano. To Anatole France, who accused her of lacking imagery, the philosophical poetess Madame Ackermann triumphantly replied: "No imagery? Have I not THE SHIP?" A complete bard is as inconceivable without the ship as without the spring.

Many arts and crafts are plied in Graphopolis: for artisans are creators of beauty, and may sing at their work. But the country is not predominantly industrial. It is somewhat premature to condemn industry as artistically barren. Industry is a very young giantess, barely out of an ailing infancy and of a sprawling, brawling, sulky, quarrelsome childhood. So far it has made for ugliness, hardly mitigated with evidences of power. We are told that a new beauty can already be descried under the grime; but it takes very optimistic eyes to see it. Industry, as distinct from the crafts, means mass production. The maker loses his individuality: freshness, creative power, spontaneity, are ruled out of his life; and all originality is likewise eliminated from the product. Witness the short stories turned out to-day by our most approved literary factories.

It is commercial England, seafaring England, with the sturdy background of rural England, that has made England's name glorious in art and letters. It was in its commercial, not in its industrial, days, that New England was a power of the spirit. New York's intellectual supremacy has a mercantile rather than a manufacturing basis. Let us admit, then, that Graphopolis is poor in coal and iron, so that she will not be tempted to turn into Pittsburgh or Birmingham.

The crowds of Graphopolis are at home in the streets of their city; they do not rush feverishly, but they can afford to saunter and loiter. They stop for a friendly chat, they gaze at the evanescent and delightful art of window display, they have time to admire a marble statue in a public square; and, no less frankly, they feast their eyes on those living statues for whom the country is famous. They listen to some orator, poet or musician at the crossroads; they sip the ambrosia of the land at little tables set on the very sidewalks, under the trees.

There is great variety among the types you meet in Graphopolis. A few dashes of color are noticeable— ebony black, brown, red and yellow, with many shades which demonstrate that no race prejudice prevails. But these picturesque notes are the exception: the enormous majority of the inhabitants belong, broadly, to the same race; and that race, needless to say, is our own. Asia and Africa each have their Graphopolis, friendly and independent.

The coexistence in any large number of widely different breeds creates such harrowing problems that no Utopia could settle them or survive them. Almost inevitably, pride, oppression, jealousy, resentment would spring up. One race, in all probability, would isolate itself in splendid conceit and quasi-mystic snobbishness, thus stunting its own intellectual growth and mutilating its human sympathies: a superior caste is never more than the pitiful fragment of what it might have been. Yet we might conceive of conditions similar to those which prevail in Hawaii, where stocks from all parts of the world mingle with almost complete freedom. The literary results of miscegenation in Alexander Dumas and Burghardt Du Bois are decidedly encouraging. Perhaps in Graphopolis eugenics will have reached such a point that various bloods can be exactly dosed for the procreation of a great dramatist, a lyric poet, a sculptor, or an inspired cook; while race mixture would be sternly prohibited when the result is likely to be a synthetic-syndicated humorist.

Graphopolitans, as we visualize them, are white. But they are not all blonds. Complexions may be olive, amber, magnolia, ruddy and even pinkish; only the chalky pallor induced by artificial means will be under the ban. Hairs may range from Venetian red to raven black, through all the tints of bronze and gold: sonneteers would not be happy without dark ladies as well as ladies fair. Stature may be *petite* or impressively tall; figures slender or majestically rotund: we could not think of banishing G. K. Chesterton. On the whole, there may be a slight predominance of the Mediterranean type; but Nordics will not feel out of their element. Alpines specialize in plodding research and dismal realism: we have Mrs. Gertrude Atherton's word for it, and she has it on the authority of Madison Grant, who had it from Houston Stewart Chamberlain, who had it from Gobineau, who had it from God himself: so the chain of evidence is perfect. Alpines will have their modest place in the general scheme; but no book of poems will be allowed to appear if the author's cephalic index is above eighty. This simple rule will avert many literary calamities.

These people speak a sonorous, highly inflected, strongly accented language, full of idioms, allusive phrases, veiled metaphors, quaint survivals and delightful absurdities. They love it so that they revel in playing with it: they are great punsters, and they are constantly coining new words, logical or fanciful, pregnant with thought or merely musical. They rejoice in the possession of many dialects and forms of slang, closely related enough to remain mutually intelligible, but different enough to give a racier tang to any man's speech. Purism and standardization are frowned upon as inartistic: teachers in elementary schools strive to release the latent originality of their students in matters of spelling and syntax. The Graphopolitans, like the Greeks and like Shakespeare, are not vitally interested in the speech of other nations: they have too rich a fund of their own. They realize, further, that polyglottism is not conducive to literary excellence: neither university professors, nor *concierges* in cosmopolitan hotels rank very high as creative artists. A simple, practical, artificial language is used for business, for scientific purposes, for international relations, and even for those branches of literature in which logical thought is of more importance than form. The literary tongue is held too sacred for such commonplace or utilitarian services.

In politics as well as in religion, Graphopolis is pluralistic, or, in simpler parlance, tolerant. A goodly proportion of the population owe allegiance (including a very light contribution towards the upkeep of the court) to King Wenceslaus XI, who is known as a good sport, and represents the gorgeous tradition of a thousand years. His annual procession through the streets of the city on the fifth of November is a magnificent pageant. Others pay tribute to Emperor Tamburlaine XXIII, a mild little scholar who, by immemorial custom, never moves without an escort of wild horsemen. Still others do homage to Queen Cleopatra XLV, the winner of a beauty contest; and not a few join the strict, austere organization known as the Anarchistic Brotherhood. It makes little difference, as the mere business of the State is transacted by managers, mostly Alpines, independent of king, queen, emperor, or grand Anarch.

The managerial State lives at peace with all its neighbors; but the king and the emperor occasionally wage war against each other or against foreign foes. The populace looks forward to these contests with the keenest delight. The ringing challenges, the Pindaric poems and battle hymns, the enthusiastic meetings or rallies on the eve of the strife, the departure of the gaily-clad heroes for the Field of Glory, add enormously to the enjoyment of life. Pacifists who would suppress that supreme form of entertainment are summarily condemned, by such authorities as Elie Faure, as the enemies of art and poetry. The Field of Glory is a large and wild tract reserved for that purpose within convenient distance of Graphopolis; from neighboring hills, and from specially built towers, the whole population can follow the magnificent spectacle. The return of the conquering host, laurel-wreathed, with a golden nimbus in the sunset fire, is a sight never to be forgotten; but connoisseurs aver that a defeated army, slinking in, ghost-like, in the dead of the night, produces a subtler and more profound effect.

In religion, all creeds are welcome, except scientific determinism, which spells artistic death. Graphopolitans are good pragmatists: all faiths are valid if they *work*— that is to say if they enhance the enjoyment of beauty. Hellenism, Hebraism and Christianity alternate in popular favor, and at times blend rather prettily. Some artists claim that without Paganism there can be no salvation, and they are seen devoutly prostrate in the fanes of Aphrodite. But it is usually conceded that Christianity offers a more dramatic setting for human destiny, and casts a richer glow round the mysteries of birth and death. The notion of sin, in particular, is considered as a marvelous, an inexhaustible artistic device. Frankly acknowledging the services of æsthetes to the true faith, the Graphopolitan Church has beatified Baudelaire and James Branch Cabell. We need hardly say that a notable number of Graphopolitans are orthodox devil-worshippers.

There are classes, although there are no castes, in Graphopolis: several aristocracies, several clergies, a vast *bourgeoisie* with many subdivisions, and tiers upon tiers of "masses." These classes are definite enough: a man knows without a doubt whether he belongs to the upper middle class or the lower nobility; but interpenetration is not absolutely barred. The classes are in constant rivalry, and even in conflict, but not at war. A system of airtight compartments between the social ranks would be detrimental to culture; but the total abolition of class distinction, if it were possible, would be even more deadly. For art as such thrives only on a class basis: whatever is universally enjoyed ceases to exist for the genuine æsthete, and "popular" literature is a fallacy. The creation and appreciation of art are essentially methods of securing admission among an élite.

The Graphopolitan social scale is established on the basis of literary taste—from the highest aristocracy who, in the nursery, read James Joyce's latest, to the lower middle class, who can barely rise to the level of *The Little Minister*. The chief interest in Graphopolitan life is the breathless attempt of each class to catch up with the one immediately above. As soon as an élite is overtaken, it ceases to be an élite, and its proud place is assumed by another group, which, in its turn, will strain every nerve to keep ahead in the chase. It is the national game. Fads, cults, shibboleths may be resorted to in order to baffle pursuers. But it is considered poor sportsmanship to take refuge in total incomprehensibility: it is as bad as shooting the fox, which, to the British, is the sin against the Holy Ghost.

Artists enjoy the picturesqueness and dramatic possibilities of the social ladder, with clusters of men fighting for a precarious foothold at every rung. Poets move up and down at will: they associate with kings or beggars, and consciously relish the paradox of both situations. Each class has a traditional costume, a code of ethics, a manner of speech of its own, which are carefully preserved *in fiction*. In real life every one is aiming to imitate the oddities of some other class, above or even below, and the result is delightfully confusing.

There are marriage laws in Utopia, and they are extremely strict. Without them, half of the world's tragedies, and four fifths of its comedies, would cease to exist. These laws are part of the indispensable conventions of dramatic or narrative art. Judging by the precedent of the most purely *artistic* civilization that ever bloomed, that of the Troubadours, we may surmise that in Graphopolis poets will love with special ardor every wife not their own. The honor of the Graphopolitan husband will be satisfied if the verses inspired by his wife are of sufficient merit: G. B. Shaw gave us an adumbration of such a state in his skit *How he lied to her Husband*. For worthless poetry the only redress is an exchange of visiting cards, seconds, and bullets. For a woman to be sung by three bad poets in succession gives the husband sufficient ground for divorce without alimony. A chivalrous custom provides that the woman should have the first chance of using a love affair for literary purposes: the man's version can appear only six months later. A quaint statute, honored mostly in the breach, prohibits addressing the same intimate poems to more than five lovers.

What think you of such a world: Cabell, Valle Inclán, d'Annunzio, exquisite company of exiled prophetic Graphopolitans? Would you find in it enough color, chivalry, adventure, and that tang of sorrow which makes life doubly sweet? Or will you spurn a world visibly made to your order, because it would rob you of the divine discontent and the transcendental scorn which mark you as poets?

Chapter 23

LITERATURE IN UTOPIA

FOR literature such as we now enjoy it, Utopia would be a lethal chamber. Our art needs inequalities, contrasts, catastrophes, reactionary yearnings, millennial hopes, abysmal despairs, the subtly pungent odor of decay, and mystic premonitions of a far-off spring: a gloriously imperfect, capricious, almost chaotic world. With peace, with order, with justice, there would spread over the earth the pall of uniformity, mother of *taedium* and herald of spiritual death.

Needless to say that such a contingency is infinitely remote, like the cooling off of the sun. At any rate, it lies farther beyond the range of practical consideration than the exhaustion of our coal supply. Be not dismayed: for untold generations there will be enough misery and madness among men to keep poetical fires burning. When the more obvious ills are cured, more refined ones will come to light: there is ever a new peak of discontent to be climbed. So long as there is maladjustment, dissatisfaction, desire, we have not fully entered upon our Utopian heritage, and poets will have their say.

Still, we should not entertain too blind a faith in the perpetuity of human wrongs. They might fail us at any moment. The acceleration of human progress is such that the millennium might burst upon us with catastrophic suddenness. The extinction of desire might come in lieu of satisfaction, and produce the same benumbing effect. In the happy Coolidgian Age, "kickers" and "knockers" were sternly discouraged: in a world further advanced towards Utopia, discontent of any kind might be considered as the most heinous social sin. The apostles thereof would be eliminated as undesirable. Euthanasia would weed them out; eugenics would see to it that the breed remain extinct. In Utopia only those loyal and law-abiding citizens will be allowed to live whose social instincts are in perfect harmony with the organization of the State. In the Conformist's paradise, life will become purely automatic, hope disappearing along with fear.

It may be objected that literature is not merely the mirror of contemporary life. True: a Utopian world might enjoy vicariously, through art, the wickedness and distress of our age, just as the epic grandeur of the Napoleonic era was enjoyed by the peace-loving subjects of Louis-Philippe, the aristocratic calm of the Augustans by a busy plebeian public, the naïve faith of the Middle Ages by the sophisticates of the Post-Voltairian era. But if literature thus became purely retrospective, it would inevitably lose its vitality. Great art can not subsist on ghosts and make-believe. A hundred years ago, our ancestors enjoyed, romantically, knights, bandits and pirates: to-day these charming characters belong chiefly

374

to very juvenile fiction; grown-ups greet them with a smile which is wistful, but also half contemptuous.

Literature in historical setting has not completely lost its appeal, because the problems of the past are still essentially our problems. On a different scale, with different weapons, with different battle cries, the world of ten centuries ago was a world of struggle, very much like our own. In less picturesque garb, bandits, pirates and knights are still with us. But Utopian society will be vexed by none of our cares, and therefore will be thrilled by none of our interests.

When told that the people had no bread, Marie Antoinette (so runs the legend) ingenuously exclaimed: "Why don't they eat *brioches?*" She was living in an artificial Utopia, had no experience of actual suffering, and her imagination could not stretch across the chasm. Our descendants will evince the unwitting callousness of Marie Antoinette. We can not actually re-create a vanished world: we can only deck ourselves in the trappings of the past, as for a masquerade, or project our living sentiments on a picturesque antiquarian background. A literature based on the problems of a bygone age will first become superficially romantic, then purely conventional, and ultimately meaningless. This process is taking place under our eyes. The theme of the long-lost child, which delighted antiquity, the Middle Ages, and even classical Europe, has sunk to the level of cheapest melodrama. Military prowess, exploration, even the conquest of wealth and power, will go the same way: all such subjects will seem absurd when men are assigned their function in the commonwealth as the result of blood tests and skull measurements. Many of our students to-day can not understand why the Victorians made such a fuss over the loss of their orthodoxy; a book like Froude's *Nemesis of Faith* now belongs to history, not to living literature, and even the irony of Rose Macaulay in *Told by an Idiot* is too retrospective to be fully enjoyed. The problems of to-day will cast their shadows for centuries to come, just as we are still vexing our souls in this twentieth century over issues which properly belong to the Middle Ages; but the shadow will ultimately melt away altogether. The literature of Utopia will have to be founded on the problems of Utopia. If there be no problems, there will be no literature.

Utopian conditions, however, do not spell the death of *literature,* but only of a literature based upon physical adventures, contrast, surprise. In other words, they might imply simply the downfall of a superficially dramatic, or melodramatic, conception of art. In a world thoroughly conscious, organized and stabilized, the romance of accident, sudden rise, violent collapse, will cease to be significant, and therefore will cease to be interesting. Even *Œdipus Rex* might be discarded on that score. But the result would be refinement rather than barrenness: the trim garden would take the place of the wilderness. A great loss! I do not know: there is beauty in Versailles. The fear of sudden death, no doubt, gives great zest to life; at every moment you rejoice that you have been spared yet a little while; perfect security would destroy that thrill, which makes the mere fact of existence a boon. But the man who has no pestilence and no murderer to dread need not perish of boredom. He will have time to live, instead of merely begging for life. His ordered life will confess the beauty of the world's peace.

We might anticipate that, in this quieter and more spacious existence, our Utopian would have leisure for art as an exquisite luxury. Even though art should lose all deeper significance, it might retain its price as gratuitous activity, as play pure and simple. Only in Utopia is it possible for art to exist solely for art's sake. Under the present dispensation some purpose will almost inevitably be injected: even George Moore was proud that a home for unwed mothers was named after his *Esther Waters*. There is no artist who does not denounce or extoll, no artist who does not preach: the most disinterested can not refrain from denouncing the Philistines and preaching the cult of Beauty. The art that will disappear with the sordid or tragic chaos of our society is only an art of propaganda; and surely George Moore, H. L. Mencken or James Branch Cabell should be the last to plead for its retention. O bliss! In Utopia there will be no causes to serve.

No doubt literature would tend to be static in a static world. Will the thought be quite so appalling if we substitute "permanent" for "static"? What do the Classicists, and the Neo-Classicists, and most of all our Neo-Neo-Classicists, stand for except enduring values and unchangeable laws? Writers in Utopia will not be worse off than La Bruyère, who opened his book with the words: "All has been said, and there remains nothing to be said, after six thousand years of human thought." Originality of theme has absolutely nothing to do with literary merit. As Pascal remarked, although two players are using the same tennis ball, one of them places it better. Merely as a game, the combinations of words are infinitely more inexhaustible than those of chessmen.

Such a formal conception of art would lead to the worship of technique and total indifference as to subject matter. In Utopia a poet might be a prince among his peers for having brought together two unexpected epithets applied to a saucepan. In the past such conditions have invariably denoted decadence. The last poets of the Middle Ages rejoiced in metrical acrobatics, just as the last schoolmen were noted for tight rope walking over a logical abyss. The last defenders of Classicism at the end of the eighteenth century could describe the most commonplace object or happening in smoothest and most elegant verse, and managed to be perfectly definite without ever calling a thing by its rude proper name. Banville, beloved and revered by Swinburne, was the star juggler and tumbler of late Romanticism; and Jean Giraudoux among the living can give the tritest thought such unexpected piquancy that he almost deserves to live in Utopia. If all "purpose" could be banished, and form alone be sovereign, then the kingdom of Pure Poetry desired by George Moore and Henri Bremond would be at hand.

As nothing happens in Utopia, literature, after a transition period, will cease to deal with deeds, and will become entirely introspective. Long after the physical universe has been reduced to order, the heart will remain unruly and the mind mysterious. So "landscapes of the soul" and "climates of feeling" will take the place of our coarse and obvious material descriptions. Violent

378

passions, being anti-social, will long have been trained out of human nature: shades of likes and dislikes, the ghost of jealousy, the gleam of a scruple, a flicker of remorse, will be examined under a high-power microscope. Not a murder case, but the faint velleity toward the use of an expletive, may be a fair subject for a novelist of the year 3000. The psychological fiction of the French may give us an adumbration of what we have a right to expect in Utopia. Racine's tragedy *Bérénice* is a sigh in sixteen hundred lines; Marivaux "weighed airy trifles in scales made of gossamer"; Proust rediscovered his whole sensitive childhood in a bite of *madeleine* dipped in a cup of tea; and the analyst of to-morrow will out-Proust Marcel Proust as decisively as Proust himself went beyond Marie Corelli.

To our untutored taste Utopian literature would probably seem morbidly sentimental and absurdly finicky: every feeling would be isolated, magnified, placed under various lights, submitted to endless reagents, so as to be studied and enjoyed with absolute fullness. Similarly, a Texas rancher, used to guessing at a glance the weight of a live steer, would scorn the meticulous methods of the physicist, who measures a fraction of a milligramme under truly scientific conditions. The cowboy may have more native genius; but modern civilization pins its faith to the methods of the laboratory.

The possibilities of psychological romance in Utopia are unfathomable. We may take it for granted that the more obvious sentiments will have ceased to exist as fit subjects for literature: perhaps they will have ceased to exist altogether. But then we shall reach from the conscious, too clearly mapped out, into the subconscious and the unconscious. A psychological drama will take place on many planes; each new depth explored will reveal another depth still unplumbed. We could conceive of a stirring piece dealing with the obscure struggle between two embryonic thoughts, in the inmost recesses of a man's soul. The climax would be reached when the victorious idea rises to the threshold of consciousness. It might be that in the process the rivals should get inextricably entangled: the emergent thought, bearing the name of the one, would borrow most of its substance from the other: for Fate will not cease to be ironical in Utopia. The subconscious preparation of a Fundamentalist sermon implies a whole epic of spiritual warfare, more fascinating than Napoleon's titanic blundering in his Russian campaign. Our descendants will not starve for lack of fun.

If psychological training should progress in such a way as to make mind reading a common achievement and telepathy a possibility, then new problems and new techniques will open before the fictionist. Man evolved speech so as to conceal his thought: what is going to happen when that coarse mask is torn aside? The difficulty will be to *think* in such a way as to preserve inviolate the privacy of one's ultimate self. Certain thoughts will be used as smoke screens or camouflage for other thoughts. O'Neill and Pirandello are already attempting such dramas of the dark within; but their method of symbolical presentation is still crudely primitive. In order fully to fathom a novel or play of the thirtieth century, the reader will have to combine the acumen of Bergson,

Einstein and Paul Valéry. We may imagine the smile of the Utopians if they were to unearth the sophomoric subtleties of Henry James or Marcel Proust.

As Utopia reaches its perfection, even psychology may cease to offer entrancing mysteries. Not that there will ever be a lack of inner worlds to conquer: but the urge to discovery might become atrophied through premature self-satisfaction. When psychology has thus attained the definiteness and rigidity of a mechanism, it will be dead— that is to say, it will have become a full-fledged science at last. And the artists of the thirty-second or thirty-fourth centuries will feel anxious again about the future of their craft.

Idle fears once more! Long before we are seriously concerned about the exhaustion of certain sources of power, such as coal, other sources are discovered or re-discovered, such as waterfalls, the winds, the waves, the tides, the sun's rays: to-morrow we may release and harness atomic energy. Literature may face the future with like confidence. If the human mind should ever become scientifically known in its inner workings, in its relations with other minds and with the physical universe, there would still remain the boundless field of Metaphysics.

Metaphysics is to be found, evanescent or in solid nuclei, through many poetical masterpieces of the past; but it was blended with melodrama and psychology, with mere adventure and with human personalities. Now such a mixture denotes a primitive state of culture. A chemist to-day would laugh at the idea of translating the formula H_2O into a poetical masque, the courtship

of the nymph Hydrogen by the swain Oxygen: science
is direct and stark. Philosophy also may be stripped of
ornaments which are little better than puerile. The
Divine Comedy and *Faust* are grand metaphysical epics:
in an adult world, the puppet show element in Goethe's
masterpiece, the lurid popular imagery in Dante's, would
disappear altogether, like dross under an acid. The metaphysical would survive unalloyed. Could it be enjoyed
in such a form? Yes, by readers with proper gifts and
training. It is hard for a layman to realize that certain
musicians can *read* a symphony silently and derive profound enjoyment from it; that a great mathematician
can *read* pages of formulæ with perfect understanding
and intense delight. In the Utopian world, Spinoza and
Hegel will be considered, as they ought to have been
from the first, as poets, "cloud-weavers of phantasmal
hopes and fears." The destiny of the *thing-in-itself* will
thrill our great-grandchildren as keenly as the matrimonial tangles of Arthur and Evelina thrill us to-day.

The Utopian mind, after reaching the ultimate confines of its domain, might, however, refuse to venture
into metaphysics at all. What if Metaphysics were, not
the Unknown, but simply the Impalpable Inane? To
plunge into its void would be sheer suicide. "The Science of the Unknowable" is little better than an absurdity, and Herbert Spencer knew it well. This condemnation of metaphysics, if it were accepted, would
leave Mysticism unscathed. For, at all stages of human
development, there will be a feeling that cosmic life is
greater than organized science; and intuition, in the
thirtieth century, will take its flight no less boldly than

382

in the twentieth. Its expression will not be so crudely anthropomorphic: but it can never be fully scientific either. A surmise, a revelation, can only be indicated in symbolical terms. There always will be a touch of wildness in the affirmations of the mystics; for any adventure beyond the norm of experience is by definition *unsafe* and *in-sane*. The marginal ground, the debatable borderland between accepted reality and reality still in the making, will ever be the realm of dreams and fancies, intuitions and visions, and will never cease bearing poetical fruit. This as long as we see only as through a glass darkly, as long as we do not know even as we are known.

This leads us to the Supreme Utopia, when all veils are removed, and we contemplate the splendor of truth face to face: what are the possibilities of literature in heaven? According to the most approved authorities on the subject, the sole poetical *genre* to survive will be an eternal hymn of praise. Without challenging these authorities, we have a right to wonder whether their lyrical paradise be the very last stage. For the separation between Creator and creatures, implied in such a ritual, means limitation, incompleteness, and therefore longing, and therefore sorrow. Perfect bliss is inconceivable until the lost are all redeemed, and all individuals are absorbed again into the One. Then the song of praise itself will be stilled, and the absolute silence of Nirvana will prevail throughout eternity. At this extreme limit Utopia does indeed necessitate the complete extinction of all literature.

But not until then.

Let us wake up. What is the sense of all this nonsense?
Believe it or not, O practical Anglo-Saxon reader, there
is some sense to it; and since you challenge me to draw
explicitly the moral lessons of my apologue, here they
are, duly tabulated:

I. The hostility of the alleged artistic soul to industrial
and social progress is based on a fallacy. Chaos, injustice,
greed and suffering are not essential to poetry. The opposition of æsthetes to such causes as pacificism, simpli-
fied spelling, a reformed calendar, an international language, world organization, a planned economy, is
founded on a crude conception of art. Art under Utopia
will simply be more disinterested and more refined than
it is at present. Material standardization need not hurt
the soul. It simply enables us to waste less time and
thought on worldly goods, thus releasing the spirit. What
if we should all wear the same brand of clothes and
drive the same kind of automobiles? Our remote ancestors had "standardized" on nakedness and pedestrian
transportation.

II. It is not so idle as it may seem to follow as we have
done, in free yet logical fancy, certain tendencies of the
present. Some aspects of psychological literature, for instance, might easily be considered as sheer eccentricities.
O'Neill, Pirandello, Proust, Joyce, "got away with it",
at least for a season. But, for their own good and ours,
should they not remain unique? Is their art a picturesque
blind alley? Or is it destined to broaden into a main
avenue? It has been our purpose to show that, as the
gates of physical adventure were closing, our best chance
lay in the direction of an ever more searching psychology.

384

There are posers and morons among the cryptic writers of to-day; but there are men also who are pathfinders, blazers of trails, and not mere oddities.

III. The great danger which menaces all Utopias is not achievement, but stagnation. This danger is with us to-day: for stagnation is the price we have to pay for complacency. If we persuade ourselves that our Constitution, our economic régime, our religious creeds, our morals, are fundamentally and unchangeably right, then we shall have reached at a single bound Utopia in all its horror—a Utopia of conformity and dullness, worse than any cycle of Cathay. Tennyson's mid-Victorian wisdom remains true three generations later:

> And God fulfills Himself in many ways,
> Lest one good custom should corrupt the world.

It is for poets to discover new ways in which God may fulfill Himself. The Utopia just ahead, the dream born of Protest, will save us from the slough of self-satisfaction. So long as we are made to realize that this is not God's own country, there will be some hope of salvation.

Chapter 24

THE PROSPECT FOR AMERICAN LITERATURE

I

WHILE protesting as vigorously as we could against the literary jingo, we protested no less vigorously against the literary expatriate. Literature and civilization can not be divorced: the American background affects us at every turn. It is normal that we should be most interested in the life of our own country; and the natural conclusion of our survey is: "What is the bearing of all this upon American literature?"

There is another reason why we should attempt to translate our theories into strictly American terms: it is the severest test to which they could be submitted. No general idea should shrink from the plain question: "For instance?" And the more immediate our knowledge, the more definite our challenge. Rousseau started his sketch of human evolution with the liberating words: "First of all, let us brush aside the facts!" And if Taine chose English literature for the demonstration of his doctrine, it was partly because he and his readers knew it far less thoroughly than French literature. This should be a warning; we have little use for a truth which can not thrive in our home atmosphere.

"We Anglo-Saxons" (if I may quote the colored sergeant again) are not so fond of finespun theories as Taine was. But there is one case in which we appeal to "race, environment and time" very freely: as an alibi for our alleged inferiority in literature. An adopted son, I might hesitate to mention the subject. But there is no secret about it: it has become part of the American tradition.

Self-depreciation is not strictly an American fault: we have fully discovered the tonic effect of self-confidence and the educative value of boosting. We take legitimate pride in our natural resources, our enterprise, our athletic records, our wealth and health, our power of organization, our general smartness. There are only two points about which we are positively humble: diplomacy and literature. We take it for granted that we can not deal with other governments without being invariably duped—a delusion which would be amusing if it were not so dangerous: it has retarded the recovery of the world by at least a decade. And we are also persuaded that we can not beat the foreigners at the literary game. Even the apostles of American literature suffer from the same inferiority complex. The Great American Masterpiece which they herald is, like Prosperity, always lurking just round the corner. It has not come yet, because. . . . In both cases, our humble mindedness is an inverted form of pride. We are too frank and open to have our Metternichs and our Talleyrands. And we are too sensible, too practical, too manly, to take literature very seriously, like those effete Europeans.

The rest of the world, pardonably, accepts our own

verdict. If we, the most indomitable of optimists and the most efficient of advertisers, acknowledge and blazon forth our own defeat, Europe will be too courteous to contradict us. There is no inborn dislike abroad for American things: our films and our cocktails are still in great favor. But there are far fewer American books successful in Europe than European books popular on this side. While we gather Olympic palms by the armful, we lag behind minor countries among the contenders for the Nobel Prize in Literature. And our single successful champion won with a vigorous caricature of Americanism: we are still wondering whether the honor was a compliment.

Naturally, when Europeans take us at our word, we bristle up and curse their insolence. We are like Cyrano: we may freely indulge in pitiless quips about our noses, but we do not permit an outsider even to raise his eyebrow. Forty years ago, the French were loudly proclaiming—to themselves—their own decadence: but they were chagrined and indignant when the rest of the world echoed their self-criticism. It was William II himself who compared German "frightfulness" with the scourge of the Huns: but no one outside Germany was allowed to take him seriously. We alone have the right to call our brother: "Thou boob." Non-Americans are therefore requested to skip this chapter altogether.

"What is the matter with us?" There is no fault to find with our *race,* since we have not any; nor with our *climate,* since we have all kinds, mostly exceptional. The first alibi is our youth, which Oscar Wilde aptly called our oldest tradition. We are the direct heirs of

European civilization, and the Declaration of Independence did not break the chain. The Bible and Shakespeare are ours as much as they are England's. As a matter of fact, we seldom realize that we are to-day *the oldest nation in the world*. The American mind came to consciousness in the second half of the eighteenth century, and, theoretically at least, it has not altered. Materially, we have ploughed virgin soil; but our thinking is scrupulously that of the Fathers. In the last hundred and fifty years, England has been recast a couple of times; so have Italy, France, Germany. Russia, Turkey, India, China are lusty infants, rather unruly and untidy as infants are apt to be. America, in contrast, has the bland composure, the serene self-satisfaction, of a Gilbert ancestral portrait.

Our second handicap is the lack of a national language. Until we have a vernacular, we shall obscurely feel ourselves mere "colonials" and satellites. The desire for a speech of one's own is universal among nations. Sensible and progressive Norway wants to break away from Danish and make its local dialect official. Ireland is striving desperately to unlearn English, which it uses so forcibly, and revive Celtic, a wraith. A master of incisive *English* prose is advocating "an American language." The sign *English Spoken, American Understood,* which tourists claim to have seen on European shops, would point in the right direction: unfortunately, we believe that sign to be a senescent myth. The fact that the London edition of *Babbitt* required a glossary is more definitely encouraging. It is usually admitted, although not with the proper degree of pride, that many of our political leaders have discarded the use of English.

Is it a fact that no great literature can be produced in a borrowed language? Neither Alexandria nor Syracuse could compare with Athens: but their culture was more brilliant than that of any other Greek city. Few Latin writers of the first rank came from beyond the confines of Italy: but, by the time Latin civilization had spread to the outlying provinces, it already was decadent in Rome herself. Spanish and Portuguese America is no better off than we are. The French colonies offer a creditable roll of fame: but their literary sons made their careers in Paris, and did not start an autonomous colonial culture. Australian literature, like the continent itself, is semi-desertic. All this, in our opinion, only proves that precedents are of no avail when we have to deal with the unprecedented. There has never been, so far as we know, a "colony" that could compare with the United States to-day. In William Bennett Munro's neat phrase: "We can teach History, but History can not teach us." If English were an alien tongue, artificially superimposed upon native dialects, as it is in India and in the Philippines, it would probably have a paralyzing effect upon literature. But English is now healthily rooted in our soil, and has no local competitor.

If we did need "an American language" before we could produce genuine literature, our chances would be slim indeed. All the forces of modern civilization are against the formation of new local dialects: the old ones are disappearing so fast, that scholars find it difficult to register them. In the Middle Ages, two English valleys, less than a hundred miles apart, were more deeply separated than Chicago and London are to-day. Each of these cities can read every morning the latest scandal from the other; each can call the other on the 'phone; both listen to the same lecturers, the same discs, the same talkies, the same radio broadcast. Even in my youth, while I found it difficult to understand a Yorkshireman, I had no trouble with a New Zealander or a Californian.

Will America's ever fresh fountain of speech, slang, help create a new dialect? Only in a very fleeting and superficial fashion. Most of those spontaneous creations live but for a moment, and do not contribute to the permanent vocabulary. Those which survive infallibly reach London. And it is easy to prophesy that the process will be further accelerated. It used to take decades for an American joke to be understood in England; now, it is merely a matter of years.

The next two hypotheses can be neatly paired off. Our inferiority, says Irving Babbitt, is due to our neglect of standards. We have lost our sense of values, because Democracy refuses to accept enlightened Leadership. "What must one think of a country," asks one of our foremost critics, "whose most popular orator is W. J. Bryan, whose favorite actor is Charlie Chaplin, whose most widely read novelist is Harold Bell Wright, whose best known evangelist is Billy Sunday, and whose representative journalist is William Randolph Hearst?" * Salvation is to be found only in the good old ways. If we were consistent, we should all proclaim ourselves, with T. S. Eliot, Royalists, Catholics and Classicists. But

---

* *Democracy and Leadership*, p. 240.

this is only a counsel of perfection: we might get by with sound Republicanism, sturdy individualism, the Puritan tradition and compulsory Latin. A cultural heaven for Harvard professors.

But to this *fundamentalist* thesis may be opposed the *modernistic*. America has no literature commensurate with her other achievements, because she is still hampered by standards which do not belong to her own civilization. We reject feudal titles, but we piously preserve medieval reputations. We are now doing great things in architecture because we are worrying a little less about Tudor and Queen Anne, Palladian Renaissance or Louis Seize: but our literary education is still antiquarian. Our closest bids to literary greatness were not Bryant and Longfellow, but Walt Whitman and Mark Twain. Unfortunately both labored under the delusion that the literature of a vast new continent should be loose and sprawling. We might just as well assert that the literature of a small country like Scotland must be "tight", and that of Chile "elongated": all variants of the geographical fallacy.

The Neo-Humanists, we believe, are not a majority even among American professors; but they have behind them the force of a united tradition, whereas the Modernists can only express, often with absurd emphasis, vague and conflicting hopes. The result is that the sane, educated *bourgeoisie,* still the backbone of the literary public, is almost solidly fundamentalist.

The same conflict occurs in all countries. It is particularly ardent in France, where the Classics are a party issue. But nowhere, to our knowledge, is the conservative élite so contemptuous of the masses as with us, nor the masses so perfectly oblivious of the élite. There is no communication between them, no cross-fertilization. Irving Babbitt preached only to his own parishioners.

The fifth obstacle in the path of American literature is, or rather was, the heavy cost of Americanization. On account of the diversity of our origins, an enormous effort was expended in bringing us all into line. This was the first aim of our education; and, beyond our school years, it absorbed much collective and individual energy. The community striving so hard to turn all its members into Americans, the man whose chief desire was to remake himself into an American, had little spiritual power left for anything else. Our one great masterpiece was the creation of "the American type." We need not blush at the result: it is fully as good as such things can be. But it is not an artistic achievement, just because it is standardized. Good citizenship has been identified with conformity, mass thinking, mass sentiment: under such conditions, conventionality and superficiality are almost inevitable. Only a country and a man who take themselves for granted can express their souls.

We have greater faith in America than the rabid Americanizers. We should have liked America to impose only the strictest minimum of uniformity, for practical purposes; and to respect, nay to welcome, the varied traditions that the immigrants brought with them. In the slums, we strive to root out the memory of the old lands; but in the colleges, we try our best to teach the history of European civilizations. It does not pay to turn all newcomers into spiritual paupers. Had we preserved,

instead of tossing aside, our multifarious European heritage, the result would have been, not a nation superficially
homogeneous (far more homogeneous now, in externals,
than any in Europe), but an Americanism at the same
time richer in pattern and deeper in spirit. For there
were sufficient foundations for a genuine, uncoerced
Americanism. We all came to America because we felt
in us something of the American soul; and the opportunities of the new life, without any compulsion, would have
welded us all together. We have been too modest; we
have sought to make America a nation just like those of
the old world, while this might have been a new venture,
the first conscious unit of a world commonwealth.

All this is purely retrospective, and our regrets are
futile. Forcible Americanization may have been an incubus; but it is losing force. Not because we no longer
have faith in it, but because its work is done. For half
a generation already, immigration has been reduced to
a negligible point. Assimilation is no longer a pressing
problem. Henceforth, an American may dare to be himself, to think for himself, without being afraid of seem-
ing un-American. The obsession that everybody had to
be exactly like everybody else, is lifted from our minds.
If we do not choose, we shall not have to be "individual-
ists" according to the prescribed pattern, or "Protestants"
who fail to protest. This may release, for the benefit of
literature, marvelous reserves of frozen power.

That "American type" which we sought to impose
upon all dwellers in the land was created by two sets
of factors: a natural selection from the various elements
in Europe, and the physical task of subduing a continent.
The first is the more important: had the most listless of

Europeans been dumped on our Eastern coast instead of the most eager, they would have vegetated, "gone native", or disappeared altogether. But we shall take up first the material aspect, because of its comparative simplicity.

Nations, like Tennyson's God, fulfill themselves in many ways. Our way, for two centuries, was to tame the wilderness. Such a formidable challenge could not fail to absorb a great part of our national energy. When the work was practically completed, the momentum carried us into another field, which the English and the Germans had already mapped out for us: industrial expansion. Technique became the new frontier, with the same adventurous glamour as the old. Men went higher and faster, instead of plunging farther towards the setting sun.

It can hardly be denied that this led to the subordination of disinterested culture. In popular estimation, the poets are not such red-blooded he-men as the Typical American; they are constantly under suspicion of not being in fullest sympathy with their time and with their nation. Even when they are thoroughly American, they must realize that, as mere *singers,* they can not compare with the *doers.* The American epic writer is the pioneer, the discoverer of new lands, new resources, new processes.

This phenomenon is by no means unique. A similar explanation may be offered for the acknowledged inferiority, in literature, of the Romans to the Greeks:

Tu regere imperio populos, Romane, memento
(*haec tibi erunt artes*)

During the French Revolution and Napoleon's Empire, political and military activities drained all the vigor of the land. The only writers who were not feeble ghosts were in opposition. The case of Balzac clearly illustrates our point. Balzac could be summed up in one word: ambition. He had on his table a statuette of Napoleon, the god of Successful Ambition. Had he lived twenty-five years earlier, Balzac would have sought to be an administrator or a Marshal of the Empire; had he been born twenty-five years later, so as to be in the fullness of his young manhood when the Second Empire opened an era of industrial expansion, he would have tried to be a financial magnate. His ideal was Power through Wealth: the central character in the *Human Comedy* is Money. But in the cautious *bourgeois* world of Louis-Philippe, his grandiose commercial imagination was out of place. He failed in business, and his literary career was to a large extent a magnificent substitute for a vanished dream, just as Madame de Staël's career was a compensation for disappointed love. Had Balzac lived in America, he would have been Astor, Gould, Vanderbilt, Morgan, Hill, Harriman, Carnegie, Rockefeller, rather than, as he modestly styled himself, a Field Marshal of Letters.

We do not mean that all European Shelleys, had they been Americans, would have turned into Fords, and all American Chryslers, in Europe, might have been Tennysons. But many of our successful business men—I am thinking at present of a great railroad executive—might have chosen to be writers instead, *if it had been the thing,* if it had offered commensurate rewards. All gifts are not interchangeable: but the greatest of all is energy, and it can assume many shapes.

Here again, we are in all probability standing at the

end of a period: André Maurois was right in calling the Puritan, the Pioneer and the Robber Baron "the three American ghosts." The last geographical frontier is gone; and, although the frontier of technique is capable of indefinite extension, its conquest is no longer a rough-and-tumble adventure. The discoverers, in the new age, will be scientists rather than fighters; and their work will be closely coöperative, almost anonymous, instead of brilliantly individualistic. If the heroic period of material expansion be past, heroic souls will seek other forms of self-expression, and art will come into its own.

Art, for one thing, requires leisure, and hitherto we have despised leisure. The man of leisure, in our eyes, is an idler, a parasite. If it be the sign of a gentleman to scorn toil, the only American equivalent for the gentleman is the tramp. We have not yet learned the virtue of leisure: but leisure has been brutally forced upon us, in huge chaotic blocks, under the name of unemployment. We are compelled to admit that a saner distribution of leisure is needed; and, as leisure becomes a normal fact, we shall have to fill it intelligently. The exclusive predominance of the material producer is nearing its end.

We said that the American type was the result of a natural selection. This, of course, is not wholly true. Some of us were transported; some left the old country for its own good; and, just before the Great War, the shipping companies were coralling hordes of emigrants, not infallibly the most promising material: no alien was undesirable in their eyes, provided his fare be paid. But, as a rule, it took decision, energy, stamina, to break loose and try again. So we are a people of adventurers: there is nothing in our heritage that belongs so legitimately to all of us, whatever our speech or creed may have been; and nothing from which we may derive juster pride.

All this—self-confidence, optimism, vigor—is what the Pioneers brought with them; but, as Mrs. Edith Wharton says, think of what they left behind. They left behind squalor, inequality, oppression: but, at the same time, historical culture. The people who abandoned Europe for America were those who placed *something*—freedom of worship, political liberty, economic opportunity—immeasurably above the enjoyment of the storied past. They would rather be free citizens in the monotonous Prairie, nay in the desert or the swamp, than subjects in the shadow of the noblest cathedral. They may have been idealists, or materialists, or a combination of both: but, in all cases, they were not predominantly artistic.

I know many people in Europe, no less energetic than the majority of us, who would shudder at the thought of settling in America. Sheer prejudice? No: I have also known many Europeans on this side, who, in spite of brilliant success, felt themselves in exile, and returned at the first opportunity: there is something lacking in the American atmosphere without which they can not live. *We* accepted the sacrifice; we, and our ancestors before us, did not place cultural opportunities first and foremost. If there is any reality to that vague entity, the American Type, it must include a healthy dose of Philistinism along with its splendid element of energy.

Culture is not a mere accumulation of material objects: it is the sum of memories and desires. We started our national life with a very scant cultural equipment: we had left most of it behind. Scant, but not negligible: in the first half of the nineteenth century, our hoard was increasing on the Atlantic seaboard. But the two centers in which that capital of culture was accumulating both lost their predominant influence: the Old South through the Civil War, New England through the flood of immigration and the Westward movement. Typical America to-day is Middle Western: and the Middle West is now to New England what New England once was to Europe: the aggregation of those for whom cultural interests are not paramount. For a certain type, it is better to live impoverished in Boston than prosperous in Iowa.

There are forms of self-fulfillment, nobler than riches, which are more freely open in America than in Europe, and thus successfully compete with art and literature: I mean the supreme poetry of this life, love; and of the life to come, religion. The European "marriage of convenience" is a frustration which calls for a compensation in the form of literature. In a country like France, where the Roman Catholic tradition prevails; or in one where the sects are fully stabilized, as in England, certain forms of creative mysticism express themselves in lyric, drama, romance. In America, the great longing may be satisfied by creating or joining a new cult. The founders of the Latter Day Saints or of Christian Science had in them (no less than the promoters of transcontinental railways) a genius which, with different opportunities and under a different discipline, might have given us a new *Divine Comedy,* a new *Paradise Lost.* The Four-Square Evangelist of Southern California might have been our Marie Corelli: the same luxuriant imagination is found in both. The Wesleyan movement, although its followers seldom boast of the fact, was part of Pre-Romanticism. There was enough spiritual energy in England for both a religious revival and a literary awakening: in America, the religious side has taken the upper hand. We have fewer supreme poets, but we have a far greater number of strange sects. When "men of culture" affect to despise old-fashioned religion and new-fangled cults, they do not realize that millions are obtaining, through such means, the gorgeous vision, the mystic tremor, the ultimate catharsis, that the learned receive only at second-hand, and frequently not at all. The common man converted by the crude eloquence of a Salvationist may stand closer to the spirit of Dante and Milton than the grammarian and the allusion chaser.

We have enumerated no less than seven reasons for our self-confessed inferiority in literature, to wit:

1: the brevity of our national existence;
2: the lack of a national language;
3: our "democratic" departure from time-honored standards (Irving Babbitt);
4: our superstitious reverence for standards, mostly alien and outworn;
5: the heavy spiritual toll of wholesale Americanization;
6: the overwhelming task of mastering a new continent; and, consequently, the exaltation of the *doer,* the scorn of leisure;

7: the natural selection, in the formation of our people, of men who did not place culture foremost; and, as a special instance, the successful competition of romantic love and religion with art and literature.

Our conclusions, in practically every case, were far from discouraging. All these factors may have hampered America's cultural development: but not one of them operates with full force to-day. Our "youth" is far behind; Americanization and the material conquest of the land are practically complete; leisure is ours—far more of it than we want; the artistic temperament is resurgent. All our alibis are fast losing their validity. We shall have to produce masterpieces, or know the reason why.

II

"In 1593," reports Fontenelle, "a tooth of gold was discovered in the mouth of a seven-year-old boy, in Silesia . . . Horstius, Rullandus, Ingolsteterus, Libavius, wrote learned treatises on that miraculous portent, sent by God himself to comfort the Christians afflicted by the Turks. . . . A goldsmith, examining the tooth, discovered that it had been very cunningly covered with gold leaf. People first wrote books, and then consulted the expert." *

Critic, *de te fabula*. We had our sport endeavoring to explain a fact which is generally taken for granted. Why not vary our amusements by challenging the fact itself?

We shall not try to disprove American inferiority by measuring ours, point by point, with other national literatures. Dear old Saintsbury, at the close of his *French*

---

* Fontenelle: *Histoire des Oracles.*

Literature, awards France first place in a few "events", second in many others, as if he were the judge of an Anglo-French track meet. Such comparisons escape being offensive only when they are frankly ridiculous.

Neither shall we dispute the point by comparison with the past. The parallel of age with age is as delusive as that between country and country. If we were to believe the blurbs, every season would bring forth a fresh crop of "epoch-making" masterpieces: only they totally fail to make an epoch. Mass production is no argument in our favor: but it creates an unfair basis of judgment. From the past, only the best stands out: the rest is forgotten, or definitely subordinated. *Our* best is so closely enmeshed with the very good, the not so good, the mediocre, the worthless, that the boldest critics dare not attempt to disentangle the bewildering mass. And, as we have seen, old masterpieces have not merely mellowed with age, they have grown. What a century will do to *Death comes to the Archbishop,* I do not know.

No critic knows, and every critic likes to play safe. It takes an erratic and sensation-loving freelance like Papini to question the literal inspiration and inerrancy of Shakespeare. Self-respecting scholars, with a reputation to lose, will not admit in so many words that *The Faerie Queene* is intolerably inflated, and *The Vicar of Wakefield* the merest trifle. We may join in a collective revolution of taste, but we do not like to travel alone: the same cause which makes us superstitious about the past makes us over-diffident about the present. Sainte-Beuve himself was practically blind to the greatness of his contemporaries. We shall not start a new Quarrel of the Ancients and the Moderns: the old one has proved insoluble.

Our defense of the present is based, not on comparison, but on the refusal to compare. Between the modes of expression of our ancestors and those of to-day, there is no common measure. Was Alexander of Macedon a greater general than Foch? How can we tell? What would Alexander's special gifts have done under the conditions of modern technique? The conditions of literature to-day are radically different from those of a mere hundred years ago.

The change which has come upon them is twofold. On the one hand, the literary public is now boundless. In theory, it is co-extensive with the mass of the nation; in practice, it reaches—fitfully—to the very depths, and no limits can be safely assigned to it: for there is no recognized "Society" which can dictate our taste. On the other hand, the ideal of fixity is disappearing from all realms of thought. We have not abandoned the notion of permanence: but it is a living, growing permanence, which manifests itself under a ceaseless variety of appearances.

A hundred years ago, Victor Hugo had prophesied something of the kind: *"Ceci tuera cela,"* *this* will kill *that,* said Claude Frollo, the somber archdeacon of Notre Dame; the printed press will kill the cathedral. At a time when the book was too fragile, too rare, too difficult of access, to be relied upon as the universal vehicle, it was the cathedral that served as the permanent repository of a people's culture. But the printing press makes the book more imperishable in its ubiquity than the cathedral in its mountainous massiveness. The unchangeable Bible of stone becomes too costly, too cumbrous, too inadaptable. Spiritual life deserts it, and rushes eagerly, through a thousand springs, into an irresistible stream. Innumerable copies may be destroyed; many books may perish altogether; others come pouring in, and the stream sweeps on, changing at every moment, eternally the same.

Exactly what the book, according to Victor Hugo, did to the cathedral, other modes of expression, more ubiquitous still, are doing to the book. The *Classic,* the work of a lifetime, destined to endure for centuries, is a monument: the magazine, the newspaper, the radio, the talkie, are innumerable living voices. We are seeking the truth of to-day, striving to reach the men of to-day, content that the ephemeral in us be forgotten altogether. If we have added an infinitesimal particle of enduring truth, it will be true to-morrow in the words of to-morrow.

The change has already come with full force in the sciences. The great scientific classic, an authority for ever, has been left far behind. "The rate of progress in science nowadays is much too great for such works as Newton's *Principia,* or Darwin's *Origin of Species.* Before such a book could be completed, it would be out of date. In many ways, this is regrettable, for the great books of the past possessed a certain beauty and magnificence, which is absent from the fugitive papers of our time, but it is an inevitable consequence of the rapid increase of knowledge, and must therefore be accepted philosophically." *

Scientists may be resigned to the undeniable loss: but what about artists? Renan, an exquisite stylist and a worshipper of beauty, agreed in advance with Bertrand Rus-

* Bertrand Russell, *The Scientific Outlook,* p. 55.

sell: *"Immortality* does not consist in being read by posterity. We must give up such an illusion. The future shall not read us. This we know, and rejoice. So much the better for the future! We shall have led posterity beyond the need of reading us."

Beyond!

Art is the eternal frontier, and the artistic impulse is that of the pioneer. This spirit is desperately needed in American culture. We had it geographically, we still have it industrially; in things of the spirit, we cling to the good old ways, the slowly desiccating wisdom of our ancestors. Not only in Russia, in China, in Italy, do we have the sense of a venture, desperate but exhilarating, an old continent left behind, the unplumbed, uncharted sea ahead: but even in England, in Germany, in France, mankind is consciously in the re-making. America, in comparison, is a sedate country, in which everything of importance has been settled for ages, and is supposed to be settled for ever.

The task of American literature is not to sing the pioneer of the material world, the conqueror of the Western plains, the Argonaut, the builder of skyscrapers and aëroplanes. Let him be honored: but his deeds suffice to his praise. Literature is not a belated and faded imitation of life, but life itself in the experiment. Organized experience is no longer alive: mechanical laws force out and supplant the will of man. From this materialization, art offers an escape; perhaps the sole escape. Art is a flight, not from life, but from death.

405

BIBLIOGRAPHY

Acknowledgments

The preparation of these Bibliographical Notes was a family enterprise; my wife and son must be ready to accept their full share of blame for all errors and omissions.

For abundant aid cheerfully given, my heartiest thanks are due to:

Mrs. Eleanor Clement Jones, of the Harvard Psychological Clinic
Miss Edith Ronald Mirrilees, of Stanford University
Mrs. Isabel Paterson, of the New York Herald-Tribune

I would also add that several passages in this book appeared in The American Mercury, Books Abroad, The Nineteenth Century and After, *and* Scribner's Magazine. *Our thanks are hereby tendered to the editors of these periodicals, for past hospitalities, and for the exhumation permit.*

A. G.

Bibliographical Notes

The study of Literature as a social phenomenon is not so much a *subject* as a *method*. It has therefore no special bibliography: every piece of creative literature is a valid document, and many works of criticism or literary history have important contributions to offer. The purpose of this inquiry is merely to define a point of view: every reader must organize the field of his own experience. In the following notes, I have listed a few books which afford good illustrations of the various points discussed in this volume. Many of them contain extensive bibliographies. Unless otherwise indicated, the place of publication is New York, and the date that of the edition I have used. No indication is given in the case of easily accessible classics.

GENERAL INTRODUCTIONS

Moulton, Richard Green: *The Modern Study of Literature: an Introduction to Literary Theory and Interpretation,* University of Chicago Press, 1915. (A practical and stimulating guide.)

Baldensperger, Fernand: *La Littérature, Création, Succès, Durée,* Paris, E. Flammarion, 1913.

Ermatinger, Emil (editor): *Philosophie der Literaturwissenschaft,* Berlin, Junker und Dünnhaupt, 1930.

SOCIETY SURVEYED BY LITERARY MINDS

Books of this kind offer an excellent preparation for the reverse process: literature viewed by the social scientist.

Many of the Essays of Carlyle and Matthew Arnold belong to this category. Among recent works, the following will serve as specimens:

Brooks, Van Wyck: *Letters and Leadership,* The Viking Press, 1918.

Babbitt, Irving: *Rousseau and Romanticism,* Boston, Houghton Mifflin Company, 1919.

Babbitt, Irving: *Democracy and Leadership,* Boston, Houghton Mifflin Company, 1924.

Krutch, Joseph Wood: *The Modern Temper,* Harcourt, Brace and Company, 1929.

Krutch, Joseph Wood: *Was Europe a Success?* Farrar & Rinehart, Incorporated, 1934.

Lippmann, Walter A: *A Preface to Morals,* The Macmillan Company, 1929. (I wonder if Mr. Lippmann would resent being called a literary mind?)

Russell, Bertrand: *The Scientific Outlook,* W. W. Norton & Company, Inc., 1931. (Curiously prophetic of Huxley's *Brave New World.*)

Huxley, Aldous: *A Brave New World,* Doubleday, Doran & Company, Inc., 1932.

Ortega y Gasset, José: *The Revolt of the Masses,* W. W. Norton & Company, Inc., 1932.

Mumford, Lewis: *Technics and Civilization,* Harcourt, Brace and Company, 1934.

Part I The Background of Literature: Race, Environment and Time

It is impossible to give a separate bibliography for each chapter, as the topics inevitably overlap. This overlapping is in some cases due to confusion of thought. (How difficult it is to keep distinctly apart Race, Language, Nationality!) But it may also result from natural connections: economic, social, political conditions react upon one another.

WORKS ON THE SOCIOLOGICAL INTERPRETATION OF LITERATURE

The classic on the subject is:

Taine, Hippolyte: *Introduction to the History of English Literature,* Paris, Hachette et Cie, 1863. (Many editions and translations; separate edition of the Introduction, with notes by Irving Babbitt, D. C. Heath and Company.)

Taine, Hippolyte: *La Fontaine et ses Fables,* Paris, Hachette et Cie, 1861. (A good illustration of the method.)

The social point of view is implied in the title of:

Francke, Kuno: *A History of German Literature as Determined by Social Forces,* (earlier: *Social Forces in German Literature*), Henry Holt and Company, Inc., 1901.

Thorndike, Ashley H.: *Literature in a Changing Age,* The Macmillan Company, 1920.

Thorndike, Ashley H.: *Outlook for Literature,* The Macmillan Company, 1931.

Calverton, Victor F.: *The Newer Spirit: A Sociological Criticism of Literature,* Boni & Liveright, 1925. (*Newer* is amusing: but the book is not humorous.)

Ichowicz, Marc: *La Littérature à la Lumière du Matérialisme Historique,* Paris, M. Rivière, 1929. (A formidable title. "If the light that is in thee be darkness, how great is that darkness!")

Berl, Emmanuel: *Mort de la Pensée Bourgeoise: la Lit-térature,* Paris, Grasset et Cie, 1929.

THE SOCIOLOGICAL APPROACH TO AMERICAN LITERATURE

Parrington, Vernon Louis: *Main Currents in American Thought: an Interpretation of American Literature from the Beginnings to 1920.* Harcourt, Brace and Company, 3 vols., 1927–1930. (Title and to some extent method inspired by Georg Brandes's *Main Currents in Nineteenth Century Literature.* A standard work.)

Perry, Bliss: *The American Mind: American Traits in American Literature,* Boston, Houghton Mifflin Company, 1912.

Perry, Bliss: *The American Spirit in Literature: a Chronicle of Great Interpreters,* New Haven, Yale University Press, 1918.

Mumford, Lewis: *The Golden Day: a Study in American Experience and Culture,* Boni and Liveright, 1926.

Calverton, Victor F.: *The Liberation of American Literature,* Charles Scribner's Sons, 1931.

DeVoto, Bernard: *Mark Twain's America,* Boston, Little, Brown & Company, 1932.

Lewisohn, Ludwig: *Expression in America,* Harper & Brothers, 1932.

Hicks, Granville: *The Great Tradition,* The Macmillan Company, 1933.

RACE

Until the eighteenth century, the Race idea had been applied (very sporadically) to political theory, but hardly to literature. *Cf.:*

412

Barzun, Jacques: *The French Race: Theories of its Origins and their Social and Political Implications,* Columbia University Press, 1932.

Herder was chiefly responsible for the inextricable confusion between Race, Language, Nationality. *Cf.* his *magnum opus:*

Herder, Johann Gottfried: *Ideen zur Philosophie der Geschichte der Menschheit,* 4 vols., 1784–1791.

Ergang, Robert R.: *Herder and the Foundations of German Nationalism,* Columbia University Press, 1931.

For a very brief discussion:

Guérard, Albert: "Herder's Spiritual Heritage", *Annals of American Academy of Political and Social Science,* July 1934.

In the same line:

Fichte, Johann Gottlieb: Addresses to the German Nation (Purity and Primitiveness of the German Race. *Cf.* particularly Address VIII: *The Definition of a Nation in the Higher Sense of the Word, and of Patriotism*), 1807–1808.

The modern master of the Nordic Mythicists is:

Gobineau, Comte Arthur de: *Essai sur l'Inégalité des Races Humaines,* Paris, Didot, 4 vols., 1853–1855.

In the same line of passionate fuliginous thought:

Chamberlain, Houston Stewart: *The Foundations of the Nineteenth Century,* 2 vols., Dodd, Mead & Company, 1912.

Discussed by:

Hertz, Friedrich: *Race and Civilization,* The Macmillan Company, 1928.

Grant, Madison: *The Passing of the Great Race,* Charles Scribner's Sons, 1916.

Stoddard, T. Lothrop: *Racial Realities in Europe,* Charles Scribner's Sons, 1924.

Stoddard, T. Lothrop: *The Rising Tide of Color Against White World Supremacy,* Charles Scribner's Sons, 1920.

McDougall, William: *Is America Safe for Democracy?* Charles Scribner's Sons, 1921. (A great psychologist in strangely . . . entertaining company.)

For a less inspired but more reliable approach:

Ripley, William Z.: *The Races of Europe,* D. Appleton & Company, 1899 (many later editions). (Still a very convenient compilation of facts and a capital presentation of problems.)

Pittard, Eugène: *Race and History: an Ethnological Introduction to History,* Alfred A. Knopf, 1926.

Boas, Franz: *The Cephalic Index,* American Anthropologist, New York, Vol. I, 1899.

Boas, Franz: *Anthropology and Modern Life,* W. W. Norton & Company, Inc., 1928.

Anthropology leads to the still more dangerous field of:

RACE PSYCHOLOGY AND ETHNOPSYCHOLOGY

Garth, Thomas Russell: *Race Psychology: a Study of Racial Mental Differences,* McGraw-Hill Book Company, Inc., 1931.

Porteus, Stanley David: *Temperament and Race,* Boston, R. G. Badger, 1926.

Porteus, Stanley David: *Race and Social Differences,* Clark University Press, 1930.

Fouillée, Alfred: *Psychologie du Peuple Français,* Paris, Félix Alcan, 1898.

Fouillée, Alfred: *Esquisse Psychologique des Peuples Européens*, Paris, Félix Alcan, 1902.

Le Bon, Dr. Gustave: *The Psychology of Peoples, its Influence on their Evolution*, London, 1899.

Lacombe, Paul: *La Psychologie des Individus et des Sociétés chez Taine, Historien des Littératures*, Paris, Félix Alcan, 1906.

Brownell, William Cary: *French Traits*, Charles Scribner's Sons, 1908.

Cf. supra: Perry, Bliss: *The American Mind;* and *The American Spirit.*

Huntington, Ellsworth: *The Character of Races As influenced by Physical Environment, Natural Selection and Historical Development*, Charles Scribner's Sons, 1925.

Madariaga, Salvador de: *Englishmen, Frenchmen, Spaniards: an Essay in Comparative Psychology*, Oxford University Press, 1931.

PHYSICAL ENVIRONMENT

The ancestor (in modern times) of the "Doctrine of Climates" is:

Bodin, Jean: *Les Six Livres de la République*, Genève, Cartier, 1599. (First edition: 1576.)

And the most famous early exponent is:

Montesquieu, Charles Louis de Secondat: *L'Esprit des Lois*, 1748.

Huntington, Ellsworth: *Civilization and Climate*, New Haven, Yale University Press, 1915.

Cf. supra his: *Character of Races*, Charles Scribner's Sons, 1925.

Febvre, Lucien: *A Geographical Introduction to History,* Alfred A. Knopf, 1925. (Good working bibliography.)

THE COMMUNITY: POLITICAL, SOCIAL, ECONOMIC ENVIRONMENT

(a) *Literature and Democracy*

The general surveys of Society listed at the beginning of these Notes have much to contribute to this question; usually in a very pessimistic spirit.

Cf. also McDougall, William: *Is America Safe for Democracy?* Charles Scribner's Sons, 1921.

Gummere, Francis Barton: *Democracy and Poetry,* Boston, Houghton Mifflin Company, 1911.

(b) *Literature and Social Classes*

will be studied in greater detail in Parts II and III.

(c) *Literature and Economics*

Morris, William: *Lectures on Socialism:* "Art under Plutocracy", 1883; "Art and Socialism", 1884. *Collected Works,* XXIII, Longmans Green and Co., 1915.

Matthews, Brander: "The Economic Interpretation of Literary History", in: *Gateways to Literature,* Charles Scribner's Sons, 1912.

Sinclair, Upton: *Our Bourgeois Literature, the Reason and the Remedy,* 31 pp. Chicago, Kerr. No date.

Sinclair, Upton: *The Cry for Justice: an Anthology of the Literature of Social Protest,* Philadelphia, The John C. Winston Co., 1915.

Sinclair, Upton: *Mammonart, an Essay in Economic Interpretation,* Pasadena, the Author, 1925.

Cf. Calverton, Victor F.: *The Liberation of American Literature,* and Hicks, Granville: *The Great Tradition.*

(d) *Literature and (Russian) Marxism*

Strachey, John: *Literature and Dialectical Materialism,* Covici Friede, 1934. (In bulk, a pamphlet; in purport, a treatise. Strachey has little to say; but, for that little, he has an audience—favorable or antagonistic.)

Trotsky, Leon: *Literature and Revolution,* International Publishers, 1925. (A difficult, unconvincing book, but full of hints and glimpses.)

T. S. Eliot gave an interesting commentary on the above and on Calverton's "Liberation of American Literature" in his *Criterion,* January, 1933.

Freeman, Joseph, *et al.: Voices of October: Art and Literature in Soviet Russia,* The Vanguard Press, 1930.

Reavey, George, and Slonim, Marc: *Soviet Literature: An Anthology,* Covici Friede Books, 1934.

Eastman, Max: *Artists in Uniform: a Study in Literature and Bureaucratism,* Alfred A. Knopf, 1934. The former editor of *The Masses* brings a scathing indictment, not of the Socialistic, but of the Totalitarian State. In the same spirit, *cf.:*

Fabbri, Luce: *Camisas Negras,* Buenos Aires, Nervio, 1934. (Chapter V: "Las Dictaduras y la Cultura"; a fine, although partisan, contribution from an unexpected source.)

(e) *Literature and Utopia*

The problem of Literature and Society from a different time-angle:

Huxley, Aldous: "The Boundaries of the Promised Land",
London, *Fortnightly Review,* December 1930: "The
Boundaries of Utopia", *Virginia Quarterly Review,*
January 1931.

Krutch, Joseph Wood: "Literature and Utopia", in: *Was
Europe a Success?* Farrar & Rinehart, Incorporated,
1934.

This, of course, barely touches upon The Literature of
Utopia, which is boundless. *Cf.:*

Mumford, Lewis: *The Story of Utopias,* Boni and Liveright, 1922.

Russell, Mrs. Frances Theresa: *Touring Utopia; the Realm
of Constructive Humanism,* Dial Press, Lincoln Mc-
Veagh, 1932.

TRADITION

(a) *Tradition,* in the meaning of *that which survives,*
is obviously the basis of all literary history, and needs no
special illustration. However, we may mention as typical:

Wendell, Barrett: *The Traditions of European Literature.
From Homer to Dante,* Charles Scribner's Sons, 1920.

Engel, Eduard: *Was bleibt? Die Welt-Literatur,* Leipzig,
Koehler & Amelang, 1928. (Contains also a statement
and brief treatment of general problems.)

Buck, Philo Melvin: *The Golden Thread,* The Macmillan Company, 1931.

(b) The spirit of *Tradition* as *the Wisdom of Prejudice,*
a reaction against the rationalism of the eighteenth century, is best expounded in:

Burke, Edmund: *Reflections on the French Revolution,*
1790. This attitude, which was *not* traditional in Eng-

land at the time, dominated the nineteenth century. It merged with the Nationalism of Herder (q.v.) and—*longo intervallo*—with that of Maurice Barrès. On Barrès, *cf.*:

Curtius, Robert Ernst: *Maurice Barrès und die geistigen Grundlagen des Französischen Nationalismus,* F. Cohen, Bonn, 1921.

Guérard, Albert: *Five Masters of French Romance,* Charles Scribner's Sons, 1916.

(c) *Tradition* as *the Key to Order:* a very different conception from the above, although not irreconcilable with it. Already clear in:

Arnold, Matthew: *Culture and Anarchy,* 1869. Best exemplified in the Neo-Classicists, Neo-Humanists and Neo-Thomists.

Brownell, William Cary: *Criticism,* Charles Scribner's Sons, 1914.

Brownell, William Cary: *Standards,* Charles Scribner's Sons, 1917.

More, Paul Elmer: *Shelburne Essays,* Boston, G. P. Putnam's Sons, 1904 *seq.*: *The Greek Tradition,* 5 vols., 1917–1927. (Philosophical.)

Foerster, Norman: *The American Scholar; a Study in Litterae Inhumaniores,* University of North Carolina Press, 1929.

Foerster, Norman (editor): *Humanism and America,* Farrar & Rinehart, Incorporated, 1930. A collective declaration of principles, which called for the counterblast:

Grattan, Clinton Hartley: *The Critique of Humanism; a Symposium,* Harcourt, Brace and Company, 1930.

Foerster, Norman: *Toward Standards,* Farrar and Rinehart, Incorporated, 1930. Appropriately dedicated to Willa Cather and Robert Frost.

Probably the most authoritative of the Traditionalists is:

Eliot, Thomas Stearns: *The Sacred Wood,* London, Messrs. Methuen, 1920. Particularly the essay: "Tradition and the Individual Talent."

Eliot, Thomas Stearns: *Selected Essays,* 1917–1932, London, Faber & Faber, Limited, 1932.

Eliot, Thomas Stearns: *After Strange Gods,* Harcourt Brace and Company, 1934. Also the Collection of his quarterly *The Criterion;* and *The American Review.*

Many of these critics were manifestly influenced by French thought. The French leaders of the movement are Ferdinand Brunetière, Charles Maurras and Jacques Maritain. As channel of this influence *cf.:*

Babbitt, Irving: *The Masters of Modern French Criticism,* Boston, Houghton Mifflin Company, 1912. Particularly Chapter X: "Brunetière", and Chapter XI: "Conclusion", (94 pp.).

(d) *Miscellaneous Connotations of Tradition* will be found in:

Santayana, George: *The Genteel Tradition at Bay,* Charles Scribner's Sons, 1931.

Various Authors: *Tradition and Experiment in Present-Day Literature;* addresses delivered at the City Library Institute, London, Oxford University Press, 1929.

Huxley, Aldous: *Music at Night,* Doubleday, Doran & Company, Inc., 1931.

Hicks, Granville: *The Great Tradition,* The Macmillan Company, 1933.

Part II *Homo Scriptor:* The Author as a Social
Type

I. OBJECTIVE STUDIES

Can *Homo Scriptor* be studied from without? Hardly.
The purely scientific mind dealing with pure literature is
like a blind man discoursing on colors. *Cf.* however a few
notable attempts:

Nordau, Max: *Degeneration,* D. Appleton & Company,
1895. (An Epigone of the scientific-realistic age fights
a rear guard action against resurgent Romanticism.)
Attempted refutation of the above by:

Shaw, George Bernard: *The Sanity of Art: an Exposure
of the Current Nonsense about Artists being Degenerate,* London, Constable & Company, Ltd., 1911. (*Vide
infra* under "Genius and Insanity.")

Eastman, Max: *The Literary Mind; its Place in an Age of
Science,* Charles Scribner's Son, 1931. (Janus-like, and
eloquent with both mouths. Really a defense of true
literature against cults and cliques, from Neo-Human-
ism to Unintelligibility. The unfortunate hero in Huxley's *Brave New World* is a perfect example of "the
literary mind and its place in an age of science.")
The experimental approach:

Toulouse, Dr. Edouard: *Emile Zola: Enquête Médico-
Psychologique sur les Rapports de la Supériorité In-
tellectuelle avec la Névropathie. Introduction Générale,*
Paris, Société d'Editions Scientifiques, 1896. (Not
merely thorough, but absolutely exhaustive.)

Binet, A., and Passy, J.: "Études de Psychologie sur les

Auteurs Dramatiques", *Année Psychologique,* I, 1894, pp. 60–175.

Binet, A.: "La Création Littéraire: Portrait Psychologique de Paul Hervieu", *Année Psychologique,* X, p. 162.

Clark, Edwin L.: "American Men of Letters; their Nature and Nurture." *Studies in History, Economics and Public Law,* Vol. 72, Columbia University Press, 1916.

HEREDITY

Galton, Sir Francis: *Hereditary Genius,* D. Appleton & Company, 1891. (First published 1869.)

II. LITERARY DOCUMENTS

The best authority on *Homo Scriptor* is *Homo Scriptor* himself: confessions, memoirs, diaries, letters. The next best is the sympathetic study of literary men by critics who themselves belong to literature. The prototype of self-revealing documents is, of course:

Rousseau, Jean-Jacques: *Confessions* (published 1781–1788).

The literary type par excellence, the Poet, is found in its purity among the major English Romanticists. Blake, however, can not serve as a norm even of the abnormal. Both Coleridge and Wordsworth are partly obscured by a smoke screen of doctrines. The obvious Byronic pose makes it difficult to reach the true Byron. Shelley and Keats are probably the most valuable specimens; Keats at present seems the favorite.

Carpenter, Edward, and Barnefield, George: *Psychology of the Poet Shelley,* E. P. Dutton & Co., Inc., 1925.

Lowell, Amy: *John Keats,* 2 vols., Boston, Houghton Mifflin Company, 1925.

Murry, John Middleton: *Keats and Shakespeare,* Oxford University Press, 1925.

Weller, Earle V.: *The Autobiography of John Keats.* Compiled from his Letters and Essays. Stanford University Press, 1933.

Krutch, Joseph Wood: *Edgar Allen Poe: a Study in Genius,* Alfred A. Knopf, 1926.

Baudelaire, Charles: *Lettres,* 1841–1866, Paris, 1907. (If an antidote were needed against *Les Fleurs du Mal,* none better could be devised than Baudelaire's correspondence. The study of Oscar Wilde is less profitable, because the problem is befogged with irrelevant elements.)

Mumford, Lewis: *Herman Melville,* Harcourt, Brace and Company, 1929.

(After several attempts, the psychological biography of Ambrose Bierce remains to be written. Van Wyck Brooks's *Ordeal of Mark Twain* hovers between the psycho-analytical and the sociological interpretations.)

Moore, George: *Confessions of a Young Man,* Modern Library, 1917.

Moore, George: *Hail and Farewell (Ave, Salve, Vale),* 3 vols., London, William Heinemann, Ltd., 1914–1926. (Almost chemically pure as a literary type. Such purity is not an element of greatness.)

In recent literature, D. H. Lawrence has already become the center of a Golden Legend. None of the books about him compares with:

Huxley, Aldous: *The Letters of D. H. Lawrence, edited*

and with an Introduction by Aldous Huxley, The Viking Press, 1932.

As a fascinating oddity, note:

Symons, Alphonse J. A.: *Frederick Baron Corvo (Frederick Rolfe),* The Macmillan Company, 1926.

For a better understanding of the pure literary type (the disinterested creative artist), a comparison with the semi-literary may be useful:

Charteris, Sir Evan Edward: *Life and Letters of Sir Edmund Gosse,* Harper & Brothers, 1931. (The perfect "man of letters.")

Bradford, Gamaliel: *The Journal of Gamaliel Bradford, 1883–1932,* edited by Van Wyck Brooks, Boston, Houghton Mifflin Company, 1933. (The tragedy of a "man of letters" whose dream it was to be a creative artist, and who knew the difference.)

Bennett, Arnold: *The Journal of Arnold Bennett, 1896–1928,* The Viking Press, 1933. (A shrewd business man who kept account of every word and every penny.)

Rinehart, Mary Roberts: *My Story,* Farrar & Rinehart, Incorporated, 1931. (Shows how wholesome, good and clever both personality and writing can be, without any claims to "literature.")

WRITING AS A PROFESSION. SOCIAL STANDING OF AUTHORS

Putnam, George Haven: *Authors and their Public in Ancient Times.*

Putnam, George Haven: *Books and their Makers during the Middle Ages,* Vol. I: 476–1600. Vol. II: 1500–1709, G. P. Putnam's Sons, 1896–1897.

Holzknecht, Karl J.: *Literary Patronage in the Middle Ages,* University of Pennsylvania Press, 1923.

Sheavyn, Phoebe: *The Literary Profession in the Elizabethan Age,* Manchester, University Press, 1909.

Beljame, Alexandre: *Le Public et les Hommes de Lettres en Angleterre au XVIIIème Siècle: Dryden, Addison et Pope,* Paris, Hachette et Cie, 1883.

Collins, A. S.: *Authorship in the Days of Johnson,* (Routledge), E. P. Dutton & Co., Inc., 1927.

Collins, A. S.: *The Profession of Letters,* (Routledge), E. P. Dutton & Co., Inc., 1928. (Continues the account of the relationship of authors to their patrons and to publishers from 1780 to 1832.)

Vigny, Alfred de: *Stello, ou les Diables Bleus: Première Consultation du Docteur Noir,* 1832. (A romantic and profound treatment of the theme. Deserves to be better known.)

Cf. also: Part III: "The Public; Society; Groups and Cliques; Publishers."

THE ENIGMA OF GENIUS

Lombroso, Cesare: *The Man of Genius,* London, Walter Scott, 1895 and 1901. (Marked differences between the two editions.) (The vigorous restatement of a very ancient paradox.)

Türck, Hermann: *The Man of Genius,* London, A. & C. Black, Ltd., 1914. (Contains a discussion and refutation of Lombroso.)

Guilbert, Dr. Charles: *L'Envers du Génie: Gérard de*
Cf. also Nordau, Shaw, Toulouse, *supra.*

Nerval, Baudelaire, Alfred de Musset, Rollinat, Paris, Albin Michel, 1927.

Cox, Catharine Morris: *Genetic Studies of Genius:* Vol. II: "The Early Mental Traits of Three Hundred Geniuses", Stanford University Press, 1926.

Marks, Jeannette: *Genius and Disaster,* Adelphi Co., 1925.

Lange-Eichbaum, Wilhelm: *Das Genie-Problem: eine Einführung,* München, Ernst Reinhardt, 1931. *id: The Problem of Genius,* translated by Eden and Cedar Paul, London, Kegan Paul, French, Trubner and Co., Ltd., 1931.

Lange-Eichbaum, Wilhelm: *Genie, Irrsinn und Ruhm,* München, Ernst Reinhardt, 1929. (Perhaps most original and most valuable in its treatment of Fame; but the discussion of Genius and Insanity is remarkably sane.)

Part III The Public

GENERAL

The study of Literature as a branch of social psychology is not yet fully organized; the close kinship in method and spirit between evangelization, education, criticism, propaganda and advertising is hardly ever confessed. It may be advisable therefore, to approach the problem of Public Opinion through political books, and test the results in the literary field.

One of the pioneers in Collective Psychology was the ever-ebullient polygraph:

Le Bon, Dr. Gustave: *The Crowd,* London, T. Fisher Unwin, 1896.

McDougall, William: *Introduction to Social Psychology,* London, Messrs. Methuen, 1908.

McDougall, William: *Group Mind,* G. P. Putnam's Sons, 1920.

Lippmann, Walter: *Public Opinion,* Harcourt, Brace and Company, 1922.

Lippmann, Walter: *The Phantom Public,* Harcourt Brace and Company, 1925.

Dewey, John: *The Public and its Problems,* Henry Holt and Company, Incorporated, 1927.

Convenient Instruments:

Young, Kimball, and Lawrence, R. B.: "Bibliography on Censorship and Propaganda", *University of Oregon Publication, Journalism Series, I.* No. 1, March 1928.

Young, Kimball: *Social Psychology,* F. S. Crofts & Co., 1930.

Graves, W. Brooke: *Readings in Public Opinion; its Formation and Control,* D. Appleton & Company, 1928.

Childs, H. L.: *A Reference Guide to the Study of Public Opinion,* Princeton, Princeton University Press, 1934.

With special application to Literature:

General:

Schücking, Lewin Ludwig: *Die Soziologie der literarischen Geschmacksbildung,* München, Rosl, 1923.

Cf. Baldensperger, Fernand: *La Littérature, Création, Succès, Durée,* Paris, E. Flammarion, 1913.

Cf. Lange-Eichbaum, Wilhelm: *Genie, Irrsinn und Ruhm,* München, Ernst Reinhardt, 1929.

Blankenship, Russell: *American Literature as Expression of the National Mind* (suggested readings), Henry Holt and Company, Incorporated, 1931.

As special examples of the study of Fame:

Chew, Samuel C.: *Byron in England, his Fame and After-Fame,* Charles Scribner's Sons, 1924.

Blanchard, Frederick: *Fielding the Novelist, a Study in Historical Criticism.* (Vogue, recognition, fame.) New Haven, Yale University Press, 1926.

This method is far more general in Comparative Literature than in the purely national field; *cf.:*

Baldensperger, Fernand: *Goethe en France,* Paris, Hachette et Cie, 1920.

Carré, Jean-Marie: *Goethe en Angleterre,* Paris, E. Plon, Nourrit et Cie, 1920.

"SOCIETY": COURTS AND SALONS

General:

Traill, Henry Duff (editor): *Social England: a Record of the Progress of the People,* etc. 6 vols., G. P. Putnam's Sons, 1894–1902.

Turberville, Arthur Stanley (editor): *Johnson's England: an Account of the Life and Manners of his Age,* 2 vols., Oxford University Press, 1933.

And, of course, Pepys, Evelyn, Boswell, Madame d'Arblay, Chesterfield.

Beljame, Alexandre: *Le Public et les Hommes de Lettres en Angleterre au XVIIIème Siècle: Dryden, Addison et Pope,* Paris, Hachette et Cie, 1883.

Tinker, Chauncey Brewster: *The Salon and English Letters:* Chapters on the "Interrelations of Literature and Society in the age of Johnson", The Macmillan Company, 1915.

Gleichen-Russwurm, Alexander von: *Geselligkeit: Sitten*

und Gebräuche der Europäischen Welt, 1789–1900, Stuttgart, Julius Hoffmann, 1910. (A very agreeable bird's-eye view.)

Recent documents in American literature:

Atherton, Gertrude: *Adventures of a Novelist,* The Liveright Corporation, 1932.

Wharton, Edith: *A Backward Glance,* D. Appleton-Century Company, Inc., 1934. (Reveals perfect indifference of New York "Society" to literature half a century ago.)

Luhan, Mabel Dodge: *Intimate Memories.* Vol. I: "Background", Harcourt Brace and Company, 1933. (Buffalo Society was even more impervious to literature than New York Society.)

The French Salon is an inexhaustible subject. *Cf.* any standard bibliography of French Literature, Lanson, Thieme, Nitze and Dargan, etc. Classic Comedies: *Les Précieuses Ridicules, Les Femmes Savantes.* Edouard Pailleron: *Le Monde ou l'on s'ennuie,* 1881; *cf.* two recent examples:

Pouquet, Jeanne Maurice: *The Last Salon: Anatole France and his Muse,* Harcourt, Brace and Company, 1927. (Why "the last?")

Daudet, Léon: "Salons et Journaux" in: *Souvenirs des Milieux Littéraires, Politiques, Artistiques et Médicaux,* 2 vols., Paris, Nouvelle Librairie Nationale, 1920–1926.

And many indications in Marcel Proust: *À la Recherche du Temps Perdu.*

LITERARY SOCIETY: GROUPS, CLUBS, BOHEMIANISM

Allen, Robert J.: *The Clubs of Augustan London,* Harvard University Press, 1933.

Shelley, Henry Charles: *Inns and Taverns of Old London,* London, Sir Isaac Pitman & Sons, Ltd., 1909. ("Setting forth the historical and literary associations of those ancient hostelries, together with an account of the most notable coffee-houses, clubs and pleasure gardens of the British Metropolis.")

The most extensive document on the social aspects of literary life:

Goncourt, Edmond de: *Journal des Goncourt, Mémoires de la Vie Littéraire,* Paris, Charpentier, 1891 *seq.* (Several volumes still unpublished.)

Parry, Albert: *Garrets and Pretenders: a History of Bohemianism in America,* (extensive bibliography), Covici Friede, 1933.

Howells, William Dean: *Literary Friends and Acquaintances; a Personal Retrospect of American Authorship,* Harper & Brothers, 1901.

Garland, Hamlin: *Roadside Meetings,* 1930.

—— *Companions of the Trail,* 1931.

—— *My Friendly Contemporaries; a Literary Log,* 1932. All three, The Macmillan Company.

Emerson, Edward Waldo: *The Early Years of the Saturday Club,* 1855–1870, Boston, Houghton Mifflin Company, 1918.

Howe, M. A. DeWolfe: *Later Years of the Saturday Club,* 1870–1920, Boston, Houghton Mifflin Company, 1927.

Van Vechten, Carl: *Peter Whiffle, his Life and Work,* Alfred A. Knopf, 1927. (An amusing and innocuous satire of certain American cliques at home and abroad.)

Anderson, Margaret: *My Thirty Years' War,* Covici Friede, 1930. (Strenuous liveliness.)

Stein, Gertrude: *The Autobiography of Alice B. Toklas,* Harcourt Brace and Company, 1933.

Burdett, Osbert: *The Beardsley Period, an Essay in Perspective,* Boni & Liveright, 1925.

Cf. Smith, Cedric Ellsworth: *The Yellow Book; a Selection,* Hartford, Edwin Valentine Mitchell, 1928.

Cf. Beer, Thomas: *The Mauve Decade,* Alfred A. Knopf, 1926.

Rascoe, Burton: *"Smart Set" History: Introduction to "Smart Set" Anthology,* Reynal and Hitchcock, 1934.

Nathan, George Jean: *Intimate Notebooks,* Alfred A. Knopf, 1932.

Clark, Emily: *Innocence Abroad,* Alfred A. Knopf, 1931. (Little magazine *The Reviewer,* Richmond.)

THE BOOK TRADE AND ITS INFLUENCE UPON LITERATURE

Cheney, O. H.: *Economic Survey of the Book Industry,* 1930–1931, National Association of Book Publishers, 1932.

Grasset, Bernard: *La Chose Littéraire,* Paris, N.R.F. (Gallimard), 1929.

Duffus, Robert L.: *Books, their place in a Democracy,* Boston, Houghton Mifflin Company, 1930.

Swinnerton, Frank: *Authors and the Book Trade,* Alfred A. Knopf, 1932.

Page, Walter Hines: *A Publisher's Confession,* Doubleday, Page & Co., 1905.

(*Cf.* Hendrick, Burton Jesse: *The Life and Letters of*

431

Walter H. Page, 3 vols., Doubleday, Page & Co., 1922–25.)

Unwin, Stanley: *The Truth about Publishing,* London, George Allen & Unwin, Ltd.

McClure, Samuel Sidney: *My Autobiography,* F. A. Stokes Company, 1914.

Holt, Henry: *Garrulities of an Octogenarian Editor. With Other Essays Somewhat Biographical and Auto-biographical,* Houghton Mifflin Company, 1923.

Tooker, Frank L.: *Joys and Tribulations of an Editor,* The Century Company, 1924.

Whyte, Frederick: *William Heinemann,* London, Jonathan Cape, Ltd., 1928.

Doran, George H.: *Chronicles of Barabbas,* Harcourt, Brace and Company, 1935.

INDEX *

* CAPITALS: topics. *Italics:* titles of books. Small Roman: proper names.